KU-014-735

Feminist approaches to art therapy

The practice of art therapy has been slow to embrace the critical and theoretical viewpoints, including feminism, which have made a huge impact in other areas of the humanities and social sciences in recent years. Art therapists are excellently placed, however, to respond to the growing awareness that language and images have a role to play in creating and maintaining gender inequality and the pressures that can lead to mental ill-health among women.

In *Feminist Approaches to Art Therapy*, leading international practitioners in this field explore the ways in which gender issues can be addressed in art therapy and suggest that by being sensitive to the socio-cultural dimensions of women's lives therapists can become more receptive to the needs of their female clients.

Within their own specific areas of expertise the contributors challenge the over-reliance on universally applied psychological theory. Case studies illustrate how issues of class, race and gender introduce a social element into what is sometimes described as a purely personal, cathartic process. Chapters also discuss empowerment, sexuality, pregnancy and childbirth, providing a comprehensive survey of women's issues within art therapy which will prompt a reevaluation of current training and practice in this field.

Susan Hogan is Senior Lecturer in Art Therapy at the University of Derby's School of Health and Community Studies and an art therapist in private practice specialising in work with women.

Contributors: Helene Burt; Jean Campbell; Doris Abra Gaga; Susan Hogan; Val Huet; Maggie Jones; Susan Joyce; Marian Liebmann; Miche Fabre-Lewin; Deborah Lupton; Cathy A. Malchiodi; Rosy Martin; Carol Ross; Sally Skaife; Harriet Wadeson.

Feminist approaches to art therapy

Edited by Susan Hogan

85892

WITHDRAWN

SOCIAL STUDIES
LIBRARY
SOCIAL STUDIES CENTRE GEORGE ST
OXFORD OX1 2RL

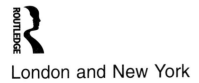

London and New York

First published 1997
by Routledge
11 New Fetter Lane, London EC4P 4EE

Simultaneously published in the USA and Canada
by Routledge
29 West 35th Street, New York, NY 10001

© 1997 Susan Hogan

Typeset in Times by Keystroke, Jacaranda Lodge, Wolverhampton
Printed and bound in Great Britain by Butler and Tanner Ltd

All rights reserved. No part of this book may be reprinted or
reproduced or utilized in any form or by any electronic,
mechanical, or other means, now known or hereafter
invented, including photocopying and recording, or in any
information storage or retrieval system, without permission
in writing from the publishers.

British Library Cataloguing in Publication Data
A catalogue record for this book is available from the British Library

Library of Congress Cataloging in Publication Data
Feminist approaches to art therapy / Susan Hogan.
    p.   cm.
    Includes bibliographical references and index.
    1. Art therapy. 2. Feminist therapy. 3. Women–Mental health.
I. Hogan, Susan, 1961– .
RC489.A7F46 1997
615.8′5156′082—dc21   96-52368
                                                        CIP

ISBN 0–415–14839–1
    0–415–14840–5 (pbk)

In memory of Sylvia June Hogan (née Young)

Fee was my mother.

She was dismissed by her doctor as neurotic.

By the time she received a correct diagnosis her cancer was too far advanced for her to be saved.

Like many women she was loving and compassionate enough to forgive the doctor and insist that I not take legal action against him for negligence as I wished to do.

This book is in memory of Fee and the thousands of women like her who have been misdiagnosed, abused and mistreated by our medical and psychiatric services.

Susan Hogan

Contents

Illustrations and tables

ILLUSTRATIONS

TABLES

Acknowledgements

Thanks are due to Edwina Welham for her patience in all her dealings with me regarding the production of this book. Thanks also to Alan Rice for encouraging me to write. My research assistant, Matt Wellard, a talented researcher and lecturer, deserves particular mention for his effort of laboriously correcting references and typing in editorial changes. Thanks also to him for editorial suggestions and straightforward comments on some of the texts including my own chapters. His perseverance, conscientiousness and generosity have been much appreciated.

Elizabeth Burns gave me the benefit of her publishing experience and helped me put together the original proposal for Routledge and I am extremely grateful to her for that assistance. Recognition of the hard work of the contributors is also called for. I know that some of them found their chapters very difficult to write.

I owe a great debt of gratitude to Phil Douglas for his vigorous and robust criticisms of the texts and for his incisive editorial suggestions. It is his rigorous help in particular which is responsible for the annihilation of excessive hyperbole in the rest of this book!

Susan Hogan
Edinburgh

Contributors

Helene Burt is an art therapist registered with both the Canadian (RCAT) and the American Art Therapy Associations (ATR). She currently teaches and supervises students at the Toronto Art Therapy Institute and has published in the areas of art therapy and ethnicity.

Helene's clinical experience includes working in the areas of addiction case management and counselling. She has also worked in an in-patient adult psychiatric unit. Her work in the area of sexual abuse has involved her in using art therapy with both victims and offenders.

Jean Campbell is a trained art therapist and art teacher. She has worked for eighteen years in clinical, community and educational settings. She has a special interest in women's creativity and health. Jean is also an active member of the Race and Culture Group (ARC) of the British Association of Art Therapists (BAAT). From 1989 to 1995 Jean was an art therapist and fertility counsellor for the fertility clinic at the London Hospital. She currently works in private practice and teaching. Jean has two major publications to date *Creative Art Groupwork* (Winslow Press, 1984) and 'Fertile Ground – The Role of Art Therapy in the Fertility Clinic', in *Infertility Counselling* edited by Sue Jennings (Blackwell Scientific Press, 1995).

Miche Fabre-Lewin is a practising multi-media artist, and registered art therapist (BAAT). A colonial upbringing in Zimbabwe, combined with a French and Jewish heritage and her passion for the savanna bush, have profoundly shaped her working practice. Miche moved to Britain to study comparative literature at the University of East Anglia in Norwich. She has worked within the National Health Service in a therapeutic community setting with young adults. She is now particularly interested in the subjects of mental health politics, gender, class, cultural identity and self-empowerment. She currently teaches art therapy at Bath City College and works as an art therapist primarily with women. Miche is also a member of the Race and Culture Group of the British Association of Art Therapists.

Doris Abra Gaga studied drawing and painting at the Canterbury College of Art and Design (1984–1987) and then completed a Masters degree in fine art at Manchester Polytechnic. She trained as an art therapist at the Psychotherapy Unit, Goldsmiths' College of the University of London and is a registered art therapist (BAAT). Doris has been practising as an art therapist since 1991. She currently works at the Alcohol, Counselling and Prevention Services in Brixton, London. Prior to taking up her current appointment she worked as a Senior Art Therapist, specialising in substance misuse and adult mental health. Doris is a member of the Race and Culture Group of the British Association of Art Therapists.

Susan Hogan completed a fine art degree in Edinburgh, art therapy training at the University of Hertfordshire and then a Masters degree in arts policy and management at City University, London. Her masters thesis was on gender, power and organisational dynamics. She then attended the University of Sydney, researching expressionism. In Australia Susan taught twentieth-century art history and theory at the University of New South Wales and the National Art School, Sydney. Her doctoral research was based at the University of Aberdeen. She is currently preparing two books: *The Intellectual Precursors of Art Therapy in Britain*, and an edited volume, *Gender Issues in Art Therapy*. Susan has taught art therapy at introductory, foundation and under- and post-graduate levels. She has latterly been involved in the development of art therapy courses in Australia and Britain.

Val Huet is a registered art therapist, former secretary, and former chairperson of BAAT. Born in Algeria and educated in France, Val studied sculpture at Camberwell School of Art in London. She completed art therapy training at the University of London at Goldsmiths' College. Subsequently she trained as a group psychotherapist at Goldsmiths' and then completed a Masters degree in art therapy there. Val worked for four years in multi-cultural community settings for Lambeth Social Services. She now teaches part-time at the University of London on their art psychotherapy and group psychotherapy courses.

Maggie Jones was born in England in 1955. She moved to New Zealand in 1986. Maggie trained first as a teacher of art and then completed the post-graduate Diploma in Art Therapy at Sheffield University. She is a registered art therapist (BAAT). She has worked in adult mental health for ten years, primarily with women. Painting remains for her a necessary, difficult delight.

Susan Joyce is a registered art therapist (BAAT) trained at St Albans (University of Hertfordshire). Susan also holds a Masters degree in women's studies from Griffith University, Queensland. She works as an art therapist in Brisbane, Australia, specialising in work with women. She has held the posts of Membership Secretary and Vice-President of the

Australian National Art Therapy Association and is currently a professional member of ANATA. Her clinical experience is varied and includes psychiatry, visual impairment and women's sexual-assault support. The latter has become her particular area of concern. Susan lectured in art therapy on the Masters degree in arts therapy at the University of Western Sydney, Nepean, and was a Visiting Lecturer to the Masters degree in art therapy at the Edith Cowan University in Perth, Western Australia.

Marian Liebmann is well known in the field of art therapy for her many publications including *Art Games and Structures for Groups* (1982), *Art Therapy for Groups* (Routledge, 1986), *Art Therapy In Practice* (Jessica Kingsley Publishers, 1990), *Art Therapy with Offenders* (Jessica Kingsley Publishers, 1994) and *Art Approaches to Conflict*. Her work is widely used in the training of art therapists. Marian has worked in education, social work and community work settings, including work with victims and offenders in the criminal justice system. She has used art therapy with many community groups, including several women's groups. She is currently working in the area of mediation and resolution and as an art therapist with the Bristol Inner City Mental Health Team. She has also used art therapy at a day centre for ex-offenders and ex-psychiatric patients and with probation clients. Marian also teaches art therapy at Bristol University in the Department of Counselling, and is a visiting lecturer on the art therapy diploma course at City of Bath College.

Deborah Lupton is Associate Professor of Cultural Studies and Cultural Policy and Deputy Director of the Centre for Cultural Risk Research in the School of Social Sciences and Liberal Studies, Charles Sturt University, Bathurst, Australia. Her primary research interests are in the socio-cultural aspects of the body, sexuality, medicine and public health, food, the media and the emotions. She has published several books in these areas, including *Moral Threats and Dangerous Desires: AIDS in the News Media* (Taylor & Francis, 1994), *Medicine as Culture: Illness, Disease and the Body in Western Cultures* (Sage, 1994), *The Imperative of Health: Public Health and the Regulated Body* (Sage, 1995) and *Food, the Body and the Self* (Sage, 1996).

Cathy A. Malchiodi is current editor of *Art Therapy: Journal of the American Art Therapy Association* and is author of *Breaking the Silence: Art Therapy with Children from Violent Homes* (Brunner/Mazel, 1997) and *Supervision and Related Issues* (1996). She was elected to the executive board of the American Art Therapy Association (AATA) for four years and served as chairperson of various AATA committees, including Membership, Ethics, Certification, and Publications. In 1991 she received the distinguished service award for her work for art therapy. She also serves on the editorial board of the *International Journal of Arts Medicine* and the

Journal of Child Sexual Abuse. Cathy has lectured in art therapy for seventeen years. She served as Locum Director of the art therapy and marriage and family counselling degree programme at California State University, Sacramento. She is the former Director of the art therapy graduate programme at the University of Utah. Cathy is currently an adjunct professor at Lesley College, and Southwestern College. She is also Executive Director of the Institute For the Arts and Health in Salt Lake City.

Rosy Martin is a photographer, designer, lecturer, workshop leader and therapist. Since 1983, together with the late Jo Spence, she has evolved and promoted a new photographic practice – phototherapy, based on re-enactment and documentation of past events and relationships. Exhibitions of her phototherapy work have been shown extensively, and venues have ranged from international galleries to community spaces. She has run workshops throughout Britain, Finland, Canada and the USA. Rosy has written and published on the subject of phototherapy for a number of years. She is widely regarded as one of the most interesting and provocative practitioners in the area of arts therapy today.

Carol Ross is both a registered art therapist (BAAT) and a trained teacher and equal-opportunities counsellor. She spent many years working in London schools as an advisory teacher for equal opportunities and has lectured in higher education on gender issues. Carol has also been involved in a variety of research projects relating to gender concerns, and has produced a number of publications. Currently she is working for Islington Learning Support Services in London as an art therapist and specialist teacher for children with emotional and behavioural difficulties.

Sally Skaife graduated from Reading University with a Fine Art degree before training as a teacher. She later trained as an art therapist at the University of London at Goldsmiths' College. She also holds a Masters degree in art psychotherapy also undertaken at Goldsmiths' College. In addition to this she has completed further training in psychotherapy at the London Centre for Psychotherapy. Sally is a registered art therapist who has served as Membership Secretary and Chairperson of BAAT. She is currently a member of the editorial board of *Inscape*, the journal of the British Association of Art Therapists. She is also a member of the Group Analytic Society. She worked as an art therapist in various London hospitals between 1975 and 1986. Sally now lectures in art therapy at the Art Psychotherapy Unit of Goldsmiths' College.

Harriet Wadeson LCSW, PhD., ATR-BC, HLM, is a Professor and Co-ordinator of the Art Therapy Graduate Programme of the University of Illinois at Chicago and director of its annual Summer Institute at Lake Geneva, WI. She is author of *Art Psychotherapy*, and *The Dynamics of Art*

Psychotherapy and editor of *Advances in Art Therapy*. She is also editor of the first book published by the American Art Therapy Association, *A Guide to Conducting Art Therapy Research*. In addition, she has published chapters in numerous texts and over sixty articles in professional journals. Harriet Wadeson is the recipient of many art awards, including a first prize from the Smithsonian Institute. She has received a Resolution of Commendation from the State Legislature of Illinois, first prize for research from the American Art Therapy Association, honorary life membership in the American Art Therapy Association (the profession's highest honour in the United States) and the Benjamin Rush Award for Scientific Exhibits from the American Psychiatric Association. One of art therapy's pioneers in the USA, Harriet Wadeson began her career in 1961 at the National Institute of Mental Health under the tutelage of Hanna Kwiatkowska, where she engaged in clinical work, research and writing for psychiatric journals. She inaugurated art therapy courses at the National Institute of Health (NFMH). Harriet holds a Masters degree in art therapy and psychology from Goddard College, and a Masters degree in social work from the Catholic University and a doctorate in art therapy and psychology from the Union Institute. Subsequently she became Director of the Art Therapy Graduate Programme at the University of Houston. In 1980 she developed the Art Therapy Graduate Programme at the University of Illinois where she is currently a professor. In addition, for twenty years she has maintained a private practice in art therapy and psychotherapy.

Foreword

Deborah Lupton

The practice of art therapy may take place on two different levels. One is the personal: the use of art, writing or performance by individuals experiencing psychological or physical trauma, distress or social disadvantage in the attempt to express visually or verbally their embodied sensations and emotions. This art may not be seen by others (beyond the therapist or perhaps others in a therapy group); its purpose is purely self-expression and catharsis. The practice of art therapy at this level, therefore, tends not to challenge the broader social and cultural conditions in which the individual finds herself constructed as 'other'. Indeed, such practices may actually work to individualise social and economic disadvantage by focusing the person's problems at the level of her personal biography and personality. The other use of art therapy is the overtly political, in which art is used to express and critique the socio-cultural context in which pain, illness, disability or social stigmatisation or inequality are experienced. This type of art is primarily designed for public display in the attempt to instigate social change. It may critique current visual and linguistic representations, seeking to overturn them or alter them. Activist art seeks to challenge dominant practices in the medical or psychiatric treatment of illness and disability, or to draw attention to the ways in which certain social groups such as women, the poor, the disabled, gay men and lesbians, the elderly, the unemployed and immigrants are routinely stigmatised and disadvantaged in the dominant culture.

In this book, both kinds of art therapy are discussed. What makes the book's focus different from previous analyses and uses of art therapy, however, and what brings the two practices of art therapy together, is its focus on feminist approaches. The use of the term 'feminism' immediately brings the book into the sphere of contestation and the political. It signals that the contributors within are not simply content with describing the practice of art therapy as a means of expression of bodily or psychic pain or distress, but are consciously working towards an approach that calls into question and addresses the notion of inequality as it relates to women's socio-cultural and economic position. While it also allows for women to express their frustrations around their position *qua* women in society by engaging in catharsis and self-expression, such an approach to art therapy has the potential to go beyond the individualised and personally thera-peutic concept of art therapy to the more overtly political, or the 'socially therapeutic' practice of art therapy. As several of the contributors point out, the practice of art therapy has been rather slow in embracing the critical and theoretical viewpoints, including feminism, that have enlivened fine art theory and scholarship as well as other areas in the humanities and social sciences. Part of this reluctance seems to be the lack of acknowledge-ment on the part of art therapists themselves of their role in contributing to the production of meaning and the reproduction of power relations in the therapist–client relationship, a role which several of the authors are at pains to highlight.

One aspect of the emerging critical approach to art therapy as articu-lated in this book which I find particularly intriguing is the relationship between self, body and emotion as they are expressed via art work, writing and performance. Artistic expression, of course, has always been centrally organised around the conveying of emotional states in ways that most academic discourse and practice attempt to avoid. Language is often constrained in conveying the meaning of pain, psychological or emotional states; it is here that visual expression can step in to fill the gap. When the potent images or performative bodily movements produced in the context of art therapy move beyond the personal, beyond the particular, to the wider domain, such art can begin to challenge the status quo:

> engaging in artistic and creative pursuits has the potential of serving several purposes for people who are ill and their supporters. Expressing their feelings and experiences creatively allows a cathartic release of the fears, confusion and anxieties surrounding serious illness, and thus fulfils a personal need. But when the work is received into the public domain, when it is exhibited, published, transmitted or screened, the personal experience of disease fulfils a collective goal of drawing attention to the ways in which linguistic and visual representations of disease constitute practices.
>
> (Lupton, 1994: 77–8)

Over the past few decades, the direction of cultural theory has undergone an important shift, moving from focusing primarily on social and political structures (evident in structuralist approaches) to an emphasis on language and discourse (the poststructuralist approach). In the 1970s, much cultural theory was dominated either by Marxist critiques, directed at exploring the ways in which elite social groups maintained their hold on power, semiotic analysis of cultural texts influenced by Barthes or psychoana-lytic approaches to cultural reproduction drawing upon Lacan's writings. By the 1990s, most areas of the arts, humanities and social sciences had experienced what has been termed a 'linguistic turn'. Such a 'turn' has involved paying greater attention to the ways in which language and discourse not simply 'reflect' reality and notions of the self, but their constitutive role. The underlying reasons for this shift include the increasing dominance of semiotics and deconstructionism, followed by poststructuralist theory. Through Foucault's writings in particular, it has come to be recognised that representation, power and knowledge are inextricably intertwined. While Marxist critics called for the untangling of knowledge from power, Foucauldian theory argued that this separation is simply not possible, given the pervasive and productive nature of power.

Discourse, as the term is used here, refers not only to verbal communication but to visual images. Discourses serve to shape representation, and therefore experience, subjectivity and understandings of the world. The words that are chosen to talk about and describe social groups, the images that portray them, are integral to the ways that individuals come to understand themselves, to construct their sense of self and embodiment, to define themselves as members of some social groups but not others. Foucault (1979), for example, has drawn attention to the process by which 'the homosexual' was constructed as a distinct sexual type in the late nineteenth century via the discourses and practices of medicine, science and sexology. People who engaged in same-sex sexual practices, until that time, were not specifically identified as 'homosexual'; with that label a new kind of subjectivity by which individuals could define themselves and others was brought into being. As Foucault notes, the discourses that defined 'deviant' or 'aberrant' sexual identities at that time were intended not simply to suppress the expression of this sexuality, 'but rather to give it an analytical, visible, and permanent reality' (1979: 44).

Feminist theory has also emerged over the past few decades as an important site for cultural analysis and critique. Feminism is, of course, a currently contested term, to the extent that many academic scholars tend to prefer to use the term 'feminisms' to denote the existence of differing approaches that may be used to draw attention to issues around women's position in contemporary societies. It is now frequently acknowledged that women are not homogeneous in their experience and that white, heterosexual, able-bodied, middle-class feminists cannot speak for all women. That is not to say, however, that women cannot be thought of as a social collective, for as Iris Marion Young argues, 'Without conceptualising women as a group in some sense, it is not possible to conceptualise oppression as a systematic, structured, institutional process' (1995: 192). The alternative is to slide into a liberal individualistic approach that suggests that we are all 'individuals' with our personalised life trajectories and choices or constraints, thereby ignoring institutionalised and structural disadvantage. It is this focus on women as a distinct social collective, Young argues, 'that gives feminism its specificity as a political movement' (1995: 193).

The insights offered by the interdisciplinary field of cultural studies are also highly relevant to a critical and theorised art therapy practice. Scholars and researchers in this field have focused on the ways in which cultural products, including elite texts but especially focusing on popular texts, contribute to the reproduction of power relations and the shaping of subjectivity. Texts ranging from romance novels, music video clips and television soap opera to policy documents, museum displays and medical and scientific literature have provided the stuff for analysis (see, for example, the chapters in Grossberg, Nelson and Treichler, 1992). Cultural studies is interested in the ways in which such texts are produced and read by their audiences or consumers as well as in analysing or 'deconstructing' the meanings of the texts themselves. In doing so, it seeks to take an oppositional stance, focusing on the politics of difference and the reproduction of socio-economic inequality through cultural texts. Cultural studies has been an important site for feminist researchers to interrogate the processes by which gender is produced and reproduced via both popular and elite cultural products and cultural institutions (see, for example, Franklin, Lury and Stacey, 1991). In its attempts to identify and critique both the symbolic and everyday aspects of culture, and in its focus on the constitutive and political nature of representation, cultural studies offers much to a critical art therapy practice.

Feminisms and cultural theory have come together to enable women to critically explore their position as gendered subjects and to attempt to identify the ways in which bodies are constructed as 'feminine' or 'masculine' through the processes of acculturation. Initially the attention of feminist critics was directed at patriarchy, or the ways in which men and the masculinist social and economic system constrains and regulates women's rights and access to equal opportunities. With the advent of poststructuralist theory and the French feminist psychoanalytic critique, this rather simplistic approach to power relations has been challenged, with a recognition of the dispersed and often contradictory nature of power and subject positions. The notion of subjectivity as fragmented, rather than unified, has also been an important theoretical advance. The poststructuralist perspective argues that individuals may think of themselves as subjects in terms of their gender at some times, but not at others, when their age, ethnicity, social class or sexual preference may be more important ways of identifying the self.

The diversity of methodological and theoretical approaches in feminist writings and practice is reflected in the chapters in this volume. One perspective favoured by several of the authors is that which takes up psychoanalytic theory to address the construction of gender identities via unconscious processes. Others are more interested in the notions of 'empowerment' and healing as they may take place through group work, or in exploring the representation and treatment of women in psychiatry and health care, both in past times and in the present. All authors, how-ever, are unified in their determination to cast a critical eye on feminine identities and the ways that women tend to be marginalised in Western societies. They raise questions about how the meanings of femininity are reproduced and constructed in art works and other forums such as medical and mental health literature, how women experience physical and mental illness and health care as gendered subjects, how such factors as ethnicity, social class and age mediate gender and how characteristics of the art therapist herself, such as pregnancy or her ethnicity, shape her interactions with her clients.

This latter preoccupation fits in with the quite recent interest in the sociology and anthropology of the body, itself influenced by both feminist and Foucauldian theory, which has directed attention towards the ways in which human bodies are constructed through society and culture (see, for example, Turner, 1984, 1992; Scott and Morgan, 1993; Shilling, 1993). In this work, the historically and culturally contingent nature of embodiment has been highlighted. The body is conceptualised as 'inscribed' or 'written on' by culture, regulating the ways in which social relations take place and are organised around gender, race and ethnicity, age and so on (Grosz, 1990). This emphasis has demonstrated that representation and discourse around the body are subject to change, sometimes as a result of direct and conscious intervention. Where once, for example, the hysterical female body, subject to the effects of the 'wandering womb', was a mainstay of European medical practice among the well-to-do in the Victorian era, this body has largely disappeared from contemporary medical epistemology. In its place is the 'pre-menstrual' or 'menopausal' feminine body, a con-struction which serves in a similar function to represent women as highly emotive, subject to unpredictable moods and loss of control due to the instability of their hormone levels.

Feminists have taken up this notion of the inscribed and unstable body, exploring its implications for how we conceptualise and live femininity and masculinity. Some have worked through these issues by using art and performance. Shapiro, for example, had used her multiple roles as dancer, choreographer, woman and academic to work towards what she describes as a 'critical pedagogy of the body' which conceptualises the body as 'a site for critical reflection and understanding of one's life-world . . . the interface of the individual and society' (1994: 65). Her dance work with her female students encourages them to reflect upon the relationship of their own bodies with culture, combining performance with writing and reading tasks. As this suggests, the body itself is not simply shaped by discourse, but is able to construct forms of recalcitrance and resistance, emerging from either the conscious or unconscious levels, generating oppositional discourses.

The emergence of critical cultural representations that highlight the discrimination inherent in dominant discourses and images around certain bodies is evidence of the spaces available to redefine discourse and practice. The advent of the HIV/AIDS epidemic, for example, has generated a lively critique of representation of the gay male body, the lesbian body, the 'at-risk' body and the body with HIV/AIDS. In such books as *AIDS: Cultural Analysis, Cultural Activism* (edited by Crimp, 1989a), *AIDS Demo Graphics* (edited by Crimp, 1990) and *Ecstatic Antibodies. Resisting the AIDS Mythology* (edited by Boffin and Gupta, 1990), gay men, lesbians, people living with HIV/AIDS and others have challenged the dominant frames of representation of risk, HIV/AIDS and homosexuality both through applying cultural theory and producing art works. As Douglas Crimp, a major exponent of 'cultural activism' has contended, the recognition that AIDS exists through social and cultural representations is important to challenge and wrest control of representation, and thus of the 'reality' of AIDS itself. This argument does not seek to challenge the embodied experience of illness, suffering and death that accompanies the syndrome, but rather points to the ways in which such phenomena are inevitably experienced through culture, for 'We know AIDS only in and through those practices' (Crimp, 1989b: 3).

Cultural activism, thus, involves using the insights of cultural analysis to protest against discriminatory and limiting representations of members of minority groups. In the context of health and illness, it allows people who otherwise are positioned as helpless or deviant by virtue of their illness to challenge this positioning. For some years, women have been using art to explore the cultural dimensions of subjectivity, gender and embodiment and engage in cultural activism. One example is Mary Kelly's *Post-Partum Document*, a collection of artefacts around the mother–child relationship exhibited by Kelly in the late 1970s. Through her art work and commentary drawing on theories of psychoanalysis, Kelly sought to expose the creativity as well as the contradictions and frustrations inherent in motherhood. The exhibition included dirty nappy liners and baby's vests, the child's hand imprints and drawings as well as linguistic analyses of the child's acquisition of language and his own early attempts at writing to document progression and change in the relationship as the child moved from the private, narcissistic dyad of the mother–child relationship to the public world. The obsessive detail of the collection of artefacts represented the mother's obsession with her child and her struggle to deal with the separation and loss of the child. In presenting the memorabilia of the child as 'art', Kelly sought to problematise motherhood, questioning the mythology of the 'mother' and highlighting the productive nature of mothering in a culture where the work performed by mothers is largely kept out of sight and stigmatised as unimportant to economic life.

The late British photographer Jo Spence (1986) is one of the best-known feminist exponents of using art as protest in her campaign against the stigmatisation and loss of autonomy over their bodies experienced by people with cancer and other serious illnesses. The chapter in this volume contributed by Spence's colleague, Rosy Martin, elaborates on the technique (phototherapy) they developed together to explore issues around multiple subjectivity, representation, illness and the feminine body. Spence, herself undergoing treatment for breast cancer, used her photographic skills and knowledge of socio-cultural theory to retain a sense of self in response to her illness and medical treatment. She found that the experience of serious illness forced her to confront the power of discourse and representation in ways that had previously not struck her. As she said in an interview:

> I think it was when I was ill that I understood for the first time what it was to be a victim. Previously, all the theory I learnt was head stuff. When I was ill, I suddenly realised that, in reading discourse theory, I was in a discourse, a medical discourse, and I hadn't understood what a discourse was before. Here I was on a production line, as the kind of fodder passing along between doctors and consultants. That was the beginning of it. I began to see how they constructed a world view through the way they worked and what I wanted was irrelevant really. I was the patient, who had to be managed, got better, but I didn't exist, other than what their discourse made me.
>
> (Quoted in Hevey, 1992: 120)

David Hevey, another photographer, has used his skills in conjunction with cultural theory to deconstruct and critique the representation of disabled people in art photography (such as that of Diane Arbus) and charity advertising. Hevey, who describes himself as disabled because of his epilepsy, sought to involve disabled people themselves in constructing their own images. In so doing, he and his participants sought to challenge the patronising images constructed by others which portrayed the disabled as dependent and helpless, needing others' charity or battling on in the face of adversity. As Hevey argues, such imagery serves to construct the disabled as 'other', as symbols of enfreakment (see Hevey, 1992).

The resonances of such work appear throughout this volume in the context of examinations of the therapist–client relationship. Psychoanalytic theory has been a central feature of feminist artists' work that challenges and confronts conventions around the feminine role and body. Sally Skaife's chapter, for example, looks at how a therapist's pregnancy has an impact upon her work with an art therapy group, using psychoanalytic theory to do so. Miche Fabre-Lewin discusses the ways in which the process of art therapy engages participants' bodies and emotions in certain tactile and spatial dimensions. Such analyses bring both the client and the therapist's body into theorising, acknowledging that art therapy and the therapist–client relationship are highly embodied practices. So, too, the art therapy discussed by contributors to the book directs the attention of participants in therapy to their own embodiment as women. One of Susan Hogan's chapters, for example, explores the emotions around the birth process, the transition to motherhood and the death of an infant, focusing on the sense of loss that women often feel. The historical role of the 'psy' disciplines themselves (psychiatry, psychology, counselling), in conjunction with those of fine art and other aesthetic enterprises, require contextual-ising in relation to the development of notions of the self, the body and the mind in Western societies so that endeavours such as art therapy may be understood as part of a broader project to locate and define subjectivity. Another of Susan Hogan's chapters, as well as Maggie Jones's contribu-tion, seek to perform this contextualising role. Other chapters show how a feminist-influenced art therapy can begin to assist specific groups of women – women on housing estates, women who have been sexually abused, women who have breast cancer, older women – to express their discontent at their life situation and begin to counter limiting and stigmatising images pertaining to their situation.

Art therapy, by definition, is directed at individuals who are in some way disadvantaged or distressed. The danger is that the practice of art therapy will do little to challenge these conditions at a socio-cultural level. This book demonstrates that an individual's sense of sorrow, loss, anger, marginalisation and oppression, or her embodied experiences of disability, impairment, abuse, pain or illness are not simply personal. These feelings, emotions and experiences arise from and are interpreted through that individual's place in culture and the social world. As this book demon-strates, a critical art therapy practice and scholarship, informed by social and cultural theory, needs to begin to engage with these ideas, moving away from the personal and towards the political.

BIBLIOGRAPHY

Altman, D. 1994. 'Psycho-cultural responses to AIDS'. In T. Gott (ed.), *Don't Leave Me This Way: Art in the Age of AIDS*. Canberra: National Gallery of Australia: 139–174.

Boffin, T. and Gupta, S. (eds) 1990. *Ecstatic Antibodies: Resisting the AIDS Mythology*. London: Rivers Oram Press.

Crimp, D. (ed.) 1989a. *AIDS: Cultural Analysis, Cultural Activism*. Cambridge, MA: MIT Press.

Crimp, D. 1989b. 'AIDS: cultural analysis/cultural activism'. In D. Crimp (ed.), *AIDS: Cultural Analysis, Cultural Activism*. Cambridge, Massachusetts: MIT Press: 3–16.

Crimp, D. (ed.) 1990. *AIDS Demo Graphics*. Seattle, WA: Bay.

Foucault, M. 1979. *The History of Sexuality, Volume 1: An Introduction*. London: Penguin.

Franklin, S., Lury, C. and Stacey, J. 1991. 'Feminism and cultural studies: pasts, presents, futures'. *Media, Culture and Society*, vol. 13. 171–92.

Grossberg, L., Nelson, C. and Treichler, P. (eds) 1992. *Cultural Studies*. New York: Routledge.

Grosz, E. 1990. 'Inscriptions and body-maps: representations and the corporeal'. In T. Threadgold and A. Cranny-Francis (eds) *Feminine/Masculine and Representation*. Sydney: Allen and Unwin: 62–74.

Hevey, D. 1992. *The Creatures Time Forgot: Photography and Disability Imagery*. London: Routledge.

Lupton, D. 1994. *Medicine as Culture: Illness, Disease and the Body in Western Societies*. London: Sage.

Scott, S. and Morgan, D. (eds) 1993. *Body Matters: Essays on the Sociology of the Body*. London: Falmer.

Shapiro, S. 1994. 'Re-membering the body in critical pedagogy'. *Education and Society*, vol. 12, no. 1. 61–78.

Shilling, C. 1993. *The Body and Social Theory*. London: Sage.

Spence, J. 1986. *Putting Myself in the Picture: A Political, Personal and Photographic Autobiography*. London: Camden Press.

Turner, B. 1984. *The Body and Society: Explorations in Social Theory*. Oxford: Basil Blackwell.

Turner, B. 1992. *Regulating Bodies: Essays in Medical Sociology*. London: Routledge.

Young, I. 1995. 'Gender as Seriality: Thinking about Women as a Social Collective'. In Nicholson, L. and Seidman, S. (eds), *Social Postmodernism: Beyond Identity Politics*. Cambridge: Cambridge University Press: 187–215.

Introduction: visions of difference

Susan Hogan

This book is an exploration of how art therapy can be seen in a social context. All the contributors have thought deeply about the construction and maintenance of gender difference in relation to their specific area of interest. The implications of a greater awareness of gender difference in the theory and practice of art therapy is explored in relation to specific client populations as well as in some more theoretical chapters.

Given that art therapy is a profession dominated by women, there have been surprisingly few publications devoted to gender issues in art therapy (notably those by Wadeson 1989, Talbott-Green 1989). Interest within art therapy in Britain in such issues as gender, race and class has been evinced by the formation of a Race and Culture Group of the British Association of Art Therapists, and several of the contributors to this book are active members of this group (Campbell, Gaga, Fabre-Lewin, Liebmann and Ross). Some art therapists have sought to address subjects which have been informed by feminist scholarship. For example Cathy Malchiodi's work on violence against children (1990). However, as Malchiodi (1996) points out, art therapists have tended to use theories from psychoanalysis (for example Schaverien 1995) rather than philosophies which might more effectively address the concerns of women. This volume illustrates that, despite a lack of literature on the subject, there is no shortage of practitioners willing to address women's issues in art therapy; indeed, it suggests a growing body of knowledge and expertise.

The title 'Visions of Difference' was chosen for this introduction to emphasise that a plurality of approaches to women's issues will be presented in the following chapters. Collectively they represent a broad cross-section of views on the position of women in art therapy. A rich diversity is displayed by the inclusion of chapters from Australia, Britain, Canada, New Zealand and the United States of America.

Diversity is evident in the range of imagery under discussion. Images are shown which were made with different intentions and in a variety of contexts.

Chapter 1 postulates that knowledge of the politics and processes of representation will help art therapists deliver a better service to their clients. This chapter examines a wide range of imagery to make the point; texts discussed range from art work intended for public display to the confidential responses of therapists to their clients' art work.

Many of the art works reproduced and discussed in this book were created within the confidential setting of the art therapist's consulting room or studio. Professional associations which regulate art therapy practice allow for such work to be displayed or published so long as the anonymity of the client is maintained. Clues to the client's identity must be removed from texts or covered over when appearing in images, and pseudonyms must be used in the place of real names. However, it is not uncommon for clients to be keen for their stories to be told; they may exhibit their own art therapy work, or, like the writer Janet Frame, whose powerful novel *Faces in the Water* describes her incarceration in an asylum, they may wish to produce art work based on their experience to critique psychiatric services or in some other way allow their suffering to be of help to others. Or, like another writer, Marie Cardinal, they may wish to record how a particular method of treatment was of benefit to them, or simply produce a testament of their experience. Whatever their motivation, clients may publish an account of their art therapy, exhibit their work, or actively encourage their therapist to do so. In written accounts of art therapy the client has the choice whether to disclose their real name or allow their therapist's account to disclose it. This book contains a mixture of texts in which the clients' identity has been revealed or concealed according to their wishes.

As Deborah Lupton points out in her foreword, some art therapy work is produced with the intention of public display. Such work might well be personally therapeutic but it also frequently seeks to challenge gender conventions or explore ideology in representations of women. The collaborative work of Rosy Martin and the late Jo Spence is a good illustration of this. Such work may be produced primarily as therapy, or primarily as art (the dividing line is sometimes unclear as in the example of Jo Spence's work), but in either case it is intended to end up on the gallery wall.

In Harriet Wadeson's chapter her client becomes an artist through her experience of making art in art therapy, and this is not unheard of. Women undergoing art therapy may produce images which are powerful and eloquent. Therefore clients may be keen to exhibit their work despite the intimate nature of the subject matter.

Diversity is also apparent in the ways authors address the subject of women and art therapy. Many of the chapters address representations of women in texts and images and the politics of feminism and art therapy. These chapters have been grouped together in the front of this book. The first three chapters in particular include an analysis and interpretation of images, many of which were produced for public display (Hogan,

Malchiodi, Jones). The following three chapters (Joyce, Burt, Fabre-Lewin) also contain a useful review of the literature. Different approaches to art therapy group work are then presented followed by individual case studies.

For several decades disciplinary boundaries have been shifting, particularly in the social sciences and the humanities. In psychology increasing attention has been paid to the social construction of illness, with psychologists straying further into territory previously occupied by sociologists and cultural theorists and vice versa. Such theorists have pointed out that women are 'pathologised' in our culture, that the defining characteristics of femininity are considered unhealthy. The effect of this upon women's mental health has been the subject of much feminist enquiry (Howell and Baynes 1981; Showalter 1985; Ussher 1992; Russell 1995).

In disciplines such as psychology, psychoanalysis, cultural studies and literary studies more attention is being paid to language and images as part of discursive practices in the production and maintenance of subjectivity (Lupton 1994: 5). Whereas art therapy was a peripheral practice of little consequence, it has now become much more relevant because of these theoretical shifts. This volume can be seen as constituting part of this general movement. These ideas are likely to halt the drift within British art therapy towards the use of reductive and universally applied dogmatic psychological models which do not represent women's lived experience or sufficiently acknowledge the socially constructed nature of individual distress. In particular, I argue in chapter 1 that drawing on cultural theory derived from semiotics and the work of Foucault (which examines the interrelation between institutions, discourses and practices) will help enrich our thinking about art therapy.

In history also there has been a move away from the emphasis on individual men of genius and large-scale historical generalisation. Historians increasingly see history as consisting of many histories spoken by many voices – variations of cultural pluralism becoming encouraged by cultural policy makers (Hogan 1992). This has had an impact on how gender is perceived; overarching definitions of masculinity or femininity have been rejected as oppressive. These new 'deconstructionist' and 'social constructionist' approaches are significant in their critique of dominant hegemonic structures such as language and accepted forms of knowledge as well as in challenging traditional disciplinary boundaries (Tong 1989: 219). Another result of this shift in thinking towards the particular has been a number of critiques of psychiatry which argue that it is quite possible for a psychiatrist to diagnose mental illness when there may be simply a clash of values between the patient and psychiatrist; and further, that the position of women rejecting dominant patriarchal 'norms' is likely to be seen as 'dysfunctional', rather than as evincing a conflict between the individual and society (Russell 1995: 33–7). Also women are more likely to be defined as in need of 'treatment' rather than 'punishment' and may as a consequence end up with longer custodial sentences. However, any generalisation made about the position of women has to take into account issues of class, race, age and geographical location as important contributory factors in how women are perceived and treated.

Psychiatry as an important gender-regulating mechanism is explored in my opening chapter. The culturally constructed nature of psychiatric illness and how this is linked to gender is illustrated through an examination of representations of women dominant in nineteenth-century medical discourses. The chapter moves on to examine representations of women in fine art, the media, psychoanalytic and literary writings. It explores how these representations are seen by different feminist groups whose analyses, I feel, could prove useful to art therapists in thinking about their work; it explains how normative roles and the construction of gender differences are embodied and sustained in various forms of representation. I argue that art therapists are particularly well placed to examine these cultural constructs and the resultant conflicting messages which can be instrumental in creating mental distress. With a greater appreciation of certain types of cultural theory, which can provide a sophisticated theoretical framework for use in art therapy training and practice, art therapists can enable their clients to explore their experience on a socio-cultural level.

As well as gender, racism is explored by British art therapists Jean Campbell and Doris Abra Gaga in their chapter 'Black on black art therapy'. This chapter poignantly describes the experience of being a black art therapist meeting clients for the first time – a moment for the client of anxiety, surprise, emotional withdrawal or intense pleasure. Issues of identification and transference start at this very moment in the art therapy process. They present a moving account of work with a black woman in which issues of racism are openly explored as part of the art therapy process. Jean and Doris also explore the context in which art therapy takes place where there is an under-representation of black women therapists.

Pregnancy and group art therapy are explored from an analytic perspective by Sally Skaife in 'The pregnant art therapist's countertransference'. The effect of her own pregnancy and the birth of her child on an art therapy group is examined with particular emphasis on the notion of 'countertransference', which is explained.

One woman's experience of giving birth to twins is examined in detail in my chapter 'A tasty drop of dragon's blood: self-identity, sexuality and motherhood'. This case study presents a vivid account of ongoing art therapy from the client's point of view. Issues around Jay's experience of the birth, her changed sense of self-identity and sexuality through pregnancy and childbirth are explored in detail along with her reactions to dominant representations of motherhood. Many of the major issues facing pregnant women and mothers of young children are evident in this chapter which illustrates the empowering potential of art therapy. The images produced are exceptional in quality and expressiveness, making this case study particularly eloquent and intriguing.

Another example of art therapy as empowering for women is given by Marian Liebmann who presents a chapter written by the women using the group. Their words and their voices describe the art therapy experience in her chapter entitled 'Art therapy and empowerment in a women's self-help therapy project'.

In 'Woman and conflict' Carol Ross explores how contention and discord can be particularly difficult areas for women to deal with. Through my own research into gender and organisational dynamics I realise that ideology about 'norms' of masculine and feminine behaviour are very much at play here in regulating behaviour. Women are conceptualised as 'emotional' and 'unstable' – both characteristics disqualifying us from senior management positions (Hogan 1991: 2). However, men are seen as 'combative' (good for management) as well as rational and logical.

Although these stereotypes are breaking down, problems do still exist. For example, if a woman displaying so-called 'masculine' characteristics, who is rational, logical and professional in her manner, comes into conflict with a senior male colleague (especially an older male colleague) who is being irrational, illogical, emotional and childish it is very difficult for colleagues, management or even union representatives to make the conceptual leap necessary to perceive what is going on and take effective action because of the reversal of entrenched gender expectations. Thus the prevention of harassment and bullying in the workplace of women by male colleagues is hampered.

Another difficulty regarding conflict, a theme that Carol Ross takes up in her chapter, is the difficulty that many women still have in speaking out in conflict situations. She explores how gender norms regulate against women being confrontational, assertive and forthright even when a situation might best be dealt with by such a response, for example in response to bullying from a spouse or employer. Traditional female roles (both at home and at work) place women in caring, supporting and nurturing roles which are often at odds with the expression of anger, disagreement or self-interest. Feelings of aggression, competitiveness and ambition may be regarded as 'unfeminine', while passivity and compliance are widely considered as female 'virtues'. Ross's chapter explores how art therapy can assist women to reconcile these contradictions and constraints to feel powerful and be assertive.

A slightly different point of view is put forward by Maggie Jones, from New Zealand, who is interested in the pictorial language used by women psychiatric patients. In her chapter, 'Alice, Dora and Constance', she speculates about how these women speak in a way that is somehow foreign to the values and suggestions with which our everyday language is laden. This is an idea borrowed from Luce Irigaray who believes 'that women's sexuality, identity and language are repressed in patriarchal cultures and that it is this repression that promotes madness . . . This silence is kept in place by the linguistic and logical processes which structure thought' (Russell 1995: 117).

Val Huet in her chapter, 'Ageing: another tyranny?', explores some of the mythology surrounding the female menopause. Germaine Greer has forcefully argued that medical intervention at menopause is an example of male professionals giving full vent to their irrational fear of women, which she carefully documents including some of the more unpleasant so called treatments such as clitoridectomy (Greer 1991: 106). Consumer culture ideology has entered the realm of personal relationships. Individuals trade in their spouses for younger models, as they might do an automobile. This behaviour though clichéd is nevertheless somehow vaguely obscene. Young women are often a trophy for the successful older man who is perhaps incapable of entering into grown-up equal relations with a mature woman and so opts for an incestuous-type relationship with someone the age of a daughter from his first marriage. Of course there is no precise agreement within feminism about such moral issues. However, older women in particular seem to be devalued in this culture. Val explores some of the pressures in Western society on women who are targeted by advertising to keep on looking young for as long as possible. She argues that older women have been badly served by psychotherapy and experience a 'double bias' against their age and their perceived sexlessness. She explores how women who often experience multiple loss at the time of their menopause, such as children leaving home, parents dying or marriage break-up, also encounter a less than sympathetic reception from the medical profession.

The historically and culturally contingent nature of ideas about embodiment has been highlighted in the foreword by Deborah Lupton. Several contributors to this volume explore these ideas further. Cathy Malchiodi takes up the theme of empowerment in her chapter about working as an art therapist with women with breast cancer. In order to demonstrate how art and the art process may be used to empower women with breast cancer, the work of women artists such as Nancy Fried, Richild Holt, Jo Spence, Hollis Sigler, Matuschka, Claire Henze, Deena Metzeger and Alica Williams, who have breast cancer or who have family or friends with breast cancer, are presented and discussed.

Psychotherapists drawing on the work of Freud, which insists that symbols are generated by sexual conflicts, have produced speculative interpretations of the work of individual artists and art objects in general based on oversimplified determinants. All human behaviour is seen as causally determined in terms of a dogmatic schema. The intellectual precursors of art therapy by no means lie only in psychoanalysis (indeed, art therapy should be seen as constituting a plurality of practices with different historical and intellectual origins), but psychoanalytic theory has influenced many art therapists. In Britain it was Ernst Jones who was to wield power and influence in psychoanalytic circles. He founded the British Psychoanalytic Society in 1919. He was responsible for inviting Melanie Klein to England, and helped both Sigmund Freud and his daughter Anna to move to Britain in 1938. The impact of Melanie Klein was felt within psychoanalysis and psychotherapy with the increasing prominence of object-relations theory. This theory was concerned with the developing infant's relationship with their mother. Donald Woods Winnicott was of particular significance to the discussion of how children differentiate themselves from the world and construct an ego and superego. During the post-Second World War period there emerged a renewed emphasis on very early childhood (pre-oedipal) development as being of central importance in the formation of psychopathology, such as 'borderline' or 'narcissistic' personality disorders (Gilman 1993: 1042). Historian Nikolas Rose described the reception of psychoanalytic ideas during this period in Britain: 'Psychoanalysis was to become a theory of development, and, what is more, a theory of the role of the mother in the development of the adjusted and maladjusted ego' (Rose 1990: 164) These ideas were propagated by the Tavistock Institute in particular. Indeed, unconscious hostility of the mother towards the infant was postulated as significant in the aetiology of later disease, and theorists such as Bowlby, who helped to popularise the idea of 'maternal deprivation', argued that if women went out to work their offspring could suffer irreparable psychological damage (Rose 1990: 165–7). In a period of post-war reconstruction in which there was a closure on a massive scale of wartime nursery provision, Bowlby's ideas were perfectly suited to the dominant ideology of the moment.

These ideas about a 'maternal complex' led to an increased regulation of motherhood which has subsequently been critiqued and called into question by sociologists and historians (Rose, 1990: 175–6). Miche Fabre-Lewin challenges an over-reliance on such theory within art therapy. In her chapter, 'Liberation and the art of embodiment', Miche concentrates on how in art therapy we can encourage awareness of our bodies, physical space, the relationship between our bodies and the art materials, gesture, proximity of the client to other group members and to the art therapist. Miche argues that in art therapy practice there is an acknowledgement of the significance of how space is depicted in the image but that much less emphasis is placed on the physicality of our bodily experience, the release of emotions through movement and noise in the therapeutic encounter. She argues that the production and evolution of the image involves a conscious relationship between the object and its maker which is also spatial, tactile and material. According to her, the image conveys more than the diagrammatic, the symbolic and the transferential. Miche postulates that we may have lost our way in art therapy by under-emphasising our physical and material existence. She argues that those art therapists who have aligned their practice to analytic psychotherapy, with its emphasis on bringing to the surface repressed unconscious material, have lost contact with their own body-consciousness. She suggests that we should question theoretical models which concentrate on redressing individual pain and disruptions in early childhood without addressing the social setting within which such postulated deprivation is generated and perpetuated. Furthermore, she suggests that through an increasing emphasis on the language of analytic thought we are losing the more human ways of interacting in art therapy.

Women have been represented in our culture as ruled by our bodies and sexuality, and seen as corrupted and corrupting, sexual, lascivious, sly, untrustworthy and a danger to the moral and social order of society (Hogan 1995). These ideas are explored in several chapters. Helene Burt in her chapter, 'Women, art therapy and feminist theories of development' shows how such ideas about women are evident in the diagnostic manuals used by art therapists in many countries (such as the *Diagnostic and Statistical Manual of Mental Disease – DSM-II-R*, or the *International Classification of Diseases – ICD*) in their work of labelling and/or subsequently treating women patients.

In Jeffrey Masson's courageous book *The Assault on Truth* he revealed the way that Freud had abandoned his initial belief in the confidences of his women patients about their childhood sexual abuse, deciding that these were mere fantasy. Since that book was written a number of studies have claimed a high correlation between instances of childhood sexual abuse (especially incest) and later mental illness. Nevertheless there has been considerable reluctance within psychiatry to embrace these research findings because they threaten the physiological model on which the profession is in part based. The advent of a backlash to these findings characterised by 'false memory syndrome' (particularly evident in the USA) which asserts that these memories are indeed fantasy is also explored in Helene Burt's chapter.

Helene in her chapter also provides a useful critique of mother–infant theories which have influenced the work of some art therapists. This is particularly useful at a time when there seems to be an increasing trend in British art therapy towards concentrating the entire art therapy process in all cases towards the reparation of early and inadequate development, with the assumption that this is a prerequisite for later mental disorder, rather than exploring the social and political dimensions of women's lives. Such an aetiology for mental distress has been questioned by feminist theorists who have emphasised other factors influencing women's mental health, such as the age and number of dependent children at home, lack of satisfying activity outside the home for women with young children and poor communication with their spouse as more important determining factors. The implication of this sort of thinking is, of course, that childcare facilities would be more appropriate than prescriptions of Valium or Prozac (Jordanova, in Russell 1995: 60). Emphasising such considerations as a strategy seems a reasonable way of demanding more child-care facilities and alerting psychiatrists and others to the obvious fact that motherhood is frequently a socially isolating and stressful experience.

Rosy Martin's impressive work in phototherapy is described in 'Looking back and reflecting'. Rosy explains her technique in which past events are re-enacted and re-experienced. This is also possible in art therapy using visual media, but in phototherapy techniques from psychodrama are employed and the subjects can *become* what they wish to explore in a very direct and tangible way. Acting various roles can enable individuals to recapture the spontaneity of fantasy play they found in childhood and to explore their multifaceted identity. The power of the images produced is a testament to the poignancy of this method.

Susan Joyce from the Antipodes provides a detailed critical analysis of research, publications, training and practice in art therapy. Her chapter, 'Feminist-perspective art therapy: an option for women's mental health – an Australian perspective', then speculates about how the emergence of feminist critiques of art therapy could inform future training programmes in art therapy and consequently influence professional practice.

This is the first edited volume to address women's issues in art therapy. The book represents a range of opinion on the subject and will, I hope, stimulate vigorous debate and further publications. It will also allow women who are thinking of engaging in art therapy as clients to get a sense of what is on offer.

We must ensure that art therapy practice continues to challenge those social and cultural conditions which pathologise women and cause distress. This can be done, as this volume illustrates, through a critical engagement with socially constructed notions of gender difference, their production and reproduction, and through an increased awareness of power relations in the client–therapist relationship. To prevent developing an over-reliance within art therapy on neo-Freudian theories (evident in some recent literature), and to encourage a more critical engagement with such theory, I suggest looking at cultural theory which is not psychoanalytically based as a stimulus for a reappraisal of how we work as art therapists. Women as potential users of art therapy services can use their clout as consumers (particularly in the sphere of private practice) to insist on gender-aware art therapy. We have to choose which art therapy practice we want – one that rests on *a priori* and reductive assumptions about subjectivity and produces dogmatic interpretations of women's art work, or an art therapy practice which is expansive and reflexive in its attitudes.

Art therapy can be oppressive (reproducing the socio-cultural content in which individual pain is generated) if it relies on reductive theoretical formulations and focuses on the individual's personality alone, as Deborah Lupton points out in her foreword. Alternatively art therapy can be empowering and liberating, allowing women to challenge their lot and critically apprehend their position in society. This book is a call for, and a reflection of, this latter approach.

BIBLIOGRAPHY

Cardinal, M. 1984. *The Words to Say It: An Autobiographical Novel*. London: Picador.

Faludi, S. 1992. *Backlash. The Undeclared War on Women*. London: Chatto & Windus.

Gilman, S. L. 1993. 'Psychotherapy', in Bynum, W. F. and Porter, R. *Companion Encyclopaedia of the History of Medicine*. London: Routledge.

Greer, G. 1991. *The Change. Women, Aging and the Menopause*. London: Hamish Hamilton.

Hogan, S. 1991. 'Women in Visual Arts Administration: Gender Power and Organisational Dynamics'. *Australian Journal of Arts Administration*. vol. 3. no. 4. Spring.

Hogan, S. 1992. 'The Cultural Melting Pot: Multiculturalism in Australia'. *Aesthetex: Australian Journal of Arts Management*. vol. 4, no. 2, pp. 77–84.

Hogan, S. 1995. 'Ars Longa Vita Brevis – Ars Medica: Exploring Interactions Between Art and Medicine'. *Inscape: Journal of the British Association of Art Therapists*. vol. 2, pp. 19–23.

Howell, E. and Baynes, M. 1981. *Women and Mental Health*. NY: Basic Books.

Lupton, D. 1994. *Medicine As Culture. Disease and the Body in Western Societies*. London: Sage.

Lupton, D. 1995. *The Imperative of Health: Public Health and the Regulated Body*. London: Sage.

Malchiodi, C. 1990. *Breaking the Silence: Art Therapy from Violent Homes*. New York: Brunner/Mazel.

Malchiodi, C. 1996. 'Editorial. Women and Art Therapy' in *Art Therapy: Journal of the American Art Therapy Association*. vol. 13, no. 1.

Masson, J. 1985. *The Assault on Truth*. NY: Harper Perennial.

Rose, N. 1990. *Governing the Soul. The Shaping of the Private Self*. London: Routledge.

Russell, D. 1995. *Women. Madness and Medicine*. Cambridge: Polity.

Schaverien, J. 1995. *Desire and the Female Therapist: Engendered Gazes in Psychotherapy and Art Therapy*. London: Routledge.

Showalter, E. 1985. *The French Malady: Women, Madness and English Culture 1830–1980*. London: Virago.

Talbott-Green, M. 1989. 'Feminist Scholarship: Spitting into the Mouths of the Gods'. *The Arts in Psychotherapy*. 16. (4), pp. 253–261.

Tong, R. 1989. *Feminist Thought*. London: Routledge.

Ussher, J. 1991. *Women's Madness: Misogyny or Mental Illness*. Brighton: Harvester Wheatsheaf.

Wadeson, H. 1989. 'In a Different Image: Are Male Pressures Shaping the 'Female' Professions?' in *The Arts in Psychotherapy*, 16 (4), pp. 327–330.

Chapter 1

Problems of identity
Deconstructing gender in art therapy

Susan Hogan

This chapter will raise a number of important questions for the practice and theoretical development of art therapy. The analysis of images in art therapy should be seen in relation to other types of representation. This should also be done with a more serious recognition and exploration of the effects of power relationships operating within society.

I shall examine contemporary representations of women. Representations include images which in this analysis are not seen as 'mirrors' which simply reflect reality; rather, representations in this usage are conventions and codes which express those practices and forms which condition our experience and therefore in part constitute our reality. I then briefly explore how these representations are seen by different feminist groups. A similar analysis could of course be made of images of men. However, this would entail a separate essay since images of women and images of men function in quite different ways.

Why is such an analysis of relevance or interest? It is relevant in the context of the therapeutic relationship in art therapy practice because representations of women (along with those of race, age, gender and socio-economic situation) all position and limit the individual and have a vital role in determining our subjective reality. These representations have a profound and demonstrable effect on the kind of treatment we may be offered (e.g. ECT or psychotherapy, drugs rather than counselling, inpatient or outpatient care) and the diagnosis we are likely to receive.[1] Art therapists must be keenly aware of the social differences attached to these distinctions. The construction of gender difference sets up different pressures and constraints for women and men. Normative roles are in various ways oppressive and can become for both sexes the source of conflict and anxiety. Because these roles and the very construction of gender difference are embodied and sustained in the images and texts that surround us in our daily lives, art therapists are particularly well placed to examine these conflicting messages.

People often give expression to their experience in metaphorical discourse, which can better conceptualise and articulate their situation. In ideological struggles metaphors are commonly used around a contested site of meaning. This can take the form of pictorial or linguistic strategies to establish one meaning rather than another. When one looks at art therapy pictures with this in mind they can be seen as providing women with a tool for carving out a self-identity which might challenge dominant or hegemonic representations or those representations connected with their particular race, class or gender status.[2]

In this chapter I aim to demonstrate how cultural theory, and feminist cultural theory in particular, can provide a satisfying and more sophisticated theoretical framework for art therapy practice than that provided by psychological theories alone. This chapter briefly surveys some dominant ideas within psychiatry about gender difference. It will then present some feminist ideas on the subject of representations of women.

In art therapy there is a triangular relationship which involves the therapist, the client and the art object. For both client and therapist the art object can be a depiction of how they see the client's position in the world. This process of representation is central to the therapeutic process. This chapter will argue for a greater awareness of the construction of gender difference in society and the way that this is maintained through images and in language in the art therapy process.

THE CONSTRUCTION OF GENDER

I use the word 'construction' deliberately. Gender is not to be taken as a given but rather as a socially derived set of meanings which are then ascribed to the physical body. A useful idea to help us think about this process of construction is that of intellectual hegemony. This is a dominant set of ideas which 'exists not only in political and economic institutions and relationships but also in active forms of experience and consciousness' (Williams 1983: 145). The dominant ideas constitute knowledge which is taken for granted or perceived as 'common sense'. My argument here will be that the meanings ascribed to gender will always be linked to the struggle for hegemony in a particular community. While some portray gender as a fixed entity dependent upon the physical aspects of being a body with certain functions I will argue that the meaning of gender is always open to challenge. The contestation comes from those who wish to challenge the dominant or established order. The hegemony and its rival is evident in representations.

Art therapists therefore need to be better informed about social theory and require a theoretical framework which will incorporate change in representations of gender. The main problem with the concept of hegemony is that it may be perceived as representing social power as unified, coherent and centralised, when clearly this is not the case. The dominant representation is the result of conflict rather than of consensus and it can only become the hegemony by suppressing other alternatives. Foucault's idea of power as 'dispersed constellations of unequal power relationships, discursively constituted in social fields of force' is a useful one to keep in mind.[3] I interpret this to mean that historical analysis should seek to expose discursive practices – in other words those regulated and organised sets of procedures and practices and statements that create and maintain definitions such as 'madness' or 'art'. The 'dispersed constellations of unequal power relationships' I take to mean competing groups or hegemonies within and constituting such discourses. The 'social fields of force' I interpret as referring to race, nationality, educational level, gender and social standing and the interconnections between these, which are embedded in and sustained by practices of representation.[4] This discussion should be located within the tradition of Western medical practice. It should also include analysis of the fine art and literary traditions of the West, as well as consideration of gender representation in the mass media. Gender representation in all of these contexts should be seen as of fundamental importance to how gender difference is perceived and how health is defined.

The construction of gender difference comes from the interaction of several discourses and the complex task of attempting to ascertain, illustrate and expose the constructs at play is the act of deconstruction. The suggestion here is that the art therapist should learn to deconstruct their client's 'dis-ease'. This is, I suspect, what many art therapists are doing intuitively, but not articulating the process in these terms.

REPRESENTATIONS OF WOMEN IN PSYCHIATRIC DISCOURSE AND THE GENDERED CLINICAL GAZE

A brief examination of some of the dominant historical discourses within psychiatry on women's supposed nature and health should serve to illustrate how culturally and historically specific and subject to change such ideas are. Women have been represented historically as threatening the moral order and social stability of society. We were (and still are) portrayed as dangerous and dishonest (like children) and more controlled by our biology than are men.

Recent media attention on PMT or PMS (Pre-Menstrual Syndrome) is an interesting example of this. In a recent murder enquiry the wife was acquitted because she was suffering from PMS when she stabbed her husband to death in the kitchen of their home. The court heard that they were normally a very happy couple and 'in love' with each other. This emphasis could be contrasted with men who have abnormally high testosterone levels in their bodies before committing violent acts. I have not come across this used as a defence in court yet, whilst mention of PMS is now common as an explanation of women's violent acts.

The development of the 'clinical gaze' marked a movement away from the classificatory medicine of the seventeenth century which was based on the idea of the four humours, dating back to the medicine of ancient Greece. Foucault argued that along with this shift of emphasis within medicine a new interest arose in the pathogenesis of disease. As physicians shifted their attention from written texts to patients' bodies a central feature of medical learning became the medical examination or revealing the therapeutic 'gaze' to students. In the late eighteenth century the gaze became an amalgam of certain aspects of the mesmeric tradition,[5] and a gaze of subjugation used by the 'moral treatment' practitioners in the task of encouraging the insane person to internalise disciplinary norms.[6] In Britain it was only through embracing these Enlightenment-influenced ideas, and associated practices, that the newly created medical special-isation of psychiatry was able to gain increasing control of the formally *laisser-faire* management of madhouses.[7]

As the power of institutional psychiatry increased, the nineteenth century physician's gaze began to look for the precursors of 'disease' as well as for overt symptoms. In looking for the effects of hereditary disorder or taint almost any behaviour could be defined as evincing the precursors of malady and resulted in the confinement of middle class women. Independent acts, especially women's rights activism, were likely to be defined as 'hysterical'.[8]

A dominant discourse in the nineteenth century was that of biological determinism: the idea that shared behavioural norms, and the social and economic differences between human groups (primarily races, classes and sexes) arise from inherited, inborn distinctions. In the nineteenth century, society was taken to be an accurate reflection of biology (Gould 1981: 20). In this mode of thought women are seen as representing the most 'inferior forms of evolution' and were argued to be 'closer to children and savages than to adult civilised man'. A late nineteenth-century quotation from Le Bon goes thus: 'they excel in fickleness, inconsistency, absence of thought and logic and incapacity to reason' (Le Bon, founder of French social psychology, 1895: 104, cited in Gould 1981: 35).

In such nineteenth-century 'evolutionary theory' women were seen as representing a lower form of life along with other social groups. Certain sets of social relations existed and evolutionary theory was used to justify them. The application of evolutionary theories was simply a matter of analogy. Equated through likeness are women, criminals, children, beggars, the Irish and the insane – all of whom were lacking in social power and were likened to 'primitives' or to 'savages' (Stocking 1987: 229).[9]

Ideas about the differences between men and women were evident in psychology and physiology; some nineteenth-century theories of heredity assumed that women were responsible for the reproduction of the 'inside' (the internal viscera, emotions and piety) whilst the father was thought to be responsible for the external musculature and skeletal development, and analytic capabilities (Smith-Rosenberg and Rosenberg, 1973: 337). In the nineteenth century and until the 1920s males were seen as passing through a 'woman stage' on their way to maturity.[10] The dominant attitudes in the early Victorian era relating to gender and sex were patriarchal and repressive. As Blackstone had put it in the eighteenth century, upon marriage a wife's 'very being or legal existence' was incorporated into that of her husband, and this situation had not significantly changed by the Victorian period. Contemporary nineteenth-century medical opinion sustained the view that woman was a being 'little capable of reasoning, feeble and timid' (Stocking 1987: 197).

The prevalence of the image of the fallen woman in the nineteenth century conveys a preoccupation with the threat of uncontrolled female sexuality (Stocking 1987: 199). Charcot's hysterics represent the apotheosis of Victorian sexual containment and supervision. The hysteric represents above all else unrepressed female sexuality (Jacobus 1993).[11] For English Victorian society women represented what civilised society must overcome (Stocking 1987: 207).

The subordinate roles assigned to women have attracted an elaborate body of medical and biological justification. In the nineteenth century a variety of social characteristics were assumed to have a biological cause. In particular women were seen as having delicate muscles, which meant that they became easily exhausted, and, according to Dr Tracy in 1827, as having a 'more irritable' nervous system. They were endowed with 'greater sensibility' and were 'liable to more frequent and stronger impressions from external agents or mental influences' (Smith-Rosenberg and Rosenberg 1973: 334). Women were also considered to be more susceptible to nervous disorders because of their reproductive physiology (Bassuk 1986: 145; Doane 1986: 152). Victorian physicians believed in a theory known as 'reflex-irritation', a sympathy between all bodily organs. It was through electrical transmission along the nerves that irritation from the ovary or uterus could reach the brain and result in hysteria (Bassuk 1986: 146).

One nineteenth-century medic emphasised the supposed importance of women's reproductive organs thus: 'as if the Almighty in creating the female sex had taken the uterus and built the woman round it' .[12] Because the uterus was believed to be connected to the nervous system, shocks to the nervous system might also alter the reproductive cycle. The gestating foetus could be affected by emotional states (Smith-Rosenberg and Rosenberg 1973: 340). In nineteenth-century America orthodox medical doctrine taught that the brain and the ovaries were not able to develop simultaneously.[13] Doctors insisted that during puberty a girl's vital energies must be devoted to the development of her ovaries. In Britain Henry Maudsley (1835–1918) argued that the intellectual training of young women could have dire consequences including permanent injury to their reproductive systems and their brains.[14] Herbert Spencer justified the limitation of women's political rights on evolutionary grounds: the vital needs of reproduction arrested their individual mental evolution at an earlier age, and their characteristic mental traits (notably intuition and dissimulation) were those adapted to 'dealing with infantile life'. Spencer did not support Mill's 1867 parliamentary petition for women's suffrage in the same year as these written remarks.[15] The belief that too much education would ruin their health and reproductive capabilities made individual women's personal ambitions seem trivial in relation to their genetic responsibility. These ideas are analogous to the recent 'foetal protection' debates in which women have increasingly been discussed in terms of being a potential health hazard to their foetuses. The maternal–foetal unity is not acknowledged in this debate (Hogan 1991: 4). Smith-Rosenberg makes a convincing case that biological justifications were used in nineteenth-century America to limit women's access to further education. Showalter (1985: 18) points out that during the decades 1870 to 1910 middle-class women in Britain were beginning to organise themselves to try to gain access to higher education and entrance to the professions as well as political rights. At the same time as these demands were being made, diagnoses of female nervous disorders such as anorexia nervosa, neurasthenia and hysteria became endemic.

Images created of gender should be seen as of pivotal importance in creating definitions of female insanity. Many images of mad women, such as the etching by Brouillet, were displayed in the huge amphitheatre where Charcot gave demonstrations of women hysterics to medical audiences. These images gave the cue of what was expected to those mad women 'performing' under the gaze of these medical audiences. In the psychiatric photography of Hugh Welch Diamond photographs functioned to document signs of degeneration or insane physiognomy, and also as a therapeutic tool. The latter was a salutary reminder of personal appearance. The objectification of women in medical discourse in the late nineteenth century seems to be accompanied by a silencing of women. For example, 'If a patient . . . interrupts . . . she must be told to keep silent and to listen'. A stern disciplinarian disregard of what women were feeling seems to have become the established practice.[16]

Drawing on the work of Michel Foucault, Christopher Tilly (1990) makes the point that it is changing social conditions which gave rise to the development of discourses which justify the confinement and special treatment of individuals at any given time:

> In the sixteenth century the mad did not constitute a homogeneous social category . . . It was not the mad who were locked up on a consis-tent basis but lepers. At the end of the sixteenth century a profound shift occurred in conceptions of the mad. They now became a dangerous

category and the emptying of the vast leper houses of mediaeval Europe was accompanied by the filling of the social space – a space of confinement and exclusion – with the mad, who effectively became objects rather than subjects. But the mad were confined not as an isolated class but with all those other social categories deemed dangerous: the poor, the sick, vagabonds and criminals.

Madness was not designated a sickness but merely the converse of reason: unreason. It was alternatively conceptualised as a regression to a child like state or as a form of bestiality. The mad were not properly human and thus could be treated like animals.

Another shift in conception occurs at the end of the eighteenth century, represented by reformers such as Tuke and Pinel who released the mad from their chains. Insanity becomes regarded as an illness to be treated through medicine. The insane become segregated from other antisocial groups but Foucault argues that this was a product of political interventions rather than as a result of an advancement in the understanding of the insane. The mad began to be isolated in a specific institutional site, the asylum, not as an effect of liberal concern for their plight but because other social groups were now treated differently. It was economically inefficient to confine the poor: large populations of workers were now required to fill the factories of the industrial revolution. The criminal class, now considered even more of a menace to private property, should not be mixed up with the insane for the hope of reforming them. The birth of the asylum for the sole treatment of the mad rather than being a liberation resulted in an even more profound confinement, and the development of a special class of practitioners to deal with problems the mad posed – psychiatrists. An opposition between reason and madness was complete. Madness is no longer simply unreason but a pathology to be cured, and the psychiatrist working at his or her institutional site decides who is mad. Committal to an asylum defines someone as mad.

(Tilly 1990: 20)

Clearly medical practice embodies and perpetuates beliefs and norms linked to institutional arrangements, which are historically specific and subject to change. It is this recognition of historically specific institutional orthodoxies and their effect on the individual that has led art therapists to wish to address gender issues as part of the art therapy process.[17]

Today art therapists working with specific groups (specific racial groups, for example, or single-sex groups) attempt to integrate their practice with social theory. This has been done in a number of ways with themes in art therapy to address specific issues (blackness, single parenthood, AIDS and so on). The client is not seen as an individual neurotic but as a person negatively affected by social norms which may not be rational, constructive

Figure 1.1 Charcot lecturing on hysteria at the Salpêtrière, 1887 by André Brouillet

or positive. In such an approach to art therapy practice and theory clients can be enabled to draw strength from a clearer perception of themselves in society. In this socio-cultural or 'social art therapy' the unconscious is a metaphor, and symptoms are 'signs of social relations disguised as natural things, concealing their roots in human reciprocity' (Taussig 1980). In other words, psychiatric symptoms are socially constructed as well as individually experienced.

SOME FEMINIST IDEAS ON REPRESENTATIONS OF GENDER

I have used the plural – ideas – as there seems to be an assumption that feminist theory is homogeneous (certainly in the popular press and also in some academic work). Moreover, feminism is seen (particularly by the popular press) as being strident, always anti-male, and lacking in restraint.

It is important to recognise the complexity of theories within feminism and that there are differences within the feminist movements which should be acknowledged. However, what the groups all have in common is an interest in the position of women in society and an acknowledgement that women do not have equal rights with men. Many of the feminist groups share a common concern about the construction of gender differences and how these are institutionalised.

Within the feminist movement(s) analysis of images is diverse. For example, within feminism the image of a mother and child can, on the one hand, be attacked for reproducing notions of femininity wholly defined by motherhood; or it can, on the other hand, be argued to present a positive picture of women as mothers in a society in which this role is undervalued. The 'meaning' of the representation is generated by the reader of the image, the depiction itself, and the intertextual space of all the other images of mothers and children. The viewer/reader of the text constructs the meaning of the text, and the intended meaning of the artist/author does not hold a privileged position. However, there are preferred meanings which may be generated by actual content. Alternative meanings are therefore generated not by new content or a changed 'consciousness' but as a result of a different strategy for production of the image 'in relation to its inter-textual space' (Cowie 1977: 20) A crucial part of the identity of women is formed by the representations of women that surround us.

In an essay entitled 'Virility and Domination in Early 20th Century Vanguard Painting' Carol Duncan persuasively argued that assertions of virility and aggressive male sexuality were particularly evident in the images produced of female nudes. In contrast to John Berger, who points out the passive sexuality in the classical female nude which is painted for the male spectator/owner, Duncan goes further and points to the brutalising quality of many of the images painted by artists such as Kirchner, Heckel, Picasso and Valminick. Duncan writes of these nudes: 'these women show no or few signs of human consciousness of any kind'. They are reduced, she argues, to objects of pure flesh (Duncan 1983: 31).

Representations based on ideas about sexual differences have been critiqued not just in the media and in the visual arts, but also in scientific discourses, jurisprudence and so forth. The body is seen as the 'ground' on which socio-political determinants take hold and are realised. Received representations of the body are of pivotal importance in creating a definition of sexual difference (de Lauretis 1986: 2).[18]

Such ideas have been explored by the feminist artist Barbara Kruger. The Kruger poster (Figure 1.2) is evocative in several ways. Firstly, the overt suggestion that the woman's face is a 'battleground' conjures up the repugnant image of jack boots marching on a woman's face. She connotes this brutal image as an analogy for the abuse done to women's bodies, from female genital mutilation to the compulsory sterilisation or evisceration of female hysterics. She articulates the point that the body is the 'ground' on which socio-political determinants take hold and are realised. This particular example of Kruger's work provides a critique of the neighbouring image and is given an added immediacy and punch by both its scale and its location. It is situated next to an anti-abortion campaign poster which

Figure 1.2 'Your body is a battleground' billboard next to a pro-life
advertisement. Untitled photograph by Barbara Kruger, 1989.

depicts a disembodied foetus. The material fact of the maternal–foetal
unity is denied pictorially in the anti-abortion poster. The rights afforded
to women precisely because of this physical unity are also implicitly denied
by this sort of representation which could result in legislation reducing
women's control over their bodies.

Another photographer whose work is evocative, in a more indeterminate
way, is Elaine Pelot Kitchener. Figure 1.3 is part of a series, 'On the Cross',
depicting Australia's most glamorous city's sleazy underbelly. The photograph conjures up the idea of the body as the site of the material inscription
of the ideological. The woman depicted is being literally inscribed. She
looks drugged or drunk; he is in control, alert. An analogy is evoked for
how women are drugged (literally with prescribed tranquillisers) or metaphorically through the prevailing hegemony which acts as a 'drug' or 'veil'
that we cannot overcome or see through. The photograph is ambiguous,
perhaps the woman is one of the many prostitutes of Sydney's King's
Cross? She endures the pain of the tattoo to make herself more sexually
alluring to her clients or pimp.

In art therapy the produced images cannot be seen as just peculiar to the
individual. Nor can the art therapy context be seen as somehow neutral
space. The context and the images produced are part of a larger system of
meanings.[19]

Because psychology has influenced art therapy, feminist theorists who
use psychological formulations to explain the subject's gender identity and

Figure 1.3 'On the Cross', *King's Cross*, 1989 by Elaine Pelot Kitchener

its production and reproduction are relevant to this discussion. Nochlin (1989: 32) put it thus: 'The need to comply to be inwardly at one with the patriarchal order and its discourses is compelling, inscribing itself in the deepest level of the unconscious, marking the very definitions of the self-as-women in our society.' An example of such a patriarchal discourse is the assertion that the male gaze is considered to be *the* erotic discourse. This being so, other modes of perception about eroticism are rendered peripheral or hard to grasp. Although the imperative of the male gaze has subsequently come under fire as an inadequate response to the complexity of visual experience, such thinking resulted in Griselda Pollock's argument that there is a contradiction or tension between the woman as artist occupying the masculine position as the subject of the look and the traditionally feminine position of being the object of the look (Pollock 1988: 86).[20] Certainly, to take this idea further, I would argue that women can experience what might be called 'collective masochism'. It would seem that women experience erotic stimulation from fantasies which contain elements of degradation, submission, sexual force, rape, brutality and loss of control in a way that men do not generally. This is *not* to suggest that erotic stimulation might be gained from these things in 'real life'. On the contrary, women who would find sexual domination or being sexually submissive abhorrent in 'real life' may respond erotically to the idea of male forcefulness or self-degradation in fantasy. Thus representations of women

Figure 1.4 Life class, 1905, Chicago Art Institute

are internalised by women.[21] Griselda Pollock also argues that if women are unable to produce a different way of looking then they must assume a masculine position or masochistically enjoy the sight of women's humiliation (Pollock 1988: 85). This is an idea supported by Ussher (1991: 182) who writes that 'women live in a culture where men's power is eroticised through romantic fiction, pornography and film – and we cannot deny that many women find it erotic, and, indeed, many feel guilty for doing so'.

There is a binary opposition in the way that men and women are depicted as – active versus passive, looking or being seen, being a voyeur or an exhibitionist, being the subject or the object of the work (Pollock 1988: 87). Nochlin (1989: 3–4) gives the example of *The Oath of the Horatii* by Jacques-Louis David as being quintessential of this division. Nochlin argues that this painting, composed of a group of male figures on the left side of the composition standing in vigorous postures swearing allegiance to Rome on swords held before them, and a group of drooping women (seated and swooning) on the right hand side of the picture (and taking up less space on the canvas than the men), contains the ideology that strength and weakness are the natural corollaries of gender difference; the image, she argues, is intended to illustrate an opposition between strength and weakness. Examples of her idea of 'binary division' are very evident in modern advertising, which typically depicts men in taut, erect poses and women in languid, floppy poses. The woman as a consumer item, often depicted in a laid-out manner or in a passive pose, is very evident in many examples of advertising.

In terms of medical discourse women may also be seen as the object of the male gaze. Mary Anne Doane asserts that at the foundation of psychoanalysis is the assumption that there is an intrinsic pathology in womanhood. Citing Phyllis Chesler (1972: 75) she points out that

> Although the ethic and referent of mental health in our society is a masculine one, most psychoanalytic theoreticians have written about women. It is thus as an aberration in relation to the unattainable norm that the woman becomes narratively 'interesting', the subject for a case history. A narrativisation of the women which might otherwise be fairly difficult is facilitated by the association of women with the pathological ... There is a tendency to 'medicalise' the woman.[22]

This idea is also supported by Bassuk's research on the Victorian 'rest cure', which recommended that the women patients become less hysterical and more obsessional. She writes: 'the obsessional characteristics of masculinity were more desirable than the emotional and expressive style of women' (Bassuk 1986: 144).[23] It is therefore clear that women are represented both as intrinsically pathological and as the subject of male power and control.

Several feminist groups criticise representations of women displayed as sex objects or as passive rather than active agents. Excessive femininity is also criticised for pragmatic reasons (putting on make-up wastes time, high-heeled shoes debilitate women) but the underlying idea is that women should not be preoccupied with making themselves into decorative objects for the male viewer. There has been a tendency, therefore, to reject traditional female/feminine modes of dress.

Representations of women in misogynistic crime-thriller material and pornography as raped, murdered, beaten, tortured and so on are extensions of how women are portrayed in 'normal' life (as passive, unable to defend themselves, and as sex objects for the male viewer/taker). Portrayals such as the recent novel *American Psycho*, in which a women is cut up with a chain-saw for the sexual gratification of a male, are the extreme manifestations of a continuum which extends into everyday life. Women are cut up in advertising all the time, just as they are routinely raped and murdered on television and in films. Bits of women's bodies are seen on the back of buses, on trains, billboards, posters and in all media to a much greater degree than are chopped-up images of men. The chopping-up of women is therefore considered to be perfectly natural in the context of advertising; it is only when the metaphor is relocated that it becomes potentially abhorrent.

Figure 1.5 is a photograph of a butcher's shop window. The pig-woman wears only stockings and lies plump, voluptuous. Her pose echoes those used in classical paintings of nudes. She is sexually available and she is also a piece of meat ready for carving up. The pig-woman will be mutilated

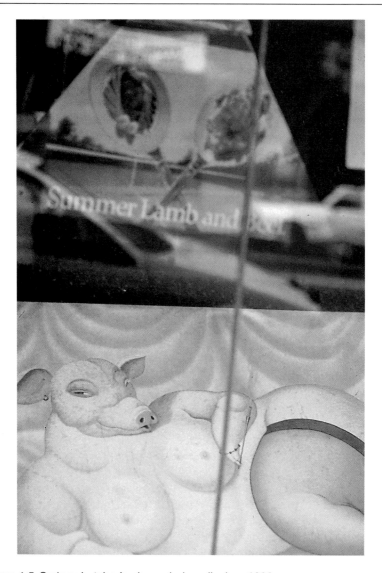

Figure 1.5 Sydney butcher's shop window display, 1992

by the butcher's knife. This is reinforced by the context as behind the pig-woman appear posters of bloody cuts of red meat and the butcher's chopping-blocks. This photograph is a particularly plain illustration of how women are portrayed as passive and unable to defend themselves and as sex objects for the male viewer/taker/consumer. There is a distinct connotation of impending sexual violence, created by the location, in this particular example.

Drawing on the work of deconstructionist philosophy, Nochlin (1989) makes the important point that in representations of women 'ideology' manifests itself as much by what is unspoken, unthinkable, unrepresentable as by what is articulated in a work of art or advertising.[24] So we can start to think about the absence of images of women working in certain fields, or defending themselves against male violence, or example. Locating absences in representations of women has been a preoccupation of some feminist groups and is evinced in some artistic strategies. Provocative challenges have also been made to accepted notions of gender by both male and female artists such as Della Grace or Joel-Peter Witkin. This particular example of Grace's work has been subverted by the *Guardian* newspaper's ridiculing title 'The Bearded Lady', with its connotations of circus freaks.

Another feminist strategy, one not so helpful to art therapy practice in my view, has been a move towards essentialism. This has been particularly evident in literature with the development of *l'écriture féminine* or 'writing in the feminine'. This movement has drawn on the work of Roland Barthes, neo-Freudian Jacques Lacan and the deconstructionist philosopher Jacques Derrida. Writers such as Hélène Cixous have attempted to disrupt the patriarchal symbolic order embedded in language. However, since gender is contingent and subject to changing definition, essentialist strategies are intellectually problematic, in my view. Rather I agree with art historian Linda Nochlin, who makes the same point as Raymond Williams, Hebdidge and others that 'ideology' functions to veil overt power relations making them appear to be part of the natural, eternal (or hegemonic) order.

Womens claims to equality and power are largely symbolic (tokenistic or mythic). Because of woman's impotence she has become symbolically very powerful (representing various essences in different cultures) and women are quick to draw upon symbolic representations in art therapy sessions. For example, men are often depicted as both coming from and returning to woman (Mother Earth). Whilst identification with the symbolic might be argued to be potentially empowering, remaining in the realm of the symbolic might serve as a palliative. The novelist Angela Carter offers a harsh critique of the women's movement's fascination with mythic versions of women:

> If women allow themselves to be consoled for their culturally determined lack of access to the modes of intellectual debate by the invocation of hypothetical great goddesses, they are simply allowing themselves to be flattened . . . All the mythic versions of women, from the myth of the redeeming purity of the virgin to that of the healing, reconciling mother, are consolatory nonsenses . . . Myth deals with false universals, to dull the pain of particular circumstances.
>
> (Carter 1979: 5)

Figure 1.6 Lesbian photographer Della Grace – 'The Bearded Lady', 1995

Figure 1.7 Man with Dog, Mexico, 1990 by Joel-Peter Witkin

TOWARDS A FEMINIST ART THERAPY

Advances in cultural theory have disrupted practice in many disciplines and will inevitably cause a review of art therapy procedures, despite their limited impact to date. The reason for this apparent unwillingness to engage in self-reflection may be fear that current practice within art therapy is, if not untenable, then deeply flawed and cannot be held up to detailed scrutiny.[25]

In my view, art therapy should be a reflexive and self-critical discipline. Otherwise, instead of helping individuals to explore their crises, we will unwittingly obscure and overlay them with our own interpretations of psychological theory. (Therapists providing interpretations of their clients art work along fixed theoretical lines are either imposing their own fantasies or that of a theorist onto the patient's art work, or more likely a mixture of both.) What I suggest, to avoid this pitfall, is a fundamental return to the notion of individuality. I am arguing against the application of universal theories and putting forward the idea that an examination of the particular circumstances of an individual should be enabled in art therapy. This analysis should not be done in a theoretical vacuum but in relation to representational systems, institutional and discursive practices which create our understanding of subjectivity, illness, insanity and health. Such a renewed focus on the individual (as the site of suffering and distress) liberates art therapy from developing an over-reliance on, and rigid adherence to, set theories and *a priori* categories of meaning inherent in theoretical orthodoxy, which can obscure as much as illuminate human suffering.

Although there isn't an orthodox or 'standard' art therapy but rather a plurality of approaches in use today, there has been a shift in recent years in Britain towards placing more emphasis on the transference and counter-transference in the relationship between the art therapist and the client (Dalley 1994: 2). Whilst an acknowledgment of the effect of the therapist upon the situation is to be welcomed, some of the theories associated with psychoanalytic psychotherapy must be open to question since they have particularly negative implications for women.[26] Some of these negative theoretical assumptions are explored in later chapters (Burt, Huet, Jones, Joyce, Campbell and Gaga) so I will not dwell on them at length here.

As I have illustrated, feminist interventions seek to expose power relations between the sexes, the social construction of gender difference and the role that representations play in the construction of gender difference. Pollock (1988) insists that gender difference is produced by an interconnecting series of social practices and institutions of which families, education, art studies, galleries and magazines are a part. These ideas are very important to art therapy practice because a critical analysis of how representations are constructed and the effect that this has on women should inform the art-therapeutic process. For example, because the body is often the 'ground' on which socio-political determinants are realised, women often experience great ambivalence about their own physical bodies. A greater awareness of the construction of representational systems within art therapy training and practice makes this an understandable reaction of women rather than a neurotic one. As the female body is a hotly contested site of meaning it is hardly surprising that women are confused about their bodies. The individual woman is more likely to come to terms with her body with a greater awareness of these systems of representation. This shift in perspective in art therapy theory will result in changes in art therapy practice. For example, more analysis of the current position of different social groups could become part of the art therapy process.[27] This can be achieved through analysis of representations of these groups. This need not be difficult and theoretical, but could, in the first instance, simply provide the opportunity for individuals to express their feelings about images, texts, the media and so on – a process not so very different from what feminists used to call 'consciousness-raising'. (I mean this in its most positive sense, as a critical and analytic exploration of the constraints of gender, rather than the acquisition of set beliefs.) If there is a desire on the part of the client then further critical analysis of representations of gender could form part of the therapeutic process.[28] At the very least the art therapist should be willing to explore with the client the details of their here-and-now socio-economic existence, rather than steering the art therapy to an examination of early childhood experiences which are viewed through a lens of reductive theory (or an interpretation of any material which arises in these terms), or to an analysis of group dynamics which avoids dealing with all the presenting issues. Whatever the specific techniques used, the art-therapeutic process must be capable of enabling women to understand, question and challenge the social and cultural conditions which are responsible for definition as 'mad' or 'deviant'.

What constitutes reality and how it is perceived can mean for the client the difference between incarceration and liberty; the difference between ongoing torment or emotional release. Some art therapists working today are using rigid and inflexible psychological and developmental theories in their work and applying these to their clients' art work and behaviour. As a result they are imposing ridiculous, arid, outdated and often misogynistic ideas about psychic development onto their patients. These art therapists are busy manufacturing metaphors from their clients' art work, analysing the process and interpreting the art work in a way which reflects their own (not their patients') sense of reality and particular theoretical persuasion. Dorothy Rowe points out:

> In dynamic psychotherapy there is a hierarchy, just as there is in psychiatry. The psychotherapist is superior, and the patient inferior. The

psychotherapist, by virtue of his knowledge, training and special insight has access to truths above and beyond the capacity of the patients. The psychotherapist's truths have a higher truth value than the patient's truths. The psychotherapist interprets the patient's truths and tells him what they *really* mean.[29]

Are those art therapists working with a model of the Oedipus complex or using the notion of the Kleinian 'paranoid-schizoid position' (at which a client may supposedly be arrested), who couch their interventions in these terms, actually helping their patients at all? Worse still, is the art therapist working to an agenda and not making this evident to the client? In simple terms, are such art therapists just making confused people more confused through their use of strange interpretative schemas which do not correspond with the client's sense of reality? I am not suggesting that this confusion is merely the inability of the patient to understand the peculiar and jargon-ridden language favoured by some therapists. Are art therapists exacerbating their clients' suffering by *overlaying it with their own version of reality?* I suggest they are and that this constitutes in extreme cases a form of psychic abuse. How can we reconcile such an explanation of internal 'reality' to the idea that subjectivity is formed by our social context? If we agree it is formed by our social context, then are art therapists who are working in the former paradigm (using dogmatic concepts from psychoanalysis) abusing their clients – or at best subjecting them to thoughtlessness and lack of acknowledgement? Catherine McKinnon points out the danger of this very forcefully in her criticism of psychoanalytic theory for its failure to acknowledge childhood sexual abuse as real rather than fantasy. Speaking of psychiatric writings, she describes the 'fantasy' not as the women's but as the 'elaborate alibis for the perpetrators, and their fantastic theoretical constructions of the victims' accounts . . . The fantasy theory is the fantasy.' Of Freud and his contemporaries she says that 'they appear to have shared a mass sexual hallucination that became a theory that became a practice that became a scientific truth because men wanted it that way' (in Masson 1986, xiv–xv). She calls for a new paradigm of the psyche.

Art therapist John Henzell noted a tendency in art therapy and psychotherapy which he refers to as a 'reductive psychodynamics'. He writes:

The creation of an image is a work of the imagination . . . It is always, particularly if it is a poetic image, a work without precedent. If in our research and practice we insist too much on the degree to which expression is disturbed by the psychological antecedents so powerfully demonstrated by psychoanalysis, we will miss what these demonstrations miss. The work of the therapist, because it feels an obligation to reduce this disturbance, to explore its origins, and expiate suffering, too often overlooks the felicity with which the patient makes his or her meaning felt.

(Henzell 1995: 199–200)

I think that Henzell is being rather tentative here. Art therapists often miss the point and negate the self-expression of their clients by imposing a reductive theoretical perspective onto the art work.

The imposition of 'reductive psychodynamics' or rigid theoretical constructs from psychoanalytic psychotherapy onto the art therapy client has resulted in the writing of some seductive fiction which poses as 'scientific' writing. This fiction plots an inner world of infantile experience acted out in art therapy, and is full of metaphorical illusions, analogies and symbolic meanings. These writings (usually case studies) have tremendous poetic appeal. They are particularly alluring since they claim to tell what is *really* going on in the client's mind and art work. They are particularly dangerous because of their tendency to pathologise any resistance to this procedure.[30] This is condescending enough but such fictions are completely abstract and remote when seen in the context of people's lives – from the site of suffering, of abuse of power, social isolation, powerlessness, poverty and deprivation, institutionalised violence, racial hatred and misogyny, discriminatory practice and thwarted ambition, guilt and shame.[31]

Ralph Pickford, who practised art therapy before formal training existed, interpreted his clients' pictures.[32] Pickford also suggested that pictures already produced, to which the patient could 'free associate', provided both an opportunity for therapy (through a process of regression and integration of repressed material) and diagnosis. The pictures he argued could be interpreted to illustrate unconscious conflicts. It is worth giving a detailed example of his work as it represents a particularly clear illustration of dogmatic interpretation: first, an example of a child's response to a picture at the Notre Dame Child Guidance Clinic in Glasgow:

> The child didn't know what a key was, but put the bright thing in her bag, and when they came home her mother couldn't find the key, but a big dog came and knocked her down and the key fell out and the door was opened.

Pickford interpreted this to reveal:

> a complex system of conflicts, including resistance at the phallic level against the father's sexuality, which is expressed in the fantasy that the little girl did not know a key. This is a defence by unconscious denial. It is coupled, however, with the wish to rob the mother of the father's penis by putting the unknown bright object into her own bag or womb, and guilt over the wish . . . The dog is the punitive super ego.[33]

Another story told by a different child about another picture in the series is as follows:

> This little boy stole apples from the farmer's orchard and was chased, but escaped only to have a tummy-ache. So he never stole apples again.

On the face of it a simple moral tale about the perils of theft. Pickford's interpretation finds her:

> stealing the father's apples – his sexuality . . . Stealing apples has a repressed genital meaning, and 'tummy-ache' is its consequence in the form of a fantasy of incestuous pregnancy . . . The wish to rob the father of his sexuality is also a wish to swallow his sexual organs. Instead of being fully displaced to the vaginal form of swallowing, which would be normal for a girl . . . Her enuresis was an unconscious expression of the wish for masculinity.[34]

His second interpretation finds the subject 'trying to be boyish'. However the principle actor of most adventure stories in this period were boys. The third-person singular pronoun was conventionally 'he'.[35] There is no attempt made by Pickford to access the effects of cultural norms upon his subjects. All of the interpretations have a monotonously similar quality usually involving some aspect of penis envy with female patients or oedipal dilemmas with boys. Such a blinkered use of psychoanalytic theory is positively harmful in my view.

Here is an example of a Kleinian art therapist explaining a client's image of a witch (a culturally potent symbol redolent of misogyny):

> At root it came from her perception of a split-off bad part of her 'internal object' . . . Paddy shot a fearful glance at me, as if she had just recognised me as the bad witch, and as if she was experiencing me in the same way that the infant part of herself has experienced the persecuting mother. When I put this to her she became quite frightened and moved away to a table at the far end of the room . . . the witch mother image had been made real. In order to escape these feelings of persecution Paddy's ego attempted to transfer her 'projected sadism' from something of her own creation . . . [36]

It is just possible that Paddy's fear was due to the strange interpretation of the therapist who seemed not to be interested in what she was really trying to express. That the art therapist became convinced of her own interpretation through 'empathy' with her client is evidence of possible veracity. However, there are great dangers to working with fixed theoretical models in this way, as I hope I have illustrated.

Art therapy in Britain has failed to respond positively to theoretical developments – particularly those which would entail the sort of awkward self-questioning I have just illustrated. This leaves the profession largely ignoring social context (the context in which people become defined as mad). A critical analysis of the operations of power linked to race, class and gender has not formed a sufficiently significant part of art therapy training. More disturbing still is that there is general ignorance about how race, class and gender serve as signifying systems. That this does not take a central place in the training of art therapists, even though it is of fundamental importance to how health is defined and self-identity is formed, is somewhat surprising.

This chapter has, I hope, illustrated that such a critical analysis of representations of gender should be absolutely central to the training of art therapists, that lack of awareness of gender issues can lead unwittingly to abuse or lack of acknowledgement of women clients.

CONCLUSION

In conclusion, there are a number of feminist approaches to representations of women. These range from an affirmation of images of femininity which do not critically examine the nature of the feminine to an outright rejection of such imagery. Femininity is seen by many feminists as an oppressive definition encouraging self-enfeeblement and dependency as 'normal'. More than this, violence against women can be seen as a natural result of certain aspects of feminine and masculine behaviour. These aspects of femininity include passivity, inability to assert and defend oneself and women as objects for the gratification of the male gaze which is considered to be part of normal socialisation. Medical practice reflects norms and social beliefs about women which are historically specific and subject to change. I have suggested that a critical analysis of art therapy practice should keep this in mind. Secondly, these norms and beliefs inscribe themselves in the deepest level of the 'unconscious'.[37] Thirdly, gender can be viewed as a signifying system. In other words that representations of gender articulate rules of social relationships. Changes in the organisation of social relationships correspond to changes in representations of gender. The idea of woman's unstable subjectivity continues to situate her as the object of medical discourse.

There is also a challenge to the categories of 'man' and 'woman' because the meaning ascribed to these categories is in a constant state of flux. The very meanings of the categories of 'woman' and 'man' are argued to be created by representations (images and texts). Analysis of images should take place in the intertextual space of all images of women. Images should also be seen as containing multiple meanings; they retain alternative, denied, or suppressed definitions.

ACKNOWLEDGEMENTS

Many thanks are due to sociologist Mike Hepworth for his encouragement, advice and reading suggestions and careful evaluation of this chapter. I also wish to thank cultural theorist and anthropologist Mary Douglas for her stringent criticism and forthright suggestions for improving this text; I am greatly indebted to her. Thanks are also due to medical historian David Smith for supplying me with an unpublished paper and for his support. I appreciated Rosy Martin's helpful comments on this chapter also. Final thanks are due to the Routledge readers for their constructive criticism.

NOTES

1 See Howell and Baynes (1981) for some statistics on how gender and class determines diagnoses and treatment options.
2 The value of collaborative phototherapy work by Jo Spence and Rosy Martin has been described thus: 'by exposing the underlying ideological bases of metaphorical and iconographic images of illness, the politics of representation are uncovered and a space emerges for passiveness to give way to active agency and the opportunity to express one's views' (Lupton 1994: 78).
3 See de Lauretis (1986) for an analysis of Foucault's work.
4 Pierre Bourdieu's work (1989) explores this subject with a great degree of sophistication.
5 Gilman, 1993: 1031.
6 Foucault, 1965: 264.
7 Jan Goldstein (1993: 1353–5) cogently argues that the Parliamentary Select Committee of 1815–16 was of pivotal importance in psychiatry embracing moral treatments. The select committee had been set up to investigate allegations of maltreatment within asylums. The testimony of one doctor in particular, Thomas Monro Bethlam, was highly publicised. In his testimony Monro admitted that the physical treatments he used (bleedings, purges etc.) had little effect and that it was the moral management of patients which was curative. Goldstein argued that it was this publicity which necessitated those members of the British medical profession who were interested in exercising control over insanity to find ways of accommodating moral treatment methods within their therapeutics. The historian Andrew Scull (1979) also provides a detailed analysis of this period.
8 Professor G. S. Rousseau points out that the work of physicians in relation to early hysteria was in distinguishing between real and false witches – those with 'real' ailments rather than signs of possession by Satan (1993: 99).
9 Evolutionary theory is a diachronistic analysis of how species evolved and was used with out justification to back up synchronistic hypotheses.
10 E D Cope (1887: 159) cited in Gould, 1981: 117–18.
11 Hysterics were not exclusively women. Jean Martin Charcot (1825–1839) found evidence of hysteria in men. However, men did not suffer from the 'grand hystérié' which was a prolonged convulsive seizure. Male hysterics had been conceptualised as feminine (emotional like women) as early as 1828 by George Burrows.
12 This and several other similar quotations by nineteenth-century physicians and gynaecologists are provided by Bassuk, 1986.

13 Smith-Rosenberg and Rosenburg, l973: 340.

14 See Showalter, 1985: 12.

15 Spencer, 1873: 340–8, cited in Stocking, 1987: 205.

16 Robert Brundell Carter, 1853, cited in Showalter, 1985: 158.

17 I am using Foucault's idea of discursive practice, as discussed by numerous authors including Ussher (1991: 22) as a highly organised and regulated set of practices and statements which serve to create and maintain definitions of madness or of gender. This has a history (genealogy) and a set of rules 'which distinguishes it from other discourses establishing both links and differences'. It is with this understanding of dis-ease that the art therapist should set about her or his work.

18 In an essay entitled 'Virility and Domination in Early 20th Century Vanguard Painting' Carol Duncan persuasively argues that assertions of virility and aggressive male sexuality were particularly evident in the images produced of female nudes. In contrast to John Berger, who points out the passive sexuality in the classical female nude which is painted for the male spectator/owner, Duncan goes further and points to the brutalising quality of many of the images painted by artists such as Kirchner, Heckel, Picasso and Valminick. Duncan writes of these nudes 'these women show no or few signs of human consciousness of any kind'. They are reduced, she argues, to objects of pure flesh (Duncan 1983: 31).

19 However the application of *a priori* categories to provide analysis of images is deeply unsatisfactory.

20 Marcia Pointon (1991) criticises the work of John Berger as too simplistic and not responding to the layers of signification inherent in classical works of nudes such as Palma Vecchio's Venus.

21 This is a dominant part of our culture ranging from the Hollywood movie in which the male character steals a kiss from the resistant woman who then melts into his arms as a result of his forcefulness to hard core pornography or snuff movies in which women are dismembered before, during or as part of the sexual act. That these representations are internalised by women accounts for the prevalence of women who say that they enjoy pornography and watch it with their partners. That women enjoy pornography in this way has been used as an argument against censorship though such women are simply inured to their humiliation.

22 Showalter (1985) argues persuasively that although psychoanalysis had an interest in what women had to say (unlike conventional psychiatry of the period) that it became codified in the interests of Freud's emerging psychoanalytic system. This point made by Showalter is elaborated by Jeffrey Masson (1993) in his study 'Dora and Freud'.

23 It is worth noting that the rest cure also had a punitive aspect that its founder, Silas Weir Mitchell, noted himself. Such total rest could become 'bitter medicine'. Secondly, weight gain, was important in the cure. Showalter's excellent ground-breaking book describes this as 'pseudopregnancy' (Showalter 1985: 205) and similar to later insulin treatments which also resulted in enforced rest and massive weight gain. Though Showalter does not explore the compatibility of each of these cures with Freudian thought, it is interesting in this context to note her remarks about Freud's later works on women's sexuality: 'In coming to terms with her "castration" in early childhood, the girl had three possible paths of psychic development: sexual fear and withdrawal; defiant competition with men, and possible homosexuality; or the happy resolution in which she switched affection from her mother to her father, changed her libidinal object from

female to male, repressed her "masculino, active, clitoral sexuality", and finally *accepted an infant, particularly a male infant, as a substitute for the phallus'* (Showalter 1985: 199, italics added).

24 Pollock in her book *Vision and Difference* argues that many of the public spaces associated with modernity were not freely available to 'respectable' bourgeois women of the nineteenth century. She also noted that women were represented according to location so that 'In spaces marked out for visual and notional sexual consumption the bodies are in evidence, laid out, opened out to view while drapery functions to reveal sexualised anatomy' (Pollock 1988: 73).

25 I am using this assertion as a point of argument. As this book illustrates, art therapists are more than willing to examine their practice and think seriously about the meaning of gender, though this tendency is not particularly evident in much recent British literature on art therapy.

26 Two recent referendum results indicated that the membership of the British Association of Art Therapists (BAAT) did not wish to change their professional title from 'art therapist' to 'art psychotherapist'. This is a clear indication that the majority of art therapists conceptualise their work as a distinct practice apart from psychotherapy even though the term psychotherapy is defined very broadly by the professional association thus: 'the term "psychotherapeutic" is understood to mean the engagement in a therapeutic alliance between therapist and client and the interpersonal relationship that is central to this process' (Core Course Requirements Document produced by BAAT TEC).

27 I am not recommending rigid adherence to certain theoretical ideas, feminist or otherwise, but a critical analysis and debate about representational systems.

28 As Professor G. S. Rousseau points out, some illnesses can be conceptualised as 'diseases of civilisation' which are closely linked to social conditions and 'gender based pain' (1993: 94).

29 Rowe (1993: 13), foreword to Jeffrey Masson's *Against Therapy*.

30 Former psychotherapy clients have recorded they did not appreciate the 'ritual humiliations of an interfering stranger' (presumably a Freudian or neo-Freudian therapist) asking about their 'sex life' and 'your relationship with your father' and importantly 'pathologising any resistance to this procedure'. Letters page, *Weekend Guardian* 28 October 1995, p. 10.

31 Art therapists mesmerised by reductive theory are particularly keen on proffering crude interpretations – seeing phallic symbols in objects such as candles, walking-sticks, trees (in almost anything in fact). Thankfully they are a tiny minority within art therapy. Women and women art therapy students quite rightly do not want some male therapist's phallic fantasies projected onto their art work; indeed such behaviour is abusive.

32 Waller's account in her 'Becoming a Profession' makes clear that Pickford regarded himself as an art therapist (1991: 78).

33 Pickford, 1963: 32.

34 Pickford, 1963: 30.

35 Many feminist writers now use 'they' instead of 'he' or get round the problem by writing in the plural form.

36 Weir, 1987: 112.

37 This word unconscious is used metaphorically. As Rosy Martin puts it: 'There is no essential self which precedes the social construction of the self through the agency of representation'. See her chapter in this volume.

BIBLIOGRAPHY

Bassuk, E. L. 1986. 'The Rest Cure', in Sulieman, S. (ed.) *The Female Body in Western Culture: Contemporary Perspectives*. Cambridge, MA: Harvard University Press.

Baudelaire, C. 1863 'The Painter of Modern Life', in Frascina and Harrison (eds) *Modern Art and Modernism A Critical Anthology*. London: Harper and Row.

Beilharz, P. (ed.) 1992. *Social Theory*. London: Allen and Unwin.

Berger, J. 1972. *The Past as Seen from a Possible Future: Selected Essays and Articles*. London: Penguin.

Berrios, G. E. and Freeman, H. (eds) 1991. *150 Years of British Psychiatry 1841–1991*. London: Gaskell.

Boas, G. 1940. 'The Mona Lisa in the History of Ideas'. *Journal of the History of Taste*. April: 207–224.

Bourdieu, P. 1989. *Distinction: A Social Critique of the Judgement of Taste*. London: Routledge.

Bourneville, D. M. and Régnard, P. 1887. *Iconographie Photographique de la Salpêtrière*, vol. 1. Paris: Bureaux du Progrès Médical and Adrian Delahay.

Carter, A. 1979. *The Sadeian Woman*. London: Virago.

Carter, M. 1990. *Framing Art. Introducing Theory and the Visual Image*. Sydney: Hale & Iremonger.

Cowie, E. 1977. 'Women, Representation and the Image'. *Screen Education*. Summer, no. 23: 15–23.

Curthoys, A. 1988. *For and Against Feminism: A Personal Journey into Feminist Theory*. Sydney: Allen and Unwin.

Dalley, T. 1994. 'Editorial Introduction'. *Inscape. The Journal of the British Association of Art Therapists*, vol. 1.

de Lauretis, T. (ed.) 1986. *Feminist Studies Critical Studies*. Basingstoke: Macmillan.

Dijkstra, B. 1986. *Idols of Perversity: Fantasies of Feminine Evil in Fin-de-Siècle Culture*. Oxford: Oxford University Press.

Doane, M. A. 1986. 'The Clinical Eye: Medical Discourses in the "Women's Film" of the 1940's', in Suleiman, S. (ed.) *The Female Body in Western Culture: Contemporary Perspectives*. Cambridge, MA: Harvard University Press.

Duncan, C. 1983. 'Virility and Domination in Early 20th Century Vanguard Painting'. *Artforum*. Dec.: 30–39.

Foucault, M. 1967. *Madness and Civilisation. A History of Insanity in the Age of Reason*. London: Tavistock.

Freud, S. 1983. *Sigmund Freud. New Introductory Lectures on Psychoanalysis*, vol. 2. Harmondsworth: Penguin.

Gilman, S. L. 1993. 'Psychotherapy', in Bynum, W. F. and Porter, R. *Companion Encyclopaedia of the History of Medicine*. London: Routledge.

Gilman, S. L., King, H., Porter, R., Rousseau, G. S. and Showalter, E. 1993. *Hysteria Beyond Freud*. Berkeley: University of California Press

Goldstein, J. 1993. *Psychiatry* in Bynum, W. F. and Porter, R. *Companion Encyclopaedia of the History of Medicine*. London: Routledge.

Gould, S. 1981. *The Mismeasurement of Man*. London: Norton.

Grosz, E. 1990. *Jacques Lacan: A Feminist Introduction*. London: Routledge.

Henzell, J. 1995. 'Research in the Particular: Epistemology in Art and Psychotherapy' in Gilroy, A. and Lee, C. 1995. *Art and Music Therapy and Research*. London: Routledge.

Hogan, S. 1991. 'Women in Visual Arts Administration: Gender, Power and Organisational Dynamics', in *Australian Journal of Arts Administration*. Vol. 3. No. 4. Spring.

Howell, E. and Baynes, M. (eds) 1981. *Women and Mental Health*. New York: Basic Books.

Jacobus, M. 1993. 'Narcissa's Gaze: Morisot, Narcissism and the Filial Mirror'. Conference paper, Association of Art Historians. Nineteenth Annual Conference, London.

Lake, M. 1988. 'Women, Gender and History'. *Australian Feminist Studies*, Summer nos. 7 and 8.

Lupton, D. 1994. *Medicine as Culture. Disease and the Body in Western Societies*. London: Sage.

Masson, J. 1986. *A Dark Science: Women, Sexuality, and Psychiatry in the Nineteenth Century*. New York: Farrar, Straus and Giroux. Preface by C. McKinnon.

Masson, J. 1992. 'Dora and Freud' in *Against Therapy*. London: HarperCollins.

Nead, L. 1992. *The Female Nude*. London: Routledge.

Nochlin, L. 1989. *Women, Art, Power and Other Essays*. London: Thames and Hudson.

Oppenheim, J. 1991. *Shattered Nerves. Doctors, Patients and Depression in Victorian England*. Oxford: Oxford University Press.

Perkin, J. 1993. *Victorian Women*. London: John Murray.

Pickford, R. 1963. *The Pickford Projective Pictures*. London: Tavistock.

Pointon, M. 1991. *Naked Authority: The Body in Western Painting, 1830–1908*. Cambridge: Cambridge University Press.

Pollock, G. 1988. *Vision and Difference*. London: Routledge.

Porter, R. 1987. *Mind Forg'd Manacles. A History of Madness in England*. Cambridge, MA: Harvard University Press.

Rabinow, P. (ed.) 1984. *The Foucault Reader*. London: Pantheon.

Ross, C. (ed.) 1992. *Therapy is Political*. Race and Culture Group of The British Association of Art Therapists.

Rousseau, G. S. in Roberts, M. M. and Porter, R. 1993. *Literature and Medicine during the Eighteenth Century*. London: Routledge.

Rowe, D. 1993. Foreword to J. Masson, *Against Therapy*. London: HarperCollins.

Russell, D. 1995. *Women, Madness and Medicine*. Cambridge: Polity Press.

Scott, J. W. 1988. *Gender and the Politics of History*. New York: Columbia University Press.

Scull, A. 1979. *Museums of Madness: The Social Organisation of Insanity in Nineteenth-Century England*. London: Allan Lane.

Showalter, E. 1985. *The Female Malady. Women, Madness and English Culture 1830–1980*. London: Virago.

Smith, D. 1995. *Foucauldian History of Dentistry*. Unpublished paper supplied by author.

Smith-Rosenberg, C. and Rosenberg, C. 1973. 'The Female Animal: Medical and Biological Views of Woman and Her Role in Nineteenth-Century America'. *Journal of American World History*, vol. 60, no. 2: 332–356

Stocking, G. 1987. *Victorian Anthropology*. London: The Free Press.

Taussig, M. 1980. 'Reification and the Consciousness of the Patient'. *Social Science and Medicine*, vol. 148. no. 3: 3–13.

Teich, M. and Porter, R. 1990. *Fin de Siècle and Its Legacy*. Cambridge: Cambridge University Press.

Tilly, C. 1990. *Reading Material Culture*. Oxford: Basil Blackwell.

Ulrich, L. T. 1990 'Of Pens and Needles: Sources in Early American Women's History'. *Journal of American History*, No 77. June: 200–207.

Ussher, J. 1991. *Women's Madness: Misogyny or Mental Illness*. Brighton: Harvester Wheatsheaf.

Waller, D. 1991. *Becoming a Profession*. London: Tavistock/Routledge.

Weir, F. 1987. 'The Role of Symbolic Expression in its Relation to Art Therapy: A Kleinian Approach', in Dalley, T. *et al. Images of Art Therapy: New Developments in Theory and Practice*. London: Tavistock.

Williams, G. L. (ed.) 1976. *John Stuart Mill on Politics and Society*. London: Fontana.

Williams, R. 1983. *Keywords*. London: Flamingo.

Chapter 2

Invasive art[1]

Art as empowerment for women with breast cancer

Cathy A. Malchiodi

INTRODUCTION

The statistics regarding breast cancer in the United States continue to be disheartening: currently, one in eight women will develop breast cancer within her lifetime (Rennie, 1993). The rate in the United Kingdom is equally as high, and breast cancer is the main cause of death for women between the ages of thirty-five and fifty-four (Faulder, 1993). Although most cases occur in women over fifty, there has been an alarming increase in the number of cases in younger women. Like the international crisis of Acquired Immune Deficiency Syndrome (AIDS), the prevalence of breast cancer is beginning to touch the lives of almost everyone either through direct experience, or the diagnosis of a family member or friend.

In response to a problem of epidemic proportions, women have taken a cue from AIDS activism and have also begun to organise, lobby and publicise the issue of breast cancer. Some of these campaigns have involved challenging the lack of public funding for breast cancer research, highlighting the disparities in funding between that allocated for breast cancer and other more rare forms of cancer and AIDS (Rennie, 1993). However, current breast cancer activism has taken shape in other ways. Women, particularly artists and writers who have had breast cancer, have begun to speak out about their illnesses, describing the experience of the disease in either images or words. Visual artists such as Nancy Fried (in Dreifuss-Kattan, 1990), Richild Holt (in Dreifuss-Kattan, 1990), Jo Spence (1986) and Hollis Sigler (1993), performance artist/activist Matuschka (in Ferraro, 1993), and writers/poets Audre Lorde (1980), Claire Henze (1987), Deena Metzger (1983), Treya Killam Wilber (in Wilber, 1991), and Terry Tempest Williams (1991), are a few of many examples of artists and writers directly confronting breast cancer through the arts.

This chapter discusses the works of some artists and writers who have explored and confronted breast cancer through visual art, literature and poetry in order to familiarise art therapists with this material for use with clients with breast cancer. The multidimensional aspects of breast cancer are also presented as they relate to the content of the works produced by these artists and writers. Resources for visual art and writing by women with breast cancer are also included to assist art therapists in obtaining this material to help women with breast cancer address, explore and confront the disease and to provide patients with empowerment, inspiration and hope.

THE USE OF ART THERAPY AND ART EXPRESSION WITH CANCER PATIENTS

Art therapy has been used in medical settings with cancer patients in a variety of ways. In general, it has been utilised both as a diagnostic tool and as a vehicle for psychotherapy (Malchiodi, 1993). Over the last two decades art therapists have contributed clinical observations and research on the use of art therapy with a variety of medical populations, including cancer patients (Barron, 1989; Dreifuss-Kattan, 1990; Minar, 1992; Minar et al., 1991). Others have explored autogenic (relaxation and guided visualisation) methods in conjunction with art (Lusebrink, 1981, 1990) and general connections between art expression and health (Lusebrink, 1990; Malchiodi, 1992, 1993, 1994).

Clinicians and researchers outside the field of art therapy have also explored the use of art (particularly drawing) with individuals with cancer (Achterburg 1985; Achterburg et al., 1994; Achterburg and Lawlis, 1984; Simonton et al., 1978). These researchers have focused on the meaning of images drawn by people with cancer and how to use these images to induce physical change and to encourage the individual to become active in his/her own health care. For example, the patient might be instructed to draw an image of cancer cells or tumours, and then to visualise or draw an image of those cells being destroyed in some way. This methodology may provide a consistent measure of how an individual is dealing with the cancer (succumbing to it, or fighting it), but in terms of empowering the person to actually fight off the illness, the technique is contentious. For people who have recurrences of their cancers, the experience may indeed have the opposite effect, resulting in a feeling of failure to overcome their disease and casting doubts on their own personal abilities to get well.

Art therapy with women with breast cancer has mainly addressed the psychological consequences of the disease (Dreifuss-Kattan, 1990; Minar, 1992; Minar et al., 1991) and to some extent, mind/body paradigms (Barron, 1989; Malchiodi, 1993). Psychological aspects of the illness are important in treatment; however, there are additional goals for art therapy with women with breast cancer. Although art can be used as a tool of psychotherapy to achieve insight, interest in making art in therapy by cancer patients is often motivated by additional factors. For example, when confronting mortality, a cancer patient often responds with a profound search for wholeness and a desire to re-examine one's life story (Leshan, 1989). Hence, an individual with a life-threatening illness often uses art as a way to summarise life experiences. More importantly, it is often a way for the seriously ill person to reclaim personal power, to create a lasting visual legacy, and to say, therefore, 'I am' and 'I exist'.

MULTIDIMENSIONAL ASPECTS OF BREAST CANCER

In using any intervention with women who have had breast cancer, it is important to understand that breast cancer is a disease which has complex effects both physical and emotional, and for this reason each woman has a different experience of the disease. A diagnosis of breast cancer involves not only the emotional consequences of serious illness, but is also compounded by invasive surgical intervention (e.g. mastectomy or lumpectomy) and treatments (e.g. chemotherapy which may result in hair loss, and/or radiation which may add to disfigurement). These medical procedures are often life-saving, but also involve loss of a breast, disfigurement and other body changes. Other losses may arise as well, particularly in interpersonal dimensions; the experience of breast cancer may cause changes in relationships with her spouse, partner, family, children and friends and may have an impact on career and life goals. The deepest losses may be the most intangible, however. Women who are diagnosed with breast cancer (or anyone diagnosed with a life-threatening illness) assume that they have a future, when suddenly they find themselves no longer able to count on continued life and subsequently experience a loss of control over their life. Cancer becomes a turning point (LeShan, 1989), often forces a review of one's life, and inevitably changes the course of one's existence. Although a woman with breast cancer may yearn to return to the time before the illness took hold, eventually she has to come to terms with a new type of existence.

In addition to addressing issues of grief and loss, the therapist may also find that women connect their experience of breast cancer to any or all of the following:

Reactions to the medical community

The medical community, although its purpose is to assist in recovery and cures, may be viewed negatively by many women, and may not be seen as either understanding or adequately addressing women's health care or emotional needs. Women may unfortunately experience a doctor who is insensitive to women's feelings about their bodies and confusing in their presentations of options for treatment. For example, during radiation treatment for breast cancer, a woman reported that when she asked to be covered with a sheet, 'the technician told me "There is no modesty in a hospital. Only 80-year-old women get upset over this." I went home and that statement ate me all night, like a cancer.'[2]

Photographer and activist Matuschka (1994) notes after her mastectomy:

> When I was diagnosed with cancer, I thought I had just been handed my finality papers and I cried without interruption for two days. I expected to live at most 18 months [her mother died of breast cancer at forty-one years] . . . My doctor recommended a mastectomy. I made the most of my last days, as Venus de Milo, photographing myself each day and making plans to document my operation and follow-up treatment. While I was undergoing chemotherapy, my surgeon told me that I hadn't really needed a mastectomy in the first place. 'You could have done with a lumpectomy'.[3]

These women's descriptions underscore both the insensitivity and often contradictory information that health-care professionals may give patients. In Matuschka's case, she used the experience to become an activist on the issue of breast cancer, but for other women anger, depression and feelings of victimisation, and other powerful emotions may emerge in reaction to medical treatment.

Frustration with identifying a cause for the cancer

Women may feel victimised by their environment since diet, pollution and even high power lines have been linked to breast cancer. Unlike AIDS or other illnesses, women who develop breast cancer do not know how they acquired it since genetics, hormones, pesticides, food additives, or other environmental influences may play a role (Love, 1991). Writer Terry Tempest Williams (1991) has had two breast cancer biopsies and a borderline malignancy. Her mother, both grandmothers, and six aunts have all had mastectomies. Terry describes above-ground atomic testing that she believes contributed to her family members' cancers:

> The bomb. The cloud . . . We were driving north, past Las Vegas. It was an hour or so before dawn, when this explosion went off. We not only heard it, but felt it . . . We pulled over and suddenly, rising from the desert floor, we saw it, clearly, this golden-stemmed cloud, the mushroom. The sky seemed to vibrate with an eerie pink glow. Within a few minutes, a light ash was raining on the car.[4]

In addition to looking for an outside cause for cancer, many women look inward for a reason they developed breast cancer. Some look to 'new age' books and tapes for answers. New age is a term that is frequently used in the US to describe emerging paradigms or philosophies, particularly in the areas of health and well-being. One of the more common new age beliefs familiar to people who have been diagnosed with a life-threatening illness is that illness is a lesson and that we experience diseases for reasons in addition to genetic predisposition, exposure, or mere accident. Another philosophy that has emerged involves the idea that repressed anger or other emotions may cause cancer and that we bring illnesses upon ourselves to some extent. These ideas, although meant as explanations for why a cancer has occurred, are often troubling to patients, and may cause unnecessary feelings of guilt and self-blame.

Artist Hollis Sigler, a survivor of breast cancer who is discussed at length later in this chapter, described the following feelings in one of her paintings called *Maybe It Was Something I Ate?*. She wrote 'The guilt of responsibility – could I have wished this on myself? In this culture, which places so much emphasis on the individual, it is seen as a personal failing if one has a disease. What did I do wrong? Can I make it right again?'.[5] The image Sigler created to describe her feelings includes a delicately drawn chair in the centre and five balloons above it with images of things that could have caused her cancer: alcohol, high power lines, junk food, pollution, or fat intake. In addition to the idea of self-blame and self-responsibility, the artist also conveys a similar message of concern over environmental causes present that may inadvertently cause breast cancer.

Feelings about being a survivor versus a victim

Although a diagnosis of breast cancer is frightening, it is a disease that can be survived. Medical interventions and other developments over the last decades have demonstrated that cancer is a disease that can be overcome, especially with early detection and medical treatment. In addition, several longitudinal studies have been conducted to assess the characteristics of long-term survivors of cancer, particularly breast cancer. For example, Greer *et al.* (1990) conducted a study of breast cancer patients, finding after five, ten and fifteen years that patients who had initially been determined and had a 'fighting spirit' had the highest survival rate. Those whose response to the disease was hopeless and helpless had the lowest survival rate.

It is important for art therapists to understand that most women who have experienced cancer prefer to be called survivors, rather than victims. The term 'survivors' had been originally used to describe individuals who were abused as children in order to convey an identity based on positive adaptation, rather than a passive, victimised status (Haller and Alter-Reid, 1986). Although some women who have had breast cancer may not care about the semantics of being called a 'breast cancer victim' or a 'breast cancer survivor', it is important to know that many women prefer the latter, seeing it as positive and hopeful and contributing to recovery.

USING CANCER-RELATED ART AND WRITING WITH CLIENTS WITH BREAST CANCER

Breast cancer patients, as other patients with cancer, approach their illnesses in a variety of ways. Some focus on psychological changes, others focus on life changes that bring about a greater sense of meaning or purpose to living, and still others want to know that recovery is within the realm of possibility. By introducing the art and writing by women with breast cancer there is a possibility to address all these dimensions in therapy, thus giving each woman an opportunity to achieve specific goals through viewing and discussing her art in a socially supportive setting. Although not specifically addressed in this brief chapter, this art and writing can also serve as a catalyst for art-making by women with breast cancer, serving as an inspiration to them and as a model for expression.

This cancer-related art serves several specific purposes. First, introducing this cancer-related visual art and writing initiates the idea that it is acceptable to make autobiographical art: that is, art that is very personal, celebrates the individual's experience, and places the personal on the same level as the political. Many women who come to art therapy either through cancer support groups or for individual therapy have preconceived ideas about what art is or should be. Their last experiences with art-making may have been young children or adolescents in school art classes where there were rules about what art should be. Art may have become defined as pieces in museums or galleries, or as having a certain style, format, and content. By seeing cancer-related art and reading poetry and prose written by women with breast cancer, the idea of art as autobiography is conveyed and also serves as an inspiration for art-making and writing about personal breast cancer experiences.

Secondly, cancer-related art provides the direct opportunity to explore the parameters of the illness: the losses, the trauma to the body, the decision-making process, the medical establishment, and other aspects of the disease previously mentioned. There is an opportunity to confront one's own fears and questions about the experience of breast cancer through looking at the art or reading and discussing the literature; in this sense, the works can be considered personally empowering. Empowerment, particularly in feminist models, emphasises raising consciousness and a focus on group process to promote active change. The latter is important in light of recent studies on the importance of social support with women with breast cancer. Spiegel *et al.* (1989) and Fawzy *et al.* (1993) suggest that social support of a group may be life-extending, life-enhancing and empowering. In Spiegel's study, women with metastatic breast cancer who participated in support groups doubled their survival time when compared to people who did not participate in support groups.

Lastly, as an art therapist who has not had the direct experience of breast cancer (only indirectly in knowing family or friends with the illness), I chose to use these works with clients because I felt that the images could express ideas that I could not. Since I have not had breast cancer, it is presumptuous of me to try to know or be an expert on the experience of women who had the personal experience of the illness. The artists and writers I have mentioned, on the other hand, know the experience intimately and can convey feelings and responses more authentically than I ever could; their works also offer the obvious added bonus to art therapy of using images and poetry to describe that experience.

The last part of this chapter briefly highlights some of the major visual artists, writers and poets who have used their art forms to respond, explore, confront and address their own and/or family members' experiences of breast cancer.

BREAST CANCER ACTION GROUP: HEALING LEGACIES

A leader in the United States in the area of making public the visual work of women who have had breast cancer is the Breast Cancer Action Group (BCAG). Founded in 1991, it is an organisation committed to the eradication of breast cancer through educational programmes, collaboration with other agencies, and exhibitions of visual, performing and literary arts. In 1993, the BCAG began the Healing Legacies project; subsequently, in 1994, the Women's Caucus for Art (WCA), an organisation of women artists, curators, educators and other professional women in the arts throughout the US joined in co-sponsorship of the project. 'Healing Legacies' now consists of a slide registry representing both professional and non-professional artists who have had breast cancer. Works are continuously solicited through arts and breast cancer organisations and through publicity about individual exhibits. The collection contains photography, painting, mixed media, sculpture, fibreworks and poetry; it also includes performance pieces, lectures and workshops about the exhibit, art and art therapy. Each work is accompanied by a brief biography about the woman's experience with the disease and her artistic process. Agencies and institutions may use parts of this collection for a fee. Art therapists are referred to the address at the end of this chapter for additional information.

Two examples are included here to show the diversity of the collection. Figure 2.1, *Grief Masks I–IV*, is a sculptural piece by Paulette Carr, describing the nightmare of breast cancer. Carr is an eight-year survivor of breast cancer and began making art two years after her mastectomy. Figure 2.2, Mastectomy Quilt, is a fabric appliqué and quilt by Suzanne Marshall. Marshall used the quilt as her art form to explore cancer for several reasons, the most obvious being that a diagnosis of cancer is something of a puzzle to be solved, reminiscent of the puzzle-like pieces of a quilt.

Figure 2.1 Grief Masks I–IV by Paulette Carr

Matuschka and invasive art

Artist, activist and performance artist Matuschka is one of the most well-known names among visual artists who have explored breast cancer through the arts. She was diagnosed with breast cancer at the age of thirty-seven. Her mother died of the disease at the age of forty-one. Matuschka has used the word 'invasive' in conjunction with her photographs and art. The term 'invasive' is often used in conjunction with a poor prognosis for cancer. Invasive cancer means one that has spread, often with the result of metastasis or a terminal prognosis. Its implication is therefore negative, implying that one will die from the disease. However, Matuschka has changed the definition of the term to mean the spread of breast cancer awareness through her photographs, images, and activism.

An image created by Matuschka caused a great deal of controversy when it appeared on the cover of the *New York Times Magazine* in the summer of 1993. The photograph, called *Beauty Out of Damage* is a self-portrait of the artist in a gown cut away to show her mastectomy scar.

Figure 2.2 Mastectomy Quilt by Suzanne Marshall

There was both outrage and positive feedback from women concerning this image. Some women felt that the image violated their privacy in that now people would know what a mastectomy really looked like. Others thought that the image would prevent women from getting checked for cancer out of a fear that the photograph showed how a woman would end up if she received a diagnosis of breast cancer. On the positive side, many women with breast cancer were pleased that the media had finally published a photograph of a woman who looked like them. Although the photograph openly portrayed the physical reality of breast cancer and surgery, it also presented it in a positive light.

Other images created by Matuschka focus on the idea of activism and self-esteem in the struggle with a breast cancer diagnosis. For example, *Vote for Yourself* presents a positive image of a torso which has undergone breast surgery to convey the underlying themes of self-esteem, self-confidence and empowerment. The artist states:

> Two years after my surgery, when I had realised that I had missed my own funeral and was feeling better than ever . . . I decided I was ready to return to making self-portraits. But the challenge was enormous: how

could I 'minus one' show my asymmetrical body and bring it to the level of my earlier work without provoking pity? When men come home from war bandaged and broken, they are considered symbols of strength, even sexy. Could I actually show a mastectomy woman who looks beautiful, who has pride and dignity? A picture evoking not self-indulgence, but power and strength?

Figure 2.3 Beauty out of Damage, 1993 by Matuschka

Figure 2.4 Vote for Yourself, 1991 by Matuschka

Matuschka's work, although controversial and confrontational, generates a great deal of discussion about issues of personal empowerment, body-image, society's perspectives on women and the challenge of life after mastectomy. Art therapists who use her work with women with breast cancer should use it sensitively with their female clients, especially with women who have been newly diagnosed and are working with initial feelings of loss and grief. However, undoubtedly Matuschka's images can generate discussion on issues surrounding breast cancer and she is personally inspiring to many women.

Hollis Sigler: *Breast Cancer Journal: Walking with the Ghosts of My Grandmothers*

Hollis Sigler is a visual artist who created a body of work called *Breast Cancer Journal: Walking with the Ghosts of My Grandmothers*. In 1985, Hollis Sigler was diagnosed with breast cancer. She had a mastectomy and underwent chemotherapy and radiation treatments. In 1992 the cancer was found again, this time in her bones. The recurrence of the cancer caused her to come forward and publicly acknowledge her own cancer by painting a series of works on the issue of breast cancer. The reference to the 'ghosts of my grandmothers' refers to the history of the disease which dates at least back to the Greek civilisation.

Sigler's work before and after breast cancer could be considered feminist in style in that she includes her personal experience as a woman, elevating home, domesticity and household objects. Sigler is an important artist for women with breast cancer not only because she honours the everyday experiences of women, but also because she has used her art to convey her anger about how society reacts to breast cancer. She observes that 'Only when women with mastectomies refuse to pretend normalcy will the silence be broken. The world will know we are many.'

Sigler explores all dimensions of cancer and her feelings surrounding it and her images are familiar to women since they often include themes of home and family. The material and style of her work is somewhat naive and child-like, often executed in oil pastel, a material common to art therapy sessions. Sigler's work, although confrontational, is less controversial than Matuschka's in content, but no less powerful. For these reasons, Sigler's work may be an appropriate group of images to initially introduce to women with breast cancer in art therapy or other cancer support groups.

Other visual artists

There have also been group shows, such as the recent 'Body & Soul: Contemporary Art and Healing', that have included art made by women with breast cancer, among others. The works in this particular show explore the links between art and healing. Included in this show are sculptor, Nancy Fried, who uses her ceramic work to convey her experience of breast cancer (see Figure 2.5), and Regina Kelley, an artist who had breast cancer and who worked in hospice care for many years and developed visualisation techniques as well as art exercises to utilise with physical and emotional pain. Kelly's own art relates closely to her interests in healing and caregiving. Other pieces in this collection focus on physical illnesses in general and art as a source for healing. (An address for a catalogue on the 'Body and Soul' exhibit is listed at the end of this chapter.)

Figure 2.5 The Flirt by Nancy Fried

Writers and poets with breast cancer

Whilst the focus of this chapter is on art-making in response to cancer, writing may be used in conjunction with art therapy. Creative writing and poetry can convey the experience of breast cancer; written work is an excellent catalyst for ideas and discussions. Also, writing has proven to be an effective adjunct to medical treatment. Pennebaker (1990) has found that people who regularly write about traumatic experiences make less visits to the doctor and have stronger immune systems than those who do not. With this finding in mind, it may also be appropriate to ask clients to write about their art as an additional component of the creative process.

Several important books have been written by women who have had breast cancer. Treya Killam Wilber, in collaboration with her husband, Ken Wilber (1991) wrote a journal of their lives after her diagnosis of breast cancer. In it she and her husband courageously explore their feelings and fears about cancer, their relationship, the medical community and health-care providers (including alternative medical practitioners they used), spirituality, death and dying. Treya Wilber touches on many of the same issues of breast cancer that the artists previously mentioned do. Like Hollis Sigler and many other women who develop breast cancer, Treya explores the reasons why she may have developed breast cancer, noting:

> too much animal fat in my diet when I was younger and too much coffee, worrying about my real purpose in life; internal pressure to find

my calling, my work, a period of major life changes and stress and depression I went through a few years ago, during which I cried almost every day for two months, failure to more vigorously pursue a spiritual path, like meditation.[6]

She also confronts her own fears about recurrence:

If I was responsible for the cancer this time around I might do it to myself again . . . I almost wish that I could see the whole thing as something that accidentally happened to me, perhaps because of a genetic predisposition or X-ray treatments . . . Now if I get depressed my will to live and my white cell count may go down.[7]

Treya and Ken Wilber's book is a difficult one to read, since it ends with her death and her process of dying is vividly described. However, it is an important work for survivors of breast cancer because it describes not only all aspects of a woman's experience with cancer, but also how it affects a spouse and caretaker (in this case, her husband, Ken).

Two other writers are also noteworthy and should be included in any collection of cancer-related writing. One is Audre Lorde, an African-American feminist author of *The Cancer Journal*, a seminal piece of literature exploring the physical and psychological consequences of breast cancer as well as society's lack of understanding of the illness. Another writer previously mentioned who examines the issue of breast cancer in a different manner is Terry Tempest Williams (1991). Her book *Refuge: An Unnatural History of Family and Place* interweaves Williams's experience of her mother's death from cancer with her interest in nature and the environment.

Lastly, Deena Metzger, a survivor of breast cancer, is an important feminist poet in the area of writing about breast cancer. Although she has written a great many other works, her collection of poems, *Tree*, illustrates how writing can be used for personal transformation and to give form to the experience of cancer. Metzger has written a book specifically as a resource for learning how to relate personal stories through journal-writing, story-writing, poetry and other experiential exercises, demonstrating the use of one's imagination as the major force in healing. Exercises in her book may be a helpful adjunct to art therapy sessions where writing is involved.

CONCLUSION

This chapter has provided a brief introduction to the art and writing of women with breast cancer. It is evident from these works that creative expression had helped these women to reframe the experience of the disease and to find new meaning for their lives after cancer. The value of the images and words of these survivors is in their inspiration to others, particularly to women who are currently struggling with breast cancer.

As with using any intervention, art therapists must be sensitive to the content of the works they present to their clients. Some women may not be ready to come to terms with the issues of disfigurement, recurrence, or mortality that many of the artists and writers convey. However, for the most part, the art and writing of women artists who have had breast cancer helps women newly-diagnosed to see themselves as survivors, rather than victims of tragedy. More importantly, these creative works can also assist women in developing a sense of self in the face of loss and in combating the sense of isolation by experiencing the images and stories of other women who have had breast cancer.

RESOURCES

Breast Cancer Action Group: Two Church Street, 3rd Floor, PO Box 5605, Burlington, VT 05402, USA; 802-863-3507. This organisation can also help with information on Matuschka and Hollis Sigler.

Body and Soul: c/o Decordova Museum and Sculpture Park, Lincoln, MA 02214, USA.

NOTES

1 The term 'invasive art' is respectfully borrowed from artist/activist Matuschka.
2 Ferraro,1993: 25.
3 From 'I am One Woman' gallery notes.
4 Williams, 1991: 283.
5 Sigler, 1993: 8.
6 Sigler, 1991: 49.
7 Sigler, 1991: 50.

BIBLIOGRAPHY

Achterburg, J 1985. *Imagery in Healing*. Boston, MA: Shambhala.
Achterburg, J., and Lawlis, G. 1984. *Imagery and Disease*. Champaign, IL: Institute for Personality and Ability Testing.
Achterburg, J., Dossey, B., and Kolkmeier, L. (1994). *Rituals of Healing*. New York: Bantam.
Barron, P. 1989. 'Fighting Cancer with Images', in Wadeson, H. (ed.) *Advances in Art Therapy*. New York: John Wiley.
Dreifuss-Kattan, E. 1990. *Cancer Stories: Creativity and Self-Repair*. Hillsdale, NJ: The Analytic Press.
Faulder, C. 1993. *The Nation With the Highest Death Rate Debates Prevention, Ms.*, 3 (6), 58–59.
Fawzy, F., Fawzy, N., Hyun, C., Elashoff, R., Guthrie, D., Fahey, J., and Morton, D. 1993. 'Effects of an early structured psychiatric intervention, coping and

affective state on recurrence and survival 6 years later'. *Archives of General Psychiatry*, 50, 681–689.

Ferraro, S. 1993. 'The Anguished Politics of Breast Cancer', *The New York Times Magazine* 15 August, 25–27.

Greer, S., Morris, T., Pettingale, K. and Haybittle, J. 1990, 'Psychological Response to Breast Cancer and fifteen-year outcome', *The Lancet*, 1, 49–50.

Haller, O., and Alter-Reid, M. 1986. 'Secretiveness and Guardedness: A Comparison of Two Incest Survivor Samples'. *American Journal of Psychotherapy*, 4, 554–63.

Henze, C. 1987. 'Poems by Claire Henze', in Regents of the University of California (ed.) *Confronting Cancer Through Art*. Los Angeles: Jonsson Comprehensive Cancer Care Center at the University of California.

LeShan, L. 1989. *Cancer as a Turning Point*. New York: Dutton.

Lorde, A. 1980. *The Cancer Journals*. San Francisco, CA: Spinsters.

Love, S. 1991. *Dr. Susan Love's Breast Book*. New York: Bantam.

Lusebrink, V.B. 1990. *Imagery and Visual Expression in Therapy*. New York: Plenum.

Malchiodi, C. 1992. 'Art and Medicine', *Art Therapy: Journal of the American Art Therapy Association*, 10. (2), 66–69.

Malchiodi, C. 1993. 'Medical Art Therapy: Contributions to the Field of Arts Medicine', *International Journal of Arts Medicine*, 2 (2), 28–31.

Malchiodi, C. 1994. 'Commentary on "Art for Recovery": Using Art to Humanize the Medical Milieu', *International Journal of Arts Medicine*, 3(1), 24–25.

Matuschka. 1994. 'I am One Woman' (gallery notes for travelling exhibition). Cincinnati, OH: YWCA.

Metzger, D. 1983. *Tree*. Berkeley, CA: Wingbow Press.

Metzger, D. 1992. *Writing for Your Life*. New York: HarperCollins.

Minar, V. 1992. 'Living with Cancer: Images of the Hurter and the Healer', in *The Art Therapist: Artist, Teacher, Clinician, Healer*. Mundelein, IL: AATA, Inc.

Minar, V., Erdman, J., Kapitan, L., Richter-Loesl, S. and Vance, L. 1991. 'Confronting Cancer through Art: A Collaborative Effort by Hospital, Patient and Therapist', in *Image & Metaphor: The Practice and Profession of Art Therapy*. Mundelein, IL: AATA, Inc.

Ostriker, A. 1993. 'Mastectomy Poems'. *The American Poetry Review*, 12–15. May/June.

Pennebaker, J. 1990. *Opening up. The Healing Power of Confiding in Others*. New York: William Morrow.

Rennie, S. 1993. 'Breast Cancer Prevention', *Ms*. 3 (6), 38–46.

Sigler, H. 1993. *Breast Cancer Journal: Walking With the Ghosts of My Grandmothers*. Rockford, IL: Rockford College.

Simonton, O. C., Simonton, S., and Creighton, J. 1978. *Getting Well Again*. Los Angeles, CA: J.P. Tarcher.

Spence, J. 1986. *Putting Myself in the Picture*. London: Camden Press.

Spiegel, D., Bloom, J., Kraemer, H., and Gottheil, E. (1989). 'Effect of Psychosocial Treatment on Survival of Patients With Metastatic Breast Cancer', *The Lancet*, 2, 888–891.

Wilber, K. (1991). *Grace and Grit: Spirituality and Healing in the Life and Death of Treya Killam Wilber*. Boston: Shambhala.

Williams, T. T. (1991). *Refuge: An Unnatural History of Family and Place*. NY: Pantheon Books.

Chapter 3

Alice, Dora and Constance from the eve of history

Maggie Jones

WHO ARE THEY?

> We practitioners go on mythologising, deriving our tough minded empirical facts from an extraordinary form of fiction: the case history, the recalling things past case history, the write-up, by means of which the details of a life are composed into a story, receive a vision, and thereby a mythical person becomes the personification of a fate which issues in to the therapeutic process.[1]

I would like to introduce this trio of women: Alice, Dora and Constance. They are certainly remarkable. They have been analysed and circumscribed by many before me and will no doubt be viewed and considered by others to come. These women are therefore placed and pictured within the frame of my discourse yet may not be bound by it for they live in the past, present and future; they are the stuff of mythology and allegory. Yet they exist. Moreover, they persist. Their very persistence lies in their fashioning, their subjection to translation and simultaneously in the inviolable problem of their failure to be known. They therefore persist as a mystery and as a riddle.

> Throughout the ages the problem of woman has puzzled people of every kind ... You too will have pondered over this question in so far as you are men; from the women among you that is not to be expected, for you are the riddle yourselves.[2]

The legacy of such invective from a not insignificant writer is central to the purpose of this exploration. The legacy did not of course have its genesis in Freud – woman as a riddle and by extension as harpy, whore, Madonna, witch, goddess – has been the object of man's gaze and puzzlement since he began writing history.

In the course of considering woman as she has been inscribed, described and prescribed by Freud it is necessary to reflect upon on what basis such observations were founded, I will make a leap backwards along the linear contour of Western Christian history to Eve and the event of the struggle over knowledge, temptation and expectation. Freud tells us in his lecture on the psychology of women that 'we must take care not to underestimate the influence of social conventions, which also force women into passive situations'. He does not however elucidate this but acknowledges that 'the whole thing is still very obscure'. Feminist writers have taken us further in being able to acknowledge the relationships between gender, consuetude and psychology.

Eve was necessary as a mother but was instrumental in the downfall of man. Essentially then from such a beginning by the very nature of and virtue of being a woman she became responsible for the life and the threat of expulsion (or death?). To make sense of what it is to be woman is to call upon all our senses, experiences and images and place them within an historic, bio-social, cultural and linguistic context. Such a context is informed by others than ourselves. As women we imagine the truth of our own experiences, until relatively recently, has been interpreted and recorded largely from a male viewpoint. There has been of course, throughout time, the brave lone voice of a woman standing her ground, and making her mark. Such voices are vital.

Often we turn to fiction to supply a truth that is otherwise too raw for acceptance, for through fiction we may be reassured of a reality one step removed. Through art therapy and the making of images a woman is given an opportunity to make her mark in her own fashion. Through imagery we may be artful with ourselves, express that which is too hard for words and, finally, to feel less obliged to mean what we say. It is difficult to be precise with imagery: with its fluid vocabulary it is easier to develop one's own sense of space and meaning. For woman then, there is the possibility of finding her own language of expression and making her own sense of this.[3]

Marie Cardinal in her story *The Words to Say It* says,

> what it meant to be a woman was to have a vagina. Until then I have never questioned the notion of femininity, that specific quality of being human having to do with breasts . . . and whose role on earth is to be the servant of the Lord, the diversion of the fighting man and the mother. Dressed, scented, embellished like a shrine, fragile, precious, delicate, illogical, bird-brained, available, the hole is always open, always ready to receive and give.[4]

Her story is of pain and self awareness within her own life. The words she found and issued to say it are courageous and womanly. In sharp contrast Bruno Bettleheim, who provides both preface and afterword to her words, within one sentence applauds and negates her. He says, 'Reading this book leaves one with great admiration for the author and restores one's faith in man.' He repeatedly refers to her as 'this girl' although she was twenty-seven years old at the time of her writing.[5] There is much encouragement to feel like a niggardly nit-picker when one draws to attention a comment

such as this, yet I believe that we serve ourselves poorly if we underestimate the significance of linguistic power and fail to note its values.

How do we define ourselves without being subjected to the descriptions
of a divisive language or without being made object within the space the
language creates? Lewis Carroll created Alice to amuse the young Liddell
girls. Alice becomes Carroll's Muse. Through her creation, the creator
finds his expression. By placing her in Wonderland he has permission
to comment on above-ground values and to take her safely through
some extraordinary experiences and transmutations. As Alice grows and
shrinks, and encounters that for which her above-world experience has
not prepared her, she asks, 'Who in the World am I?'[6] Her sense of
meaning is challenged as is the sense of self she thought she knew.
Judith Bloomingdale in 'Alice as Anima', says 'Alice herself is Carroll's
Beatrice – the Muse of his Comedy. Her fall down the rabbit hole is that
of Eve – Adam's soul-mate or *anima.*'[7] She continues her theme: 'Jung has
defined the *anima* as the archetypal image of woman that compensates the
masculine consciousness of every man.' Just as Eve might be regarded as
Adam's anima, Bloomingdale associates Alice's fall down the rabbit hole
with her transformation from being an autonomous person to becoming
Carroll's *anima.* Is this how women are animated?

By making the association of Alice with the Jungian concept of anima,
Judith Bloomingdale points to an image of woman which becomes the
epitome and container of all of man's wildest dreams. We become
'Everywoman', fashioned from a rib and made to serve like Eve; pure and
suffering in love like the Virgin Mary; wise and transcendent like the Mona
Lisa. When we fail to deliver, or conversely when we do meet man's so
called 'baser' needs, then we become the antithesis of these splendid,
bloodless images: we are witch, whore and harpy.

Alice, however, is living in the age of reason and attempts to apply her
above-ground worldly logic (*animus* – the image of man that compensates
the feminine consciousness) to the mystery and 'otherness' of Wonderland.
The voice of Carroll's masculine logical self reverberates through Alice as
she wrestles with the difficulty of her predicament. As she falls, 'down,
down, down, would the fall never come to an end?', she enters into (as
Virginia Woolf described it) 'that terrifying, wildly inconsequent, yet
perfectly logical world where time races, then stands still; where space
stretches, then contracts. It is the world of sleep; it is also the world of
dreams'.[8] It is just as well that Alice is able to think through her experiences
and endeavour to make sense of them.

There is indeed a dreamlike quality in Alice, although at times it is the
dream of monsters, of a world thought to be known no longer making
sense. A world where an understanding and use of language is insufficient
when applied to immediate experience; where the strangeness of the
Wonderland world and the necessity to survive within it requires a staunch

belief in what one 'knows' to be true, set against the apparent truth of the circumstances. Alice holds fast to her own linguistic-logistical truth but must also exist for the duration within another less known and changeable truth. She must become bi-lingual in her moral-logical understanding as well as her language, whilst remaining true to her own opinion. Alice struggles with this as she 'stubbornly persists in her attempts to relate their disordered actions to her notions of sanity'.[9] She struggles with the chaos and madness of her experience. What is madder than 'an attribute without a subject'?[10] What has Alice experienced that she might use to make sense of a grin without a cat? How do women make sense of, know ourselves, when we are subject to definition by man?

Luce Irigaray in 'The Looking Glass from the Other Side' recreates an Alice and draws a commentary on the experience of any Alice, all Alices. In this intense mimetic observation from the 'other' side, Irigaray plays upon the inside-outsideness of women's experience of being in the world:

> Up to now, that's what has controlled the limits of properties, distinguished outside from inside, differentiated what was looked on with approval from what was not. Made it possible to appreciate and recognise the value of everything, to fit in with it, as needed.[11]

The looking glass from the other side poses the question, 'How am I to know my own mind?'

> You've heard them dividing me up, in their own best interests. So either I don't have any 'self', or else I have a multitude of 'selves' appropriated by them, for them, according to their needs and desires.[12]

Just as Bruno Bettleheim rearranges a woman's experience to that of a girl, a doctor wrote in the notes in 1951 of a woman (with whom I conversed in 1993 when she was seventy-three) 'a markedly inadequate woman' and then, a little further on, 'this woman feels an intense loneliness'. What I wonder did he know of her experience? For me to come closer to her experience and self-description, firstly I had to recognise that there was a disjunction between the image of her created by the recorded observations of the 'professional' and that which I was hearing from her about herself. I know that still, in 1993, she constructed herself into 'I' and 'Me' – two selves – in order to be able to contain her pain and nightmares. She was still struggling with the bi-lingual necessity of expressing her own feeling self while endeavouring to make sense of this using the predominantly male language of the medical world. I consider that she had survived by protecting herself unselfconsciously with the 'I'–'Me' device which ensured that she was never again wholly open and available to the scrutiny and commentary of others. The use of plasticine enabled her to find an expression which did not depend on the dilemma and confusion. Her images bypassed the long-standing dichotomy, and symbolically 'I' and 'Me' became united without words.

The inhabitants of Carroll's Wonderland accept what in the above-ground experience Alice perceives as chaos. Lewis Carroll's 'masterpiece' may be seen as a clever 'exposure of the relativity of order' – a weaving of fantasy and reality perhaps.[13] It suggests that what mankind 'typically desires is not an adjustable frame of meaning, but an unambiguous and permanent order'.[14] We see through the pages of *Alice* a challenge to the convention that verbal communication is potentially logical and unambiguous. Meanings are turned upside down. If we do indeed find some uneasy solace in this possibility and savour our arm-chair romance with fiction, it would also appear that some fictions inspire us more than others. *Alice in Wonderland* has so far lasted the distance and has been translated into many languages other than English. Martin Grotjahn says, 'such books as Lewis Carroll's "Alice's Adventure in Wonderland" lead to an artistic and testing regression; they open a temporary guilt-free and relatively anxiety free communication to the unconscious. Necessary regression and sublimation are achieved more easily and with healthier results when the communication with the creative unconscious is kept alive, free, and open.'[15] Thus it may follow that Alice asks us to keep an open mind. Alice is not a matter of belief or disbelief in a logical sense, but an opening to many possible worlds of our own creating. A Victorian child created by a pathologically shy Victorian man, she is subject to his imagination but also available to ours.

As the reader, my imagination will allow the possibility and limitation of my self in my experience. Roland Barthes expands upon the necessary 'death' or disappearance, of the author in order that the text may be read untarnished and more truthfully by the reader.

> Linguistically, the author is never more than the instance writing, just as 'I' is nothing more than the instance saying 'I'. Language knows a 'subject' not a 'person' and this subject, empty outside of the very enunciation which defines it, suffices to make language 'hold together', suffices, that is to say, to exhaust it.[16]

If this approach of 'it is the language which speaks, not the author', is to be considered, there are for Alice and Dora many changes of pace and emphasis.[17] If we adopt the practice of reading intransitively we may free Alice and Dora from their respective authors and simultaneously release their authors from the responsibility of their words, beyond the acknowledgement that it was 'so and so' who actually wrote the words.[18]

What does this mean for the authors and subjects of the case study and in particular the recording of case notes in hospital files? What is the reader to make of the comment, 'a markedly inadequate woman'? The doctor had long ceased to have more than even a passing reference to the woman, yet he safely appears as the author of those words. If the file is destroyed the immediacy of the words may vanish but the memory lingers on. An effect has been achieved and confirmed through subsequent readers who add to and upon what may be assumed to be a responsible and accurate observation. She, like Dora, now wears the mantle and carries the properties of the reader's response.[19] In a sense her fate has been decided. Do we thus dare to be the authors of another's fate? It would seem so through the copious files in the mental health service.

Alice asks 'What will become of me?' in response to her apparently uncontrolled growth and also when she grapples with the curious other realities she encounters.[20] There is throughout the book an implicit understanding that her experiences are, and that she is herself, a fiction and, by extension, ultimately non-threatening. Of the many characters Alice encounters, the Duchess provides some interesting inverted commentary on the state of morality in Wonderland. 'Everything's got a moral, if only you can find it.'[21] This approach to the matter of morality appeals to me because it requires some questioning rather than directly accepting a given and presumably correct standard. The language is rearranged, but not so that it makes no sense. We may make sense of the Duchess saying, 'Take care of the sense and the sounds will take care of themselves', although this is not our usual sense or practice.[22] The emphasis of this being that we should think about the meanings of what is contained in the language that we use.

Another exchange that deserves noting here is Alice's meeting with Humpty Dumpty in *Through the Looking Glass*. Humpty Dumpty is a rather puffed-up sort of fellow. As he converses with Alice, he primps himself with his wit. They engage in a dialogue which has within it a dispute over terminology. From Alice's accepted sense of the meaning of things, she argues with his application of meaning. When this dispute seems to be going nowhere, Humpty Dumpty, in order to rest his case, says, 'When I use a word it means just what I choose it to mean – neither more nor less.' Alice retorts, 'The question is, whether you can make words mean so many different things.' 'The question is,' said Humpty Dumpty, 'which is to be master – that's all.'[23]

The emphatic nature of Humpty Dumpty's assertion has some resonance with the struggle I have experienced in hearing the truth of women's stories being told by themselves in a mental health service. This is set against the prescriptive and diagnostic interpretation of disorder as catalogued by those of a medical persuasion who seek to put linguistic parameters around individuals' experiences. Alice experiences distortion of time and space and witnesses much cruelty and aggression in her visit to Wonderland but we are finally assured that it was but a dream. However, whilst innocent Alice lingers lovingly in our heart, Freud's Dora receives no such apotheosis. We may rest assured that the girl-child-like qualities of Alice will endure.

Dora too has been the subject of much attention. Alice is a fantasy but engages in the dilemma of encountering the all too real distortions of human reality; Dora, while real – though not really Dora – is exposed as the all too human problem of Freud's failed understanding. Dora is the image of a young woman whereas Alice is the image of a girl as understood by Carroll. When we as a girl and then as a woman wonder about ourselves and our experiences, we have different abilities and capacities for our explorations, thoughts and feelings. Our explorations are limited by developmental stages, circumstance and the relative openness and fearlessness of our psyche. Furthermore, we are often limited by the words available to us to express our wonderings and the condition of the psyche. The psyche (or soul) is made more accessible through visual imagery. There is less concern about saying the right thing and the right word. Verbal and written discourse demands that we may both understand what the other person means. Hopefully, this would give more opportunity than Humpty Dumpty's use of language allowed for discovery of that meaning. But dialogue is linear in its composition, and thoughts, certainly feelings, are not necessarily so.

But is Dora a heroine or a victim? Dora went unwillingly to Freud at her father's insistence. It was she who decided, however, to terminate the contact with Freud, leaving him with a sense of unfinished business and dissatisfaction; that her decision to withdraw was 'an unmistakable act of vengeance on her part' and was engineered to frustrate him.[24] In this she seems to have been successful. For Freud's writing on 'Dora' has been gone over with a fine-toothed comb, extending and developing that original frustration that the analysis placed and replaced in various positions, analysing the analyst and his words. Through the vast amount of literature on Freud and Dora, beginning with Freud's original text, Dora has become a symbolic figure in the dispute over psychoanalytic meaning and interpretation. She has become both a fiction and a repository for psychoscientific voyeurism and speculation. Feminist analysis has ensured that Dora (Ida Bauer) is recognised as a woman and seen within a historic social, and psychoanalytic context, but it was Freud who made her a 'case'. We do not have Dora's autobiography. The image of Dora we have is Freud's, and others who have considered Dora have done so with knowledge and acuity which must still remain largely speculative. We do not know the reality of Ida Bauer.

Dora did not appear to ask, 'who am I?'. She may however have wondered, and well she might, 'what will become of me?'. Contemporary psychiatry is often to be found making subjects out of attributes and often voices itself in powerful and persuasive tones with an air of knowledge that is based on social correctness of behaviour and medical formulation. There is a strong inclination in psychiatry to presume greater knowledge than the client and to, like Humpty Dumpty, assume 'master-ship' of language. For women who find themselves as 'patients' of the mental health service the response to such questions may well contain descriptions of depression, psychosis, neurosis or personality disorder. The arguments of psychiatry are presented as gender-neutral yet 'what is left out of account, is the fact that ... we are calling attention to interpretative strategies that are learned, historically determined, and thereby necessarily gender inflected'.[25]

According to Steven Marcus, 'instead of letting Dora appropriate her own story, Freud became the appropriator of it.'[26] Freud is simultaneously interested in Dora from a psychoscientific line of enquiry and frustrated by her. He believed he could use her to explore his theory of Hysteria. She should do well as a servant to the savant.[27] Dora, however, thwarts him and takes her leave before he is able to satisfactorily conclude his enquiry. His vengeance perhaps then under the aegis of scientific advancement was to expatiate and execute her through his words. Freud reflects on the character of Dora's father: 'he was one of those men who know how to evade a dilemma by falsifying their judgement upon one of the conflicting alternatives'.[28] Now I do not mean to suggest that any obvious falsification was taking place but rather that 'as the case history advances it becomes increasingly clear to the careful reader that Freud and not Dora has become the central character in the action'.[29]

In his sexualising of Dora the words she is reported to have used and Freud's words to interpret them emphasise the 'at logger heads' position of the two. Freud refuses to accept that Dora is 'innocent of mind', for he has diagnosed her as an hysteric. In making the diagnosis Freud is clear. He claims *a priori* that 'It is possible for a man to talk to girls and women upon sexual matters of every kind without doing them harm and without bringing suspicion upon himself, so long as, in the first place, he adopts a particular way of doing it, and in the second place, can make them feel convinced that it is unavoidable'.[30] This comment seems well to indicate his 'master-fully', manipulative sense of gender power endorsed in the name of scientific enquiry.

How well this reflects the powerful positioning of psychiatric inter-pretation and assumption. How different is Simone de Beauvoir's viewing position:

> I shall place woman in the world of values and give her behaviour a dimension of liberty. I believe she has the power to choose between the assertion of her transcendence and her alienation as object; she is not the plaything of contradictory drives; she devises solutions of diverse values in the ethical scale. Replacing value with authority, choice with drive, psychoanalysis offers an *ersatz*, a substitute for morality – the concept of normality.[31]

Dora lives on. She has been infamed. 'To traverse Dora is to put in to question the subject: the subject of narrative and of sexual difference; the subject of discourse in literature and in psychoanalysis; the subject of desire, of interpretation, of transference.'[32] 'Dora is a text – and a woman surrounded by commentaries.'[33] 'For Hélène Cixous, the French theorist, Dora's case history has become an urtext in the history of woman.'[34]

Luce Irigaray contemporaneously brings the notion of the namelessness of both Alice and Dora together:

> ... 'she' never has a 'proper' name, that 'she' is at best 'from wonderland', even if 'she' has no right to a public existence except in the protective custody of the name of Mr X – then, so that she may be taken, or left, unnamed, forgotten without even having been identified, 'i' – who? – will remain uncapitalised. Let's say: 'Alice' underground.[35]

In speaking thus of Alice and Dora I endeavour to juxtapose two feminine creations by man. Are both fantasy or reality? Both have their origins in some kind of reality but have been removed from their own text and made famous or infamous through the text of male experience, imagining and longing. If we consider the authors of Alice and Dora, we are required to consider not only who they were (as far as historical reports and their own words may make them knowable) and their motivations for their authorship, but we must also view them within a historical, social and personal (including gender-based) context. A context is that which allows the text to be seen and placed. It provides the space in which an object may be seen or into which words may be spoken. It is possible, then, that a text may be taken out of context or that the text may be at odds with the context.

When a woman enters the psychiatric system she brings with her her own text. This text she may well be unable to speak but from the utterances she makes she is placed within a context which translates her into a framework of mental disorder and diagnosis. Her disease is then evaluated within a code of language which is specialised and removed from her experience. Her own text may well be so far removed from that of those who diagnose her as to render her unheard. Charlotte Perkins Gilman, like Marie Cardinal, finds herself as text as she describes her own experience in *The Yellow Wallpaper*. Her story demonstrates the alienation of her own text in a situation in which she becomes powerless in all but her imagination.

The Yellow Wallpaper is a woman's story which demonstrates 'the inaccessibility of female meaning to male interpretation'.[36] In the story the narrator is 'shut up' in a room and into her own mind and imagination. She is told by her physician husband that she must rest and do nothing. Specifically she must not write:

> But John has cautioned me not to give way to fancy in the least. He says that with my imaginative power and habit of story-making, a nervous weakness like mine is sure to lead to all manner of excited fancies and that I ought to use my will and good sense to check the tendency. So I try.'[37]

In her room, which was not the room of her choosing, she seeks to find a way out of her situation. Weighed down by the overbearing restrictions on her imposed by the voice of reason and masculine rightness, she finds uneasy solace in constructing a way out through the patterns of the wallpaper; through the walls which literally and figuratively imprison her.

The different and unbreachable experiences and values of the woman narrator and her husband are clear from the beginning:

> John laughs at me, of course, but one expects that in marriage. John is practical in the extreme. He has no patience with faith, an intense horror of superstition, and he scoffs openly at any talk of things not to be felt and seen and put down in figures.[38]

Finally she escapes:

> I've got out at last, in spite of you and Jane. And I've pulled off most of the paper, so you can't put me back.[39]

The author and her husband are both fluent in the English language. It is assumed that a shared understanding of meanings might follow (unlike in Wonderland). It becomes clear, however, that whilst she has an understanding of his context (in contemporary parlance: 'where he's coming from'), he is unable – and unwilling – to approach her meaning. She is thus ultimately reduced to speechlessness and voicelessness. In her silence his voice remains . . . until she escapes through her own imagery.

Although the story was written late last century, I was reminded of it recently on hearing the words of a man whose wife had been hospitalised following a manic episode: 'All I want is an efficient wife.'[40] In the text of *The Yellow Wallpaper* the narrator describes a turning point. She has succumbed to John's opposition to her writing; she has been disallowed from going out to visit people whom she feels may lift her spirits and she has endured John's reading to her after he put her back into bed. It is after these events that she begins to see a dim shape lurking behind the outside pattern of the wallpaper: 'It looks like a woman stooping down and creeping.'[41] 'From that point on the narrator progressively gives up the attempt to *record* her reality and instead begins to *read* it, as symbolically adumbrated in her compulsion to discover a consistent and coherent design amid "the sprawling outlines" of the wallpaper's apparently "pointless pattern".'[42]

The image of the creeping woman between the layers and patterns of the wallpaper is remarkably powerful. Each reader will respond to such imagery from her or his own experience and state of understanding. This is informed and coloured by culture, gender, age and so on. Although the description is made through words, it is the image of a creeping woman which has lasting potency. This image, then has become for me less ephemeral than the words used to create it. It speaks to me directly. Thus the many words which encompass this image provide the context for it, whilst the image may also exist discretely. A visual image, for example, a painting made in art therapy, may 'contain' many references and meanings in the one space.[43]

For women, in contrast to the linguistic tradition, art therapy offers a means of expression that is less readily 'male' in its vocabulary and is therefore more readily open to and able to reference the true experience of the woman. There is a more immediate sense of this being her own expression, her own language. Concomitantly there is an explicit sense of it being less easy to read and therefore less easy to interpret into another context. The image may speak for itself, reducing the possibility of the artist/client being spoken over.[44]

Art therapy is able to access a personal language for the artist/client which requires a more reflective consideration and less assumption than the more discursive verbally based communication. The strength of art therapy for women lies in the opportunity for a more truly personal expression which yet may be safely seen by another. There is always the possibility, of course, of the other viewer, the therapist, assuming that her or his interpretation is required, correct and that he or she can see through the imagery. This possibility is a perennial concern of therapy. The potential for art therapy lies in the possibility that a person's expression is valid in itself and through the safe contact with the therapist and the imagery the language is safely developed. In the images or pictures made by women, any interpretations require a sagacity that is mindful of both the personal and the wider context(s) and the language used to describe it. If, as I have suggested, an image may speak for itself – if we can but allow it – we may be allowed closer to the truth of what is being expressed. A quote from Nietzsche illustrates my point: 'Art treats appearance as appearance; its aim is precisely not to deceive, it is therefore true.'[45] With imagery, then, a truth is more immediately accessed and is less easily subdued by interpretation.

The values and exclusiveness of terminology used within certain systems and groups (often to which we pay to have access and make use, for example, the legal, justice and medical systems) is inflected with the masculine prerogative. In the face of health reforms, the language of fiscally driven management continues to emerge as a dominant force with which to be reckoned. Working within the mental health environment now requires an understanding of the language of money-speak as well as psychiatry-speak. In order to work with integrity, it is important not only to be familiar with these languages but also to sustain the openness and otherness of the possibility of art and of women. There is always pressure to join ranks with a dominant voice. Art therapy provides a voice, the strength of which is its otherness amongst accustomed formality. Art has its own, some would say subversive, power. This will continue, as art is necessary for succour and survival, to accommodate and provide a language for women where we are either required to use a seemingly foreign language or else go unheard.

I began this chapter with a quote from James Hillman and will conclude with one in which he describes the confusion of identity for women as anima:

> This soul person is the person of our moods, self reflections and reveries, of our sensuous longing beyond the sensately concrete, the spinner of fantasy who is the personification of all unknown psychic capacities that lie waiting, drawing us seductively, uncannily inward to the dark of the uncut forest and the deep below the waves. She is father's daughter and mother's daughter and my sister, my soul. She is also a worrying succubus drawing off our life's juice, a harpy with talons, a cold white wraith with mad addictions – but a nurse as well, and a serving maid, a Cinderella nymphette, vague with no history, a tabula rosa waiting for the word. And she is also the Sophia of wisdom, the Maria of compassion, the Persephone of destruction, compelling Necessity and Fate, and the Muse.[46]

Thus are all women and thus we are all Eve, Alice and Dora. And Constance. Did I not mention her? She has been there all along.

NOTES

1 Hillman, 1975: 155.
2 Freud's Lecture XXXIII, 'The Psychology of Women', in *New Introductory Lectures on Psychoanalysis*, Freud, 1949: 145–6.
3 Needless to say, as soon as a therapist is involved in this process there is always the risk of that other interpretation (through the linguistic tradition) entering in and clouding the scene. With care and the ability to make room for the unique language potential of art, this risk may be lessened.
4 Cardinal, 1993: 261–2.
5 Bettleheim, preface to Cardinal, 1993: xii.
6 Carroll 1971: 8.
7 Phillips, 1973: 438.
8 Carroll, 1971: 10; Phillips, 1973: 79.
9 Phillips, 1973: 467.
10 Phillips, 1973: 467.
11 Irigaray, 1985: 10.
12 Irigaray, 1985: 17.
13 Phillips, 1973: 465.
14 Phillips, 1973: 465.
15 Phillips, 1973: 368.
16 Barthes, 1977: 145.
17 Barthes, 1977: 143.
18 This raises an important issue for the historical silence and anonymity of women's writing.
19 I am aware that there needs to be a more thorough exploration of the relative

'purpose' of writing, though one might follow the same principles here of Barthes' author–reader commentary.

20 Carroll, 1971: 32.
21 Carroll, 1971: 79.
22 Carroll, 1971: 80.
23 Carroll, 1992: 113.
24 Freud, 1953: 109.
25 Kolodny, 1985: 243.
26 Marcus, 1990: 85.
27 It has been noted that Dora was the name of a servant known to Freud.
28 Freud, 1953: 34.
29 Marcus, 1990: 85.
30 Freud, 1953: 48.
31 De Beauvoir, 1979: 82.
32 Suleiman, 1987: 127.
33 Suleiman, 1987: 128.
34 Appignanesi and Forrester, 1993: 146.
35 Irigaray, 1985: 22.
36 Kolodny, 1985: 257.
37 Gilman, 1973: 22.
38 Gilman, 1973: 9.
39 Gilman, 1973: 36.
40 It was first published in May 1892 in the *New World Magazine*.
41 Gilman, 1973: 22.
42 Kolodny, 1985: 250.
43 'Contain' here is used to denote both the possibility and coexistence of many references and also that they may be held within the space of the paper upon which they figure.
44 I hope as a therapist I am not in the habit of 'speaking-over' unwittingly but it must be noted that it is much less likely that I would do a 'paint-over'.
45 Nietzche, quoted in Brooke-Rose, 1987: 35.
46 Hillman, 1975: 42–3.

BIBLIOGRAPHY

Appignanesi, L., and Forrester, John. 1993. *Freud's Women*. London: Virago.

Appignanesi, R. 1979. *Freud for Beginners*. London: Writers and Readers.

Barthes, R. 1977. *Image-Music-Text*. (Translated and selected by S. Heath.) London: Fontana-Collins

Bernheimer, C. and Kahane, C. 1990. *In Dora's Case: Freud, Hysteria Feminism*. New York: Columbia University Press.

Brooke-Rose, C. 1987. 'Id Is, Is Id?', in Rimmon-Kenan (ed.).

Cardinal, M. 1993. *The Words to Say It*. London: The Women's Press.

Carroll, L. 1971. *Alice's Adventures in Wonderland*. London: Oxford University Press.

Carroll, L. 1992. *Through the Looking Glass*. London: Macmillan.

de Beauvoir, S. 1979. *The Second Sex*. Harmondsworth: Penguin.

Freud, S. 1949. 'Lecture XXXIII, The Psychology of Women', in *New Introductory Lectures on Psychoanalysis*, Jones, E. (ed.). London: Hogarth Press.

Freud, S. 1953. 'A Case of Hysteria' in *The Collected Works of Freud*, vol. VII. London: Hogarth Press.

Garner, N., Kahane, S., Sprengnether Madelon, C. (eds) 1985. *The (M)other*

Tongue: Essays in Feminist Psychoanalytic Interpretation. Ithaca, New York: Cornell University Press.

Gilman, C. P. 1973. *The Yellow Wallpaper.* London: The Feminist Press.

Hillman, J, 1975. *Re-visioning Psychology.* New York: Harper and Row.

Irigaray, L. 1985. *This Sex Which Is Not One.* Ithaca: Cornell University Press.

Kolodny, A. 1985. 'A Map for Re-reading; or, Gender and the Interpretation of Literary Texts', in Garner, Kahane and Sprengnether (eds).

Marcus, S. 1990. 'Freud and Dora: Story, History, Case History', in Bernheimer and Kahane (eds).

Phillips, R. (ed.) 1973. *Aspects of Alice.* Harmondsworth: Penguin.

Rimmon-Kenan, S. (ed.) 1987. *Discourse in Psychoanalysis and Literature.* London and New York: Methuen.

Suleiman, S. R. 1987. 'Nadsa, Dora, Lol v. Stein: Women, Madness and Narrative', in Rimmon-Kenan (ed.).

Chapter 4

Feminist-perspective art therapy: an option for women's health

An Australian perspective

Susan Joyce

A feminist model of therapy has been developed and established by feminist therapists over the past two decades. However, in the field of art therapy discourse on feminist philosophy and feminist practice seems to have been absent in the literature, training components and practice. With such a void, there can be no platform for feminist art therapists to debate, challenge traditional frameworks and work towards strategies to provide a feminist art therapy practice. In this chapter I will first view and question the possible reasons for the lack of a feminist perspective in art therapy, focusing on the absence of feminist research and publications, together with the absence of feminist influence in art therapy training.

In the second half of the chapter, I look at some ideas on women and mental illness – you know, that 'disease' to which women are 'naturally' so 'prone'. For over two centuries feminists have voiced their discontent with a mental health system that is prepared to diagnose a woman as mentally ill without taking account of the social, political or cultural factors in her life. In art therapy training there is usually a compulsory component of basic psychiatry and mental health diagnosis to prepare the art therapy student to work in psychiatric institutions among other mental health professionals. Many at the end of their training believe that these diagnostic categories represent actual truths about women. Historical analysis of the discourse of women's mental illness suggests that the institution of psychiatry has been shaped as a tool to oppress women and lead them to social conformity under a patriarchal regime.

Feminist art therapists must begin to debate about how we perceive our role as professionals working with women who have mental health problems. Do feminist art therapists work *with* the mental health system, accepting the diagnoses and pharmaceutical treatments of their women clients, agreeing with the prognosis that they are clinically mentally ill? Or do we use our skills and knowledge to offer women an alternative form of treatment, by assisting them to become aware of the effects of social, political and economic oppression, the objectification and sexualisation of women's bodies and the suspicion and low value associated with the female gender?

This chapter is not only aimed at providing material for debate among art therapists and other health professionals, it is intended to serve as an informative and provocative essay for women who are interested in or have had personal contact with the mental health system.

FEMINISM AND ART THERAPY: PROBLEMS IN RESEARCH, PUBLICATION AND PRACTICE

It is surprising to find a scarcity of feminist art therapy research and publications in the available literature, journals and training components, considering the profession is predominantly pursued and occupied by women. According to Johnson, women make up 90–95 per cent of qualified art therapy practitioners.[1] Abbenante comments, 'In twelve years of practice and eight years of teaching art therapy [I] remain disturbed by the absence of feminist approach in the literature of the field'.[2]

The acknowledgement of this void in feminist input resulted in the publication of a 'special issue' in the journal *The Arts in Psychotherapy* entitled 'Special Issue – Women and the Creative Arts Therapies'.[3] Although this recognition is preferable to non-recognition, this marginalisation of women's issues by the use of the term 'special' serves to locate women and women's issues in a place that is not central. This so called 'marginal group' of 'other' applies to those whose gender is not male. In politics and policy-making, women are constantly being referred to in these terms, even when women make up 52 per cent of the world population.

In the context of *The Arts in Psychotherapy* special issue a contributor to the volume, Marlene Talbott-Green, acknowledges this concern. Talbott-Green quoting Dubois *et al.* explains that in relation to research, the presentation of a special issue by any discipline is problematic in that it isolates the subject from the rest of the field suggesting that it is not sufficiently accepted to be considered among more standard research.[4] This has the effect of the subject being 'ghettoized' within a discipline. Furthermore, after the publication of a special issue the subject was virtually dropped from further issues. Indeed, there have been no other sightings of feminist articles about art therapy since the 1989 special issue.

We cannot assume, however, that the lack of published feminist art therapy literature constitutes an absence of activity on the part of feminist art therapists. Nor can we assume that there are few women art therapists who consider themselves feminists. Talbott-Green states, 'The reality is that both creative arts and feminist therapists have a rich body of theory, research, and practice that is sound and vital to the field of psychotherapy.'[5] If feminist art therapists do exist, why is there such a lack of research and publications? Is research being conducted by feminist art therapists? If they actively conduct research, why is this work not published in the mainstream journals?

According to Talbott-Green, the reason for the lack of recognition of feminist art therapists' accumulated knowledge and experience is both political and personal. The barrier that restricts feminist art therapists from research and publication comprises:

the dominance of traditional theory, research and practice, its accepted methodology, the political structures for dissemination of this knowledge, and the cultural, social and personal biases that effectively eliminate a feminist perspective as a guiding principle.[6]

In her article 'Feminist Scholarship: Spitting into the Mouths of the Gods', Talbott-Green details five reasons that may explain the lack of authority and recognition of a feminist perspective in art therapy research publication and practice.[7] These are: (a) the misconceived drive towards professionalism by some leaders in the fields, (b) sex bias in research, (c) reverence for the knowledge in physical sciences and the desire to emulate them so as to ensure credibility and legitimacy, (d) exclusive editorial policies, and (e) a personal inability to incorporate the feminine into the psyches of individual researchers and therapists.

Although the art therapy profession is predominantly occupied by women, specialists and practitioners in the wider categories of professions in mental health are predominantly men. Milwid conducted research on thirty white middle-class women in their twenties to thirties who had a nontraditional career in a dominantly male occupied profession and who had practised for five years or under.[8] The findings revealed that although the women had no difficulty with their actual work, the stress and effort to gain professional recognition from their male colleagues became exhausting and caused anxiety. The women perceived that they had to perform in an outstanding fashion to gain the slightest credibility and had to accomplish far more than their male peers in order to be seen as a professional equal. They said that their performance in the job had to be better than excellent – it had to be perfect. One woman described her reaction of not knowing the answer to a question as a feeling of total shame and inadequacy, while her male peers felt that not knowing an answer had no consequence for them.

Milwid's research indicates the effect on women who are working in male-dominated professions. The area of research and publication has historically been mostly occupied and governed by men. Talbott-Green claims that it is the relative absence of feminist perspectives in the creative arts and therapy professions and the lack of publications that hinder the development of full professional status for women in the field.

Keeping women out of print is a strategy, conscious or unconscious, overt or covert, to isolate and insulate them from their own experience, from learning about affirming the experiences of other women, from forming bonding professionally.[9]

Within the mental health system, a hierarchy exists that places psychiatrists at the top. Psychiatrists are predominantly male and determine the very categories by which mental health or mental illness is diagnosed. Next on the ladder are the psychologists whose 'scientific' tests, measures and assessments produce the statistics of 'normality' and 'abnormality'. Further down are the 'others', the psychotherapist and those specialising in particular forms of expressive therapies – for example art therapy, music therapy and drama therapy. At the very bottom of the ladder are the nursing staff. In institutional settings the nursing staff have more interaction with the clients than other staff. The last two categories, the expressive therapists and nursing staff, are predominantly female while the areas of psychiatry and psychology are predominantly male.

The higher up the ladder, the more 'professional' and the more of an 'expert' you are perceived to be. Moreover, the further up the ladder, the more one enters the male domain. Ussher quotes Holloway, stating that the 'experts' of psychological assessment, that is, psychiatrists and psychologists, are not as objective and neutral as they claim. Instead they have been 'implicated in coercive social regulation and in reproducing social differences in favour of men, white people, Western and middle class people'.[10]

In her article, Talbott-Green suggests that women working in the mental health field as art therapists are likely to find it difficult to consider themselves to be fully professional because of the hierarchy of the 'real experts', and therefore are likely to feel less confident about venturing into research and publication.[11] She concludes by asking the women readers:

> Is your important knowledge being published and disseminated among a wide audience of mental health professionals? Might you be doomed forever to tell truthful stories never to be believed, making ecstatic utterances while others think you are mad?[12]

Research in the area of feminist art therapy must include a complete analysis of the various discourses that are handed to the profession as 'factual truths'. In other areas of therapy, feminist analysis of traditional frameworks are being turned on their head or viewed from such a perspective that they are rendered as irrelevant or in opposition to women's psychological health. For instance, Gilligan *et al.* research the period when young girls aged around eleven years, often lose their self-confidence and develop various physically and psychologically harmful relationships and practices.[13] In developmental psychology, this period is accepted as a difficult and confusing stage for the pubescent and is acknowledged as a stage of 'resistance'. However, Gilligan *et al.* have concluded that in listening to girls as authorities about girls, the understanding of resistance has been transformed and reframed as a psychological strength and a healthy mark of courage. 'Resistance' can be seen as the capacity to resist disease processes, to embark on political struggle and the wish to act on one's own knowledge. The psychological health of women depends on their ability and the strength of their resistance.

In this instance, the clinical concept of 'resistance' is turned from an inevitable negative period of confusion, non-compliance and self-destruction, to a period of strength, courage and self-determination. Gilligan believes that the study of adolescent girls offers a key to understanding women's psychological development and can offer suggestions for preventing and treating women and girls' psychological suffering. In the field of art therapy, such methods of critical evaluation and analysis are absent, and the 'truths' that the 'gods' of art therapy speak have remained accepted and unchallenged.

In reviewing the contemporary art therapy literature (much of which is included in reading lists for art therapy courses) there is no mention of feminism or feminist-perspective therapy. Currently, art therapy remains entrenched in and framed within the traditional concepts that stem from aspects of traditional psychoanalysis, psychiatry and developmental and clinical psychology. In fields such as family therapy and psychotherapy, these concepts have been critically analysed by feminist theorists, whereas in the field of art therapy these traditional concepts have yet to be examined or challenged by feminist art therapy theorists.

FEMINIST PERSPECTIVE IN ART THERAPY TRAINING

During my experience of having trained in art therapy, worked as an art therapist in various community and clinical settings, and having taught on Masters level art therapy programmes, I have found a total lack of feminist theory in the area. Despite requests and demands made by students and colleagues (and myself), there has been a sustained resistance to address this issue. Feminist theory seems to be considered a 'new concept' in art therapy, and one that is consequently overshadowed by more traditional theories of psychoanalysis, psychiatry and developmental psychology. Its absence results in leaving these other approaches unchallenged and art therapy graduates not gaining exposure to alternative theories.

Students training at Masters level in art therapy are required to understand the psychoanalytic theories of theorists such as Freud, Jung, Klein and Winnicott as a basis for understanding concepts in therapy. Some feminists have criticised such theories as patriarchal and misogynist and as continuing to perpetuate essentialist myths about women. Israel quotes Kravetz in saying that traditional psychoanalytic theories

> present women as innately passive, dependent, anatomically inferior, and emotionally immature. Motherhood is required as a universal

fulfilment. There is increasing pressure to reinforce that view of women from the conservative segments of society. Unfortunately, standards used to assess the behaviour of female clients and evaluate their distress, and formulate treatment goals are derived from such concepts. Thus the prevalence of sex bias in clinical theories is likely to affect practice.[14]

Students training in art therapy must also acquire an understanding of psychiatric diagnosis categories and terminology. While the awareness of such theories and procedures for mainstream mental health assessment is necessary in order to work in the clinical field and alongside other clinical practitioners, I would stress the need for the employment of feminist theory in conjunction with these diagnostic techniques. All diagnosis is necessarily subjective but by placing the problem within the client, under the guise of a supposedly neutral scientifically validated diagnosis, the values of the professionals are consequently concealed.[15] By omitting feminist theory from art therapy training programmes, the mental health diagnosis system continues to be perceived as a bible of unchallengeable truths for assessing women's mental health.

Given the fact that the majority of art therapists are women, why has the inclusion of feminist perspective therapy continued to be absent in the art therapy education and training system? Wadeson believes that the doctrines of clinical theory and practice have been designed by men in a patriarchal context, and that the institutions that foster theory-building are dominated by men.[16] Design and content of some art therapy training components are dictated by male academics.

Men continue to occupy the most powerful positions in graduate training. During 1992, I was invited as a visiting lecturer in the first Masters-level art therapy programme to be developed in Australia and asked to give feedback on the course content. At the time, two art therapists – one male, one female – were convening the course, but the female therapist had resigned and was due to be replaced. There were about twenty female students on the course and one male student. I had an individual meeting with the majority of the students on the course. One issue that arose for some female students was the lack of feminist components in the training schedule. During the staff feedback session I suggested that the new member of staff should be a woman because of the vast predominance of female students, and that the new tutor should have some feminist philosophy to fulfil students' requests. The general reaction of senior staff was that gender was not an issue in selecting the new tutor and suggestion of the inclusion of feminist theory in the training schedule was avoided. Shortly after this, another male member of staff was appointed and the issue of the inclusion of feminist philosophy was not further addressed.

The lack of feminist art therapists involved in the decision-making on components in the education and training of art therapists results in the continuation of patriarchal discourse as central to training and feminist analysis of such discourse together with feminist perspective as peripheral or absent. This issue, together with the problems of feminists gaining entry into this area of research and publication, and problems of feminists obtaining clinical management positions, in effect continues the promotion of patriarchal discourse and practice and excludes feminist theory, philosophy and practice in the professional arena.

STATE HEALTH SYSTEMS – HOW DO THEY SERVE WOMEN?

In Australia, a system that indirectly plays a part in the exclusion of feminist-perspective therapy practice and the promotion of patriarchal theory and practice is the state health system of Medicare. The Medicare system provides financial rebates for those on low income who use the state health system. These rebates are only available on certain medical services. In the area of women's mental health services and women's therapy needs, the Medicare rebate system provides rebates only for the services of psychiatrists. Given that psychiatry is male-dominated and focused on psychopathological causation for women's distress, the state rebate system can be seen as playing a part in the disempowerment of women by fostering their dependence on health services which reinforces and promotes patriarchy.

Women who seek therapy may have no other option than to engage with a psychiatrist in order to be entitled to the Medicare rebate, despite the availability of other therapists who may be more appropriate – for example, feminist therapists, psychotherapists or art therapists. In Brisbane, some female psychiatrists offering feminist-perspective psychotherapy have a waiting list of up to six to eight months before a new client can start therapy. Feminist psychiatrists are inundated with clients because the Medicare scheme provides financial rebates, while non-psychiatrist feminist therapists whose fees are not covered by the Medicare scheme are often unable to maintain a practice. By the Medicare scheme subsidising only the services of psychiatrists, women are limited in their choice of the type of therapy they wish to use and often restricted in the preferred sex of the therapists they wish to engage with. This limitation leaves many women with no choice but to engage in therapy with a male psychiatrist.

For female clients seeking to engage with an art therapist in an individual or group format, again the Medicare scheme can be seen as limiting women's options and choice in the type of therapy and the gender of the therapist, directing them towards male-dominated oppressive systems. Apart from the benefits of group therapy discussed later in this chapter, the group format is also a financially viable option for both women clients and the feminist therapists. The therapist can offer a therapy service in the group format at a lower cost per individual than a one-to-one session, resulting in therapy being accessible to women on lower incomes.

WOMEN AND PSYCHIATRY

Feminist literature on women and mental health has been prevalent over the past two decades. Feminists state that the category of 'women' has been constructed as deviant from the male 'norm'. The effect on individual women is that nonconformity to their social order can be easily categorised as being sick, mad or bad, through the patriarchal discourse of medicine.

The treatment of women in the mental health system has been openly criticised and attacked from the early 1970s when women who had been patients in the mental health system started to speak out, telling of their unjust treatment and negative experiences as psychiatric patients. The period from the early 1970s to mid 1980s saw a vibrant influx of feminist literature and feminist critiques on the constructs of women, women's madness and the mental health system.

Literature such as Chesler's *Women and Madness* examined how Western contemporary society routinely described female identity in terms of sickness and insanity[17]. Feminists claimed that psychiatry was based on sex-bias and sex-role stereotyping of women and that the mental health systems served to oppress and regulate women's role as subservient to men. At about the same time, there was a renewed interest in feminist critiques of psychoanalysis from various perspectives. Literature emerging during the 1970s confronted the basis and construct of psychoanalytic theory with publications such as Miller's *Psychoanalysis and Women* and Mitchell's *Psychoanalysis and Feminism*[18].

Chesler was one of the first to look intensely at the effects sexism had on women psychotherapy patients. Other major works followed for example, Tennov's *Psychotherapy – The Hazardous Cure* and Smith and David's *Women Look at Psychiatry*[19]. These critiques provided examples of the impact on psychotherapy of culturally specific assumptions about women. Broverman *et al.*'s study 'Sex Role Stereotyping and Clinical Judgement of Mental Health', was the first to document the sexist attitudes of psychotherapists[20]. Sturdivant summarises Broverman's study as finding that

> while there was little difference between adult and masculine concepts of mental health, there was a difference between the adult and female concepts of mental health. This came to be known as the 'double standard' of mental health where women could either be healthy mature adults or mature women but not both.[21]

The categories of psychopathology listed in the *Diagnostic and Statistical Manual of the American Psychiatric Association (DSM-III-R)* are based on beliefs about women's 'normality' and 'abnormality' which are stereo-typical. The psychiatric system that decides whether a woman's mental health is 'normal' or 'abnormal' has been based on ideologies of how men would like women to be, not how women actually are. Therefore if women do not conform to their assigned lot, there are convenient psychiatric categories in which to place them as pathologically mentally ill. These categories are held as 'truths' by the predominantly male-populated mental health professions.

The 'truths' which create the modern form of society are fictions and therefore themselves founded on fantasy. The 'real' therefore becomes a problematic category.[22]

In this respect, the field of psychiatry can be accused of being a blatantly systematic use of patriarchal power over women and serves to regulate and oppress women by confining them to the social order and to the male advantage.

The current trend to bring psychiatry closer to science, biology and its 'medical origins' by developing more refined systems of classification still does not address some of its basic assumptions that keep women oppressed. Traditional mental health treatment for women is based more on helping the woman adapt to her social circumstances than on 'risking a look at how the world is disastrously out of tune with human needs, particularly women's needs'.[23] According to Smith:

> Women are forced into a second hand understanding of the world. Women are trained to invalidate their own experiences, understanding, and feelings and to look to men to tell them how to view themselves. The ideas, concepts, images, and vocabularies that women use to think about their experiences have been formulated from the male point of view by universities, churches, and other social institutions.[24]

The concepts of mental illness and psychiatric theories locate the problem within the individual who is sick. Critics of psychiatry would locate the sickness within the constructs of society. The discourse of mental illness diverts the attention away from the problems within society, focusing on the individual who is suffering only as a direct result of social pressures. The labels used to diagnose someone mentally ill can be seen as a reflection of the inequalities and conflicts within society. Therefore the mental health professionals who provide individual technological solutions in the form of classification and treatment of mental illness disguise the social misery experienced by those individuals.

The concept of madness and the labelling of women's madness can be viewed as a social construct to control and maintain dominant order. Within feminist analysis Ussher concludes that

> the labelling process is seen to serve the function of maintaining women's position as outsiders within patriarchal society; of dismissing

women's anger as illness – and so exonerating the male oppressors; and dismissing women's misery as being a result of some internal flaw – and thus protecting the misogynistic social structures from any critical gaze.[25]

The psychiatric associations are continually revising the diagnostic manuals such as the *DSM*. This results in the categories becoming more refined and more inclusive of women's bodily characteristics. For instance, in the revised fourth edition of the *DSM*, it is proposed that pre-menstrual symptoms and menopausal changes will be categorised as mental illness. Critics of the inclusion of pre-menstrual symptoms argue that 'from two to eight percent of women could be diagnosed as psychiatrically ill and that all women of reproductive age are at risk of this form of "mental disorder"'.[26] A 'resurgent belief in the incapacitating effects of menstruation . . . casts an insidious shadow over all women whose normal physiological fluctuations are now deemed as excessive or incapacitating.[27]

An evaluation of the construction of medical discourse over the past two centuries illustrates that psychiatry as an institution has developed a body of knowledge concerning the categories of 'woman', 'femininity' and 'female sexuality' based on misogynous assumptions and beliefs. Through the development of psychiatry this knowledge about 'women' has provided a basis for defining women as mentally ill. The constraints are becoming narrower and more inclusive resulting in almost every aspect of women being vulnerable to the descriptions of mentally ill.

The medical discourse, in allegiance with other discourses such as law, religion and politics, has served to regulate women ensuring their confinement within the private sphere and limit their social, economic and political power. Such discourses are constructed in the interest of one gender, focusing on male supremacy, male power, male ownerships against women's best interests. The deconstruction of such discourses by feminist theorists and the analysis of power gained through such discourses are vital in the rewriting of 'women' and repositioning of women in social terms. To avoid a historical generalisation about all women, feminist theorists and feminist analysis must work within the frame of specific cultural considerations, specific historical context and specific spatial considerations.

FEMINIST-PERSPECTIVE THERAPY: FUNDAMENTAL PRINCIPLES

Because of the growing dissatisfaction with the mental health service for women, a feminist psychotherapy service started with the establishment of the Women's Therapy Centre in Britain. The founders, Luise Eichenbaum and Susie Orbach, aimed to influence other mental health services for women and aid the development of women's psychoanalytical and psychological theory. From the onset, there was a great demand for individual feminist therapy and the centre was soon well established, offering a programme of workshops: theme-centred groups, training courses for professionals and an advice and information service on psychotherapy and counselling resources for women. Women's therapy centres and training institutions now exist in several cities in the UK and USA.

The network of feminist psychotherapists involved in the women's therapy centres created a further body of work resulting in publications such as Ernst and Maguire's *Living with the Sphinx*.[28] This literature entered the theory of women's psychology and examined how theory and practice of psychotherapy could illuminate the understanding of women. This included taking up issues of power, racism and gender.

Although the development of feminist principles in psychotherapy, psychology and psychoanalysis has gained momentum over the decades, mainstream mental heath services are still firmly entrenched in the patriarchal view of women that is based on presumptions and misperceptions.

Feminist-perspective therapy rejects the sex-role stereotypes assigned to women as realities about women and concentrates on their effect in both the emotional response and the social positioning of women. In other words, feminist-perspective therapy takes into account the social and political effects of sex-role stereotyping on individual women rather than looking for a psychopathological abnormality, as psychiatry does.

In relation to women's mental health, the development of feminist theory has challenged the traditional models of treatment by saying that the method used for assessing and treating women with mental health problems exploits women's position of subservience. This leads women towards conformity by reinforcing the sex-role stereotype as 'true normality', thus perpetuating myths about women and the oppression and subordination of women. A feminist perspective perceives that the mental health professions 'serve a social function by helping to maintain sexual and other social inequalities and at the same time have the task of helping women cope with the personal consequences of these inequalities'.[29] Israel states that 'there is a basic harmful conflict between the norms of our social institutions and the expectations and social realities of women's behaviour within those norms'.[30]

In contrast to the traditional mental health profession there are several accounts and summaries outlining the basis and benefits of feminist-perspective therapy. According to Sturdivant, feminist therapy 'offers an alternative explanation, via sex-role and socio-cultural conditioning, of why things can go wrong for a woman developmentally, with corresponding implications for the interpretation of psychopathology'.[31] Israel comments that 'feminist therapy . . . frees women from the traditional sex role stereotypes, minimises the difference in power between the therapist and the client, and emphasises a person's right to self-actualisation'.[32] Ussher remarks, 'feminist practice was not developed from one particular theory of therapy: it originated from a new set of values, and a system for how these could be integrated into existing therapies'.[33] Therefore feminist therapy is seen as a philosophical approach to the practice of therapy rather than a prescription of technique and consequently can be applied to a wide range of practice.

The initial primary goal of feminist therapy was to help women overcome the effects of oppression in their own lives. The commitment was to change, not to adjustment, and to the client's definition of change, not the therapist's.[34] It was considered likely that women who engaged in this process of change might become politically aware and possibly involved in social action. Therefore the emphasis in feminist-perspective therapy was on the 'personal as political'. The emergence of literature on the psychology of women and feminist critiques of psychiatry constituted a knowledge base for new feminist practice. It must be stated, however, that the literature that formed the basis of feminist practice and principles focused on white European women, from a viewpoint of white European women, and therefore is culturally specific and cannot be appropriated cross-culturally.

In the traditional model of therapy practice the majority of practitioners were male and the majority of clients female. This involved a power relationship as the therapist was perceived as having the power of knowledge in human behaviour, and the client was considered passive and lacking in such scientific awareness. This inequality in power meant that the female client could be easily manipulated, influenced and guided towards conformity or convinced that they were mentally ill. The therapist's suggestion of medication in the form of tranquillisers to relieve distress became another tool in suppressing women's reaction to oppression, resulting in perpetuating women's position of subordination. Ussher makes the connection that:

> The abuse of power in therapy is evident in the contemporary studies on therapists (mostly male psychiatrists) forming sexual relationships with their (mostly female) clients. Quadrio's study shows that between 7–10% of male therapists form intimate sexual relationships with their female clients and that 50% of the female clients are unaware that this practice is unethical. The large majority of the female clients that become sexually involved with their male therapists have childhood sexual abuse backgrounds. According to Quadrio's study 90% of the female clients are seriously psychologically damaged as a result of the therapist's abuse of power by sexually engaging with the clients.[35]

In terms of power relations the male therapist/female client dyad is perceived as a patriarchal 'micro-culture'. Feminist therapy principles were established to create a different qualitative therapeutic relationship: not one based on dominance and control, but a way of working where the power difference is addressed and acknowledged to enable the power difference to be kept to a minimum. Addressing the issues of power in the therapeutic relationship was made a priority in the establishment of a base for feminist practice.

The strategies used to minimise the inequality of power in the therapeutic relationship have been outlined by several feminist therapy theorists (Sturdivant 1980; Gilbert 1980; Walker 1990; Rawlings and Carter 1977; Ussher and Nicolson 1992). The strategies used by feminist therapists to minimise the power inequality in therapy can be briefly outlined. In traditional therapy a client's request for information about the therapist has been interpreted by the therapist as the client's issues of distrust or as paranoiac pathological symptoms. The reluctance to disclose information and the interpretation of such requests has helped maintain a power imbalance between the therapist and client. If the feminist therapist makes explicit her personal and professional values, and her training and area of expertise, the clients have the opportunity to choose a therapist more suited to their needs rather than the therapist choosing the clients. Therefore the therapist provides a commodity and the client actively selects an appropriate service as a consumer. The power imbalance is reduced if the client is provided with information about the therapist.

Traditional therapists may resist any explanation of the process involved in therapy or the particular way in which the therapist may work. Any enquiry by the client would be seen as interpretive material for the therapist, thus avoiding the provision of such information. The myth held that if the client consciously knows the process, the unconscious material will not be revealed, has kept the therapist in the extreme position of power and knowledge over the client who is 'kept in the dark'. Feminist therapy principles developed a strong commitment to exposing and making public the therapeutic process and to being explicit about their way of working and the process of therapy. By the client having some awareness of the method and process in therapy the imbalance of power in the relationship is reduced.

With the publication of guidelines for clients' rights in therapy – for example those published by the National Organisation of Women (1978) – therapists are obliged to provide a service which is ethical and of good quality, while the client is able to make an issue of poor quality or unethical service. Feminist therapy places emphasis on the client's active participation in the negotiation of the aims of the therapy and the ongoing evaluation of the outcome of therapy. Unlike traditional therapy, this provides the client with some power of active negotiation in the desired objectives and outcomes of therapy. The traditional position of the therapist being the expert about the client is replaced in feminist therapy, with the client being the expert on and about themselves. The information from the client forms a major knowledge base for the therapist. The client's strengths and abilities are emphasised in feminist therapy, not the client's supposed psychopathology.

In feminist-perspective therapy, power-seeking techniques are replaced by techniques that enhance the client's personal power and the development of life-managing skills. The therapy process is not considered to be the only avenue for the client to develop and change. Women clients are encouraged to gain strengths (for example, assertiveness, economic independence, employment training) from other sources. In this model, the therapist is seen as accompanying the client in the process of change. Ussher states:

> An understanding of women's personal experience of power and power abuses, and use of power in the context of sexual inequality, is the starting point of empowerment.[36]

By the therapist and client acknowledging and addressing the power issues in therapy, the client may be more able to use the therapy situation to examine her experiences and issues of power in relation to her position in the social order.

The provision of feminist therapy in the form of groups for women has been shown to be an effective frame for women clients to address issues of power, socialisation and regulation. Burden and Gottlieb state that:

> a feminist approach to group work with women clients counteracts the negative consequences for women of sex-role socialisation by making explicit the impact of socialisation and social policy factors throughout the group process. The explicit nature of the approach serves to diminish the magical quality of therapy intervention and to reduce the power imbalance between women clients and the group leader.[37]

By participants sharing interpersonal issues and exploring the social determinants of problems particular to women, the position of isolation that sustains the detrimental belief that participants hold about themselves are annihilated through the group process and the sharing of experiences. Brody comments on the research conducted on feminist therapy groups for women: 'the common denominator is that there is something radically wrong with the lives of women in our culture as they have been socialised to live them'.[38] With the provision of feminist group therapy for women 'the prospects of changing this archaic programming become more hopeful'.

FEMINIST GROUP THERAPY

From the 1970s onwards, the literature on all-female therapy groups has increased, enabling a strong body of feminist analysis on group therapy for women.[39] During the mid 1970s self-help and consciousness-raising groups for women started to flourish as a means for women to support one another and adopt a position of socio-political awareness and active political change. The consciousness-raising (CR) groups were self-led or non-led and concentrated on common sources of oppression, interpersonal issues among group members and on the strength of women's group support. The format of the CR groups influenced feminist therapists in the mid to late 1970s. Group therapy evolved with a similar emphasis to the CR groups except groups were led or facilitated by a trained feminist therapist.

Feminist group therapy is now recognised as a successful arena for women to gain self-awareness and life-managing skills. 'Therapy groups for women eliminate the unconscious sexism that is present in mixed groups and provide a supportive environment in which participants can discover and experience the commonalties [and differences] of being a woman.[40] One of the tasks for women in group work is to 'counteract the dysfunctional consequences in women's general behaviour and attitude that result from a life-long reinforcement of sex-specific and subordinate roles'.[41] The feminist therapy group can provide a forum for women to gain awareness about the effects on women of sex-role socialisation and sex discrimination.

Johnson observes that 'not all women seek therapy for single problems, and not all women begin therapy with a clear understanding of the problem they seek to solve. Such women respond well to interpersonal relations group[s]'.[42] In my experience of facilitating feminist art therapy groups, I would agree with Johnson in that women who present themselves for group art therapy have a poor understanding of their issues, are confused about their 'normality', have low self-esteem and have internalised the myths about women and social sex-role stereotyping of women. Consequently, women initially attending therapy groups have presented themselves as basically sick, bad and inferior. Some women, having been through the 'mainstream' mental health system, have attached the diagnostic category given to them by the 'experts' as a true fault that lies within themselves.

CONCLUSION

As art therapists working within or outside the 'mainstream' mental health system I question our involvement and amalgamation with a system which continues to locate a psychopathological causation for a woman's mental ill-health inside the woman, rather than viewing the wider scheme of locating the problem within the social, political and economic situation in which women are positioned as inferior. The adoption of feminist therapy principles by art therapists seems to be a positive option for providing an avenue in which female clients may address issues that have resulted in them feeling sick, bad or inferior. A feminist structure views women's 'dis-ease' as a valid and realistic reaction to their subservient position in society, their limited power and options, and how they have reacted to the inherent negative myths and objectification of their gender and of their bodies.

With the absence of feminist literature on art therapy there is no collective platform from which to speak and no material to evaluate with peers. With the lack of a feminist art therapy model there is neither a theoretical nor a practical context from which to work. The aim of this chapter has been to provide some initial substance for feminist analysis, to place art therapy within a feminist context, and to inspire art therapists to engage in feminist debate and publication. In the long term, the emergence and development of feminist critiques and feminist perspectives in art therapy could inform future art therapy training programmes and consequently influence professional practice. The development of a feminist-perspective art therapy model could promote art therapy as a viable choice for women seeking therapy and provide a further option for women's mental health and psychological well-being.

NOTES

1 Johnson 1989: 79.
2 Abbenante 1993.
3 Johnson 1989: 235–238.
4 Talbott-Green 1989: 256, Dubois *et al.* 1985: 164, 188.
5 Talbott-Green 1989: 253.
6 Talbott-Green 1989: 256.
7 Talbott-Green 1989.
8 Milwid 1985: 67–73.
9 Talbott-Green 1989: 257.
10 Ussher and Nicolson 1992: 51, Holloway 1989: 132.
11 Talbott-Green 1989: 260.
12 Talbott-Green 1989: 260.
13 Gilligan *et al.* 1991:.
14 Israel 1985: 158, Kravetz 1976: 424.
15 Ussher and Nicolson 1992: 44.
16 Wadeson 1989: 328.
17 Chesler 1972.
18 Miller 1973 and Mitchell 1974.
19 Tennov 1975, Smith and David 1975.
20 Broverman *et al.* 1970.
21 Sturdivant 1980: 55.
22 Walkerdine quoted in Ussher 1991: 11.
23 Jacobsen quoted in Steen 1991: 365.
24 Smith and David quoted in Steen 1991: 365.
25 Ussher 1991: 148.
26 Cox 1994: 5.
27 Cayleff quoted in Cox 1994: 5.
28 Ernst and Maguire 1987.
29 Penfold and Walker 1984 in Ussher and Nicolson 1992: 214.
30 Israel 1985: 149.
31 Sturdivant 1980: 179.
32 Israel 1985: 179.
33 Ussher and Nicolson 1992: 214.

34 Ussher and Nicolson 1992.
35 Ussher 1991: 23.
36 Ussher and Nicolson 1992: 226.
37 Burden and Gottlieb 1987.
38 Brody 1987: xx.
39 Johnson 1987.
40 Walker 1987: 3.
41 Burden and Gottlieb 1987: 24.
42 Johnson 1987: 23.

BIBLIOGRAPHY

Abbenante, J. 1993. 'Art therapy, feminism and archetypal psychology: something's rumbling in the swamp'. Paper to 24th Annual Conference of the American Art Therapy Association, Atlanta, 16–22 Nov.

American Psychiatric Association. 1987. *Diagnostic and Statistical Manual of Mental Disorders (DSM-III-R)*. 3rd edn. revised. Washington DC: American Psychiatric Association.

Brody, C. M. 1987. *Women's Therapy Groups: Paradigms of Feminist Treatment*. New York: Springer Publishing Co.

Broverman, I., Broverman, D. M., Clarkson, I. E., Posenkrantz, P. S. and Vogel, S. R. 1970. 'Sex role stereotyping and clinical judgement of mental health'. *Journal of Consulting and Clinical Psychology*, vol. 34: 1–7.

Burden, D. S. and Gottlieb, N. 1987. 'Women's socialisation and feminist groups'. In *Women's Therapy Groups – Paradigms of Feminist Treatment*, ed. C. M. Brody. New York: Springer Publishing Co.

Chesler, P. 1972. *Women and Madness*. New York: Doubleday.

Cox, M. 1994. *Good Practices and Women's Mental Health*. Melbourne: Health Sharing: Women's Health Resources Services Publication.

Dubois, E., Kelly, G., Kennedy, E., Kormey, D., and Robinson, L. 1985. *Feminist Scholarship: Kindling the Groves of Academe*. Chicago: University of Illinois Press.

Ernst, S. and Goodison, L. 1981. *In Our Own Hands*. London: The Women's Press.

Ernst, S. and Maguire, M. 1987. *Living with the Sphinx*. London: The Women's Press.

Gilbert, L. A. 1980. 'Feminist therapy'. In *Women and psychotherapy: An Assessment of Research and Practice*, ed., A. Brodsky and R.T. Hare-Mustin. New York: Guilford Press.

Gilligan, C. Rogers, A. G. and Tolman, D. L. 1991. *Women, Girls and Psychotherapy: Reframing Resistance*. New York: Harrington Park Press.

Holloway, W. 1989. *Subjectivity and Method in Psychology: Gender, Meaning and Science*. London: Sage.

Israel, J. 1985. 'Feminist therapy'. In *Women and Mental Health – New Directions for Change*, ed. C. T. Mowbray, S. Lanir and M. Hulce. New York: Harrington Park Press.

Johnson. D. R. 1989. 'Introduction to the special issue on women and the creative arts therapies'. *The Arts in Psychotherapy*, vol. 16: 235-8.

Johnson, M. 1987. 'Feminist therapy in groups – a decade of change'. In *Women's Therapy Groups – Paradigms of Feminist Treatment*, ed. C.M. Brody. New York: Springer Publishing Co.

Kravetz, D. 1976. 'Sexism in a women's profession'. *Social Work*, vol. 21.

Miller, J. B. 1973. *Psychoanalysis and Women*. Baltimore: Penguin.

Milwid, B. 1985 'Breaking in: experiences in male-dominated professions'. In *Women Changing Therapy: New Assessments, Values and Strategies in Feminist Therapy*, Ed. J.H. Robbins and R.J. Siegel. New York: Harrington Park Press.

Mitchell, J. 1974. *Psychoanalysis and Feminism*. Harmondsworth: Penguin.

Quadrio, C. 1994. 'Sexual exploitation in professional relationships: the victim's perspective'. Conference paper 'Women and Mental Health after Burdekin', Australian Institute for Women's Research and Policy, Brisbane, 7 April.

Rawlings, E. I. and Carter, D. K. 1977. *Psychotherapy for Women – Treatment Towards Equality*. Illinois: Charles C. Thomas.

Smith, D. and David, S. 1975. *Women Look at Psychiatry*. Vancouver: Press Gang Publishers.

Steen, M. 1991. 'Historical perspectives on women and mental illness and prevention of depression in women, using a feminist framework'. *Mental Health Nursing*, vol. 12: 359–74.

Sturdivant, S. 1980. *Therapy with Women – A Feminist Philosophy of Treatment*. New York: Springer Publishing Co.

Talbott-Green, M. 1989. 'Feminist scholarship: spitting into the mouths of the Gods'. *The Arts in Psychotherapy*, vol. 16.

Tennov, D. 1975. *Psychotherapy: The Hazardous Cure*. New York: Abelard Schuman.

Ussher, J. 1991. *Women's Madness – Misogyny or Mental Illness*. Hemel Hempstead: Harvester Wheatsheaf.

Ussher, J. and Nicolson, P. 1992. *Gender Issues in Clinical Psychology*. London: Routledge.

Wadeson, H. 1989. 'Reflections-in a different image: are "male" pressures shaping the "female" arts therapy professions?' *The Arts in Psychotherapy*, vol. 1: 327–330.

Walker, L. J. S. 1987. 'Women's groups are different.' In Brody, C. M. (ed.) *Women's Therapy Groups*. New York: Springer Publishing Co.

Chapter 5

Women, art therapy and feminist theories of development

Helene Burt

WITNESSING AND VISIBILITY

The following is a quote from a woman with a history of childhood sexual abuse who used art therapy in her healing process.

> I think people are really interdependent. I think in psychiatry depen-
> dency gets a bad name lots of times. But we are really dependent on each
> other. Without any kind of therapy I would have been dead. I think
> we should give dependency a good name. It's all right. I need to show
> people visually what happened to me. And I have a real need for that.
> Art therapy allows me to do that, allows me to show myself but ... I
> want that kind of warm support. I think it's healthy to want it. I was
> brought up thinking it was unhealthy to want it but it's a normal, human
> need. I guess that's what art therapy has allowed me to do is to really
> show people visually and very clearly what happened to me and see that
> I don't have to protect anybody from it.[1]

Isabella (a pseudonym) had been in art therapy for two years and recognised the impact of the therapeutic relationship in art therapy on her
process of healing. She was able to perceive that the unique component of
the art therapy relationship is the production of a visible document of the
trauma she experienced which is witnessed by the art therapist. As all
art therapists know, it is this combination of visibility and witnessing within
the context of a therapeutic connection, which makes art therapy such a
powerful healing process. Given that the childhood trauma, which Isabella
believed led to her mental illness, took place within the context of an
abusive relationship, it stands to reason that recovery from sexual abuse
would need to take place within the context of a healing relationship.

The position of the therapist towards the client has traditionally been
viewed as one of neutrality and objectivity, a stance which discourages
emotional involvement. It was believed that the therapist would obtain a
greater sense of clarity with regard to the client's pathology when distance
in the therapeutic relationship was maintained. A closer connection

between therapist and client was viewed as disruptive of treatment and an indication of poor boundaries on the part of the therapist. In this case it was suspected that the therapist had been drawn into the client's pathological dependency.

The notion that autonomy and independence (traditionally male attributes) are indicative of mental health and that dependency and the need for closeness in relationships was less so, or even pathological, stems from the traditional developmental theory which most treatment philosophies, particularly psychiatry, are based on. Traditional developmental theories from Freud to Erickson have maintained the goal of human development to be the development of a separate, autonomous self, and therefore the goal of therapists should be to encourage 'individuation'.

With its emphasis on the experience of making the unspeakable visible to a supportive witness, art therapy is essentially a process which encourages engagement between therapist and client. However, due to the lack of attention to gender issues and feminism in the field of art therapy, art therapists are still working within the framework of formal developmental theory with its emphasis on separateness and autonomy.

This chapter will examine the origins, effects and theoretical and clinical implications of traditional developmental theories and will explain the gender bias inherent in developmental theories, ways in which it is manifested in treatment, and recent feminist reconstructions of developmental theory.

FEMINISM AND ART THERAPY

In the most recent American Art Therapy Association Membership Survey respondents were asked to identify their gender (La Brie and Rosa 1994). Eighty-six per cent of the respondents were women, 8 per cent men, and 6 per cent did not respond to the question. In a previous survey, completed four years earlier, more respondents answered this question with 92.8 per cent being women, 6.8 per cent men, and 0.4 per cent not responding to the question (Gordon and Manning 1991). It is impossible to say whether the percentage of men entering the field has actually risen. At any rate, if this represents the rate of growth of men entering the field it will be a long time before our profession can be considered anything other than a 'woman's profession'.

One of the strongest social, political and philosophical forces of the last century has been feminism. For the purpose of this chapter feminism is defined as the movement to equalise the position of women in relation to the position of men in our society. Feminism has strongly influenced the way we conceptualise the therapeutic process. Yet strangely enough, art therapy in North America exhibits a denial and ignorance of feminism quite distinct from other mental health fields. This was evident in a subject search I conducted on the CD ROM PsycLit (1/87–6/94.). I located all catalogued articles and book chapters from January 1987 to June 1994 which referenced both 'art therapy' and 'feminism'. During this six-and-half-year period, 357 articles had been written which mentioned 'art therapy'. Out of these 357 articles two also mentioned 'feminism'. Out of the 166 book chapters which mentioned 'art therapy' none mentioned 'feminism'. Wondering how this compared to other related fields I did searches throughout the catalogued literature of these fields. Table 5.1 shows the results.

Evidently art therapy can hold a claim to being the field which has paid the least attention to feminism. It has been feminism which has revealed the power differential between men and women in our society as well as the gender bias in psychological theory and practice. The profession of art therapy seems to be operating without an awareness of the socio-political structures that oppress women who work as helping professionals or are clients who utilise health care. As we shall see, this affects our work with women and, in particular, women who have been sexually abused.

Table 5.1 Search by professions of literature mentioning 'feminism' between 1987 and 1994

Search terms	Journal articles	%	Book chapters
'art therapy' and 'feminism'	2	0.6	0
'psychology' and 'feminism'	138	1.4	170
'psychiatry' and 'feminism'	14	0.5	20
'social work' and 'feminism'	30	14.9	28
'psychotherapy' and 'feminism'	99	1.2	75
'family therapy' and 'feminism'	56	1.7	31
'occupational therapy' and 'feminism'	4	0.5	0

FEMINIST THERAPY

Feminist therapy is defined by its analysis of the power differential between men and women and how this power differential is evinced socially and politically. There is not only one feminist approach to therapy; rather there are a variety of feminist therapies which respond to and expand upon existing theoretical frameworks. These include psychodynamic, cognitive behavioural and family therapy models (Dutton-Douglas and Walker 1988). However, there are a number of values and objectives which have formed the foundation for a feminist framework for therapy as I shall now explore.

An understanding of the personal as political involves acknowledging that each woman's personal experience is also influenced by the position women have in our society. The feminist therapist helps her client to see that some of her problems are socially constructed:

This feminist interpretation does not relieve women of the responsibility for engaging in efforts toward their own change, but helps them develop an awareness of the communality of women's problems ... feminist therapists empower their women clients.[2]

Encouraging women to look beyond the limited choices offered to us in a patriarchal society involves women exercising more choice in therapy. To this end, feminist therapists encourage clients to exercise more control over their therapeutic experience by being active in selecting a therapist, setting their own goals, and evaluating therapy. As well as examining the power differential between men and women and its effects on women's mental health, feminist therapists also pay attention to power as a component in the therapeutic relationship. 'The power relationship between therapist and client had been a focus of feminist therapy and achieving a more equalitarian therapist–client relationship has been a goal of feminist therapy.'[3] Feminist therapists believe in acknowledging the power they have in helping a woman reconstruct her life while maintaining that the client is her own best expert and that the client's perceptions are valid. Feminist therapists are interested in their own growth and development as well as that of their clients.

The feminist therapist values androgyny, or having the characteristics of both sexes, in that she believes that both men and women are limited by their sex roles and that both sexes can benefit by an assimilation of the characteristics ascribed to the other sex. For example, women can benefit by being more assertive and men can benefit by being more emotionally sensitive. In recognising the gender inequalities in society, a feminist therapist works towards changing the system to benefit both women and men.

Cammaert and Larsen (1988) also highlight some major ethical issues feminist therapists face.[4] Given the many different theoretical frameworks and techniques used by feminist therapists, it is important for feminist therapists to develop a clear and thoughtful model for therapy. Moreover, a feminist therapist is ethically obliged to have an awareness of new information about the psychology of women. Finally, because of the proximity of the feminist community in most centres, feminist therapists must be particularly aware of the issue of dual or overlapping roles. Feminist therapists must develop strategies to avoid harming their clients through abuse of power, lack of confidentiality, or inappropriate boundaries in the therapeutic relationship.

PSYCHIATRY

Psychiatry is one of the least feminist-informed environments. The most recent American Art Therapy Association membership survey found that the majority of art therapists work in psychiatric settings (La Brie and Rosa 1994). While feminism is not entirely denied in psychiatry, the relationship between psychiatry and feminism is a little like that of oil to water. The characteristics which are pathologised in the *Diagnostic Statistical Manual DSM-III-R* and their aetiology are based on psychoanalytic beliefs about human development and standards of mental health (APA 1987). The feminist critique of psychoanalytic theory revealed how psychoanalysis legitimised sex-role stereotypes by embedding them in quasi-scientific theories of behaviour and development like the oedipal stage of development (Sturdivant 1980; Jordan *et al.* 1991; Kaschak 1992). Even though the *DSM III-R* claims to be an impartial descriptive inventory of symptoms, it was developed by white, middle-class, heterosexual males and based on their definition of what is normal, abnormal, mental health and mental illness. The choice of symptoms was in fact not impartial. The *DSM III-R* did not have women or minorities involved in its creation (the *DSM-IV* (1994) did, but it is too little too late, the damage has been done). In the *DSM* diagnostic categories are viewed as objective truth rather than as the highly subjective constructs of the dominant group in our society which continues to oppress women, other races, cultures and sexualities. The *DSM* pathologises those issues which are problems to those in power in a patriarchal society.

Certain diagnoses are assigned much more frequently to women than men (Rothblum and Franks, 1987). These 'women's diagnoses' include Depression, Agoraphobia, Sexual Dysfunction, Simple Phobias, Anxiety States, Somatization Disorder, Multiple Personality Disorder, Psychogenic Pain Disorder, Histrionic Personality Disorder, Borderline Personality Disorder and Dependent Personality Disorder. In a study by Broverman *et al.* clinically trained therapists (psychologists, psychiatrists and social workers) were asked to determine their criteria for healthiness in men, women, and adults in general (Broverman *et al.* 1970). The researchers found that the therapists had the same criteria for men and for adults in general but quite different criteria for women. Healthy women differed in their criteria from healthy men (and also from healthy adults) by being more submissive, less independent, less adventurous, more easily excitable in minor crises, having their feelings more easily hurt, being more emotional, more conceited about their appearance, less objective, and disliking mathematics and science. The same characteristics which define 'healthy' women are the hallmarks of the 'female' diagnoses. The primary symptoms of these diagnoses – dependency, emotionality, fear of being alone – are all qualities which our society considers essential components of femininity.

BORDERLINE PERSONALITY DISORDER

A good example of gender bias in the *DSM* is the diagnostic category of Borderline Personality Disorder (BPD). The *DSM-IV* states that 75 per cent of those assigned the diagnosis are women (APA 1994). The diagnostic criteria for BPD as outlined in the *DSM-IV* includes some of the same characteristics therapists view as 'healthy' in women. Therapists see 'healthy' women as 'less independent', the *DSM-IV* notes the BPD client suffers from a fear of being alone and a need to have other people with them. The 'healthy' woman is viewed as 'more emotional', the *DSM-IV* states the BPD client suffers from 'affective instability'. The 'healthy' woman is viewed as more easily excitable in minor crises and having their feelings more easily hurt, the *DSM-IV* notes the BPD client is 'very sensitive to environmental circumstances'. This gender bias creates a link between the personality characteristics of 'healthy women' and the personality characteristics of BPD clients. We must then ask to what degree is BPD a manifestation of the condition of being *feminine* as it is defined by psychiatry and psychology.

The quality of the mother–child relationship has been viewed as the single most influential factor in the development of BPD. Much of the accepted, traditional literature concerning the aetiology and treatment of BPD clients has its origin in theory developed by Mahler (1971) who noted certain similarities between the psychological make-up of BPD adults and the separation–individuation issues of young children. Mahler used the term separation–individuation for the process whereby the infant gradually differentiates him or herself from the mother and attains the relatively autonomous status of toddler (Goldenson 1984). Mahler hypothesised that derailments in the *rapprochement* sub-phase of the separation–individuation process led to the development in adulthood of BPD. The *rapprochement* sub-phase takes place in the child's development after about eighteen months of age and represents the child's active approaches to the mother as distinct from the earlier phase in which the child was less aware of its mother's presence (Goldenson 1984). This premise was then further expanded upon by theorists like Kernberg (1975), Adler (1985) and Masterson and Rinsley (1975). A mother who was unable to meet the child's needs for acknowledgement or who could not tolerate the child's need to develop autonomy was viewed as the direct cause of BPD in her child. However, BPD aetological theory does not take into account other equally crucial relationships and life experiences in the history of the women defined as having BPD.

MATRICENTRIC RESEARCH

Birns (1985) questions the prevalent and tenacious belief that the mother–child relationship is the primary contributing factor to psychological well-being or pathology. Freud set a precedent with his statement that the mother–infant relationship was 'unique, without parallel, established unalterably for a whole lifetime as the first and strongest love object and as the prototype of all later love relations for both sexes.'[5] Birns points out the lack of evidence to substantiate this and presents current research which challenges this influential belief. Birns begins with a deconstruction of Bowlby's (1958) attachment theory the dominant model of early emotional development, by criticising the ways in which Bowlby arrived at his conclusions. Bowlby observed orphaned children being raised in an institution who were mentally and physically handicapped and concluded that this was due to the absence of mothers in the lives of these children. Bowlby also used Harlowe's experiments with monkeys from which he concluded that factors other than food provision were important in child development, particularly in his view, the mother–infant bond. Subsequent research was designed to substantiate these initial theories rather than to test them scientifically as hypotheses. Bowlby's theory was not based on actual longitudinal studies, which, through the observation of development over a long period of time, were the only type of research design which would yield valid information. In fact, longitudinal studies which have been undertaken to explore the mother–infant relationship as a predictor have shown, as in a study done from 1929 to 1957 at the Fels Research Institute, that maternal–infancy ratings do not correlate with later behaviour. The New York Longitudinal Study conducted by Chess and Thomas found that the major predicting risk factor of adult behaviour was the temperament of the child and not poor mothering.[6]

This focus on the mother–infant relationship naturally resulted in a lack of research into the significance of the father–infant relationship and other relationships in a child's development. Lewis refers to this as the 'legacy of matricentric research'.[7] Silverstein (1991) points out the failure of child development researchers to explore the effects of paternal emotional distance on a child's development. The BPD literature on parent–child relationships (Masterton and Rinsley 1975; Adler 1985) is a good example of 'matricentric research' as it focused on the mother's over-involvement but failed to explore the effects of paternal under-involvement. When paternal emotional distance has been noted (Goldberg *et al.* 1985), it is viewed as pathological rather than typical. Masterson and Rinsley were quite unabashed in their 'mother-blaming':

> This paper describes the role of the mother's faulty libidinal availability in the development of the borderline syndrome. It describes in terms of object relations theory the effects of alternating maternal libidinal availability and withdrawal, at the time of separation-individuation (rapprochement sub phase), upon the development of the psychic structure of the borderline patient . . . [8]

Research as recent as 1991 continues to utilise Masterson and Rinsley's hypothesis.[9]

SEXUAL ABUSE

'Matricentric' research also made invisible the childhood trauma many people diagnosed with BPD have experienced. For example, a history of childhood sexual abuse has been consistently found in a large majority of BPD classifications. Ogata *et al.* in their 1990 study found the incidence of sexual abuse in the population defined as BPD to be as high as 71 per cent. Nevertheless, the focus has remained on separation–individuation issues in the mother–child relationship. Saunders and Arnold (1991) in reviewing and reframing the core features of the diagnosis – primitive defences, unstable relationships, identity disturbance, inability to be alone, and self-destructiveness – demonstrate how these features are more easily understood as responses to the trauma of childhood sexual abuse. They give the example of 'splitting', which Kernberg (1975) viewed as a major defence mechanism and indicator of BPD pathology originating in the mother–infant dyad. Kernberg (1972) believed that due to excessive frustration and aggression originating with poor mothering and/or constitutional factors, the person labelled as BPD learns to split the self and others into 'all good' or 'all bad' representations. This results in weakened ego development with low tolerance for anxiety, poor impulse control, and primitive defence mechanisms.

In a deconstruction of Kernberg's theory, Saunders and Arnold (1977) point out that 'splitting' is far more likely to be generated from a patho-logical relationship between the incestuous father or other perpetrator and the child. For example, the child victim of incest is expected to integrate the polarities of the loving parent on the one hand, and the sexually abusive parent on the other. The authors note that, in this light, 'splitting' would seem more a reflection of an internalisation of the child's actual experiences of being sexually abused and therefore more of a learned response to this trauma than a defence mechanism against rage towards the mother. Here, psychiatry begins to emerge as a contributing factor to the ongoing denial and secrecy surrounding sexual abuse still prevalent in our society.

Psychiatry's lack of attention to sexual abuse as an aetiological factor in pathology, which Herman (1992) has termed the 'amnesia' of the mental health establishment, is both parallel to the secrecy maintained by the victim and the family and also a perpetuation of the secrecy which was so clearly demonstrated in Freud's suppression of the seduction theory. Secrecy around childhood sexual abuse has been maintained not only through the survivor's sense of fear and shame, but also through the protective nucleus of the family. As Schatzow and Herman state:

> With families in which incest has occurred, secrecy is the organising principle of all family relationships. Both the testimony of survivors and the clinical literature emphasise the role of the incest secret. Children

who have been sexually abused by adults outside the family also frequently keep this secret as a result of intimidation or shame. Secrecy compounds the trauma of the sexual abuse itself by isolating the victim from others, so that her own perceptions cannot be validated. Often the victim comes to doubt her own experience of reality, which is often at odds with the family's version of the truth. Many, if not most, victims of child sexual abuse reach adult life still preserving the rule of secrecy.[10]

Research has shown that childhood sexual abuse is not a rare event with the prevalence rates ranging in probability from 6 per cent to 62 per cent for females and 3 per cent to 31 per cent for males, depending on the definition of sexual abuse used (Finkelhor 1986). However, mental health professionals and the general public continue to promote the belief that childhood sexual abuse is based on the fantasy of the victim or a fantasy of the therapists who, by acknowledging the possibility of childhood sexual abuse as a causative factor in the presenting problems of their client, plants the fantasy in their client's psyche.

The False Memory Syndrome Foundation was established in 1982 by the parents of 4,000 families who claim they have been unfairly accused of sexually abusing their children (Wylie 1993). Increasingly, therapists are finding themselves in the courts accused by such parents of having planted false memories in their clients' minds. As with Freud's repudiation of the seduction theory, the so-called 'false memory syndrome' represents another backlash against the acknowledgement of sexual abuse of children in our society (Herman 1992).

Denial around childhood sexual abuse is also evident in another new 'syndrome' which has been developed to describe mothers who, while in the process of divorce, believe allegations made by their children who claim to have been sexually abused by their fathers (Weller 1992). The *Village Voice* ran a disturbing story recently about the use of 'Parental Alienation Syndrome (PAS)' which has been developed by 'pro-father' psychiatrists who have been called in as expert witnesses in custody cases. A trend seems to be developing in which the courts find PAS sufficient evidence that mothers are unfit and grant custody to fathers. Even though this is not a diagnostic category, the use of the term PAS by psychiatrists in these cases seems to be enough to pathologise a mother's belief in her child's allegations of sexual abuse by the child's father.

Signs of the disorder include: sarcastic remarks, use of answering machines to screen the father's calls, rigidity with visitation schedule, complaints about support payments, change of the child's last name to a two-name hyphenate, reluctance to move a slightly ill child to the father's home for the weekend – and false sex-abuse charges.[11]

The article gives several examples of women whose custodial rights, and in some cases visitation rights, have been removed due to their 'hysterical' behaviour as evinced, for example, in having their children examined for signs of sexual abuse by doctors. In the cases presented, sexual abuse was strongly indicated not only in the initial verbal disclosure maintained by the child, but also in the child's behaviour and symptoms. Psychiatry plays a powerful role in the continued silencing of the voices of the victims of childhood sexual abuse.

Mental health professionals who continue to understand BPD from the framework of the accepted aetiological theory with its de-emphasis of childhood sexual abuse, may not even investigate the existence of sexual abuse in a client's history. The importance of asking about childhood abuse has been emphasised by some clinicians and researchers (Alpert 1991; Lanktree *et al.* 1991; Stone 1989) and is in keeping with the feminist principle that the personal is political. This is important because of the tremendous resistance found in society and in the family and the individual to acknowledging childhood sexual abuse. Asking clients about their experience helps them to see how their problems have social as well as personal causes. Lanktree *et al.* (1991) studied two different sets of patient hospital charts. In the first set the patient was not asked by the clinician whether they had experienced sexual abuse while in the second set the patient was asked by the clinician whether they had experienced sexual abuse. They found that sexual abuse reports increased more than fourfold (from 7 per cent to 31 per cent), when patients were asked directly by clinicians whether they had ever experienced sexual abuse. They caution against assuming that this information will be readily provided.

TREATMENT IMPLICATIONS

With a focus on separation–individuation issues in the aetiology of BPD, we may contribute to the perpetuation of secrecy around sexual abuse, a trauma which has been experienced by the majority of those defined as having BPD. If we view a 'BPD client' as a woman whose mother was unable to allow her to experience a separate sense of self, we might interpret our job as therapist as helping our client begin to see herself as a separate, independent being. In doing so, we run the risk of missing the significance of sexual abuse in the development of the client's current difficulties. We could, in fact, fail ever to acknowledge the possibility of sexual abuse in the client's history. This would not make it any easier for the client to disclose her experience and would only serve to reinforce the secrecy and shame with which she has always struggled. Furthermore, we would be imposing an irrelevant theoretical model onto someone with enough problems of their own.

Focusing on separation–individuation issues, we may 'help' our client to become more independent by suggesting the need for her to begin to take more responsibility for her own behaviour and actions. Typically victims of sexual abuse believe they were to blame (Faller 1988). With her therapist emphasising her need to take more responsibility for her actions, the women defined as BPD may, on an unconscious level, interpret this as more evidence that she was responsible for the sexual abuse she suffered.

INFANTILISATION OF WOMEN AND PEJORATIVE ATTITUDES TOWARDS WOMEN DEFINED AS EVINCING BPD

Until recently the BPD literature not only overlooked the issues of gender bias and sexual abuse but also promoted an image of a childish personality whose needs were to become more mature, to individuate, to 'grow up'. Kernberg, in describing the cognitive and personality characteristics of BPD clients, uses such terms as 'primitive ego states', 'a predominance of primary process thinking', and, 'marked ego weakness'.[12].While most mental health professionals would recognise that these are clinical terms, the image is still one of an infantile personality structure and this, in itself, infantilises the BPD client. Art therapists have also used infantilising language in descriptions of BPD clients, such as in:

the adult borderline is psychologically arrested in the developmental realm of toddlerhood. One can say that they have one foot in the world, and one foot in the womb . . . [13]

This childlike presentation of the BPD client in the literature may partly have contributed to the exasperation with which many mental health professionals view this population. After all, how can we in a few months, or just a few weeks as in some cases, help a client 'grow up'?

Women have been infantilised on many levels in our society. Cantor discusses the social expectation of women to define their identities through their husbands rather than developing their own sense of identity.[14] She cites a blatant example of this in the practice of women taking their husbands' names upon marriage:

Up to now, it has been considered socially correct for women to be referred to as 'Mrs Husband's Name.' And only in 1984 did the local newspaper in Westfield, New Jersey, begin to print a bride's first name under her wedding picture.[15]

Another rather obvious indication that women's work and interests are still viewed as less serious than men's is the substantially lower salaries women receive as compared to men. This is true even when the work requires more education and/or level of skill and is reflected in the fact that in 1991 women earned only 74 cents to every dollar men earned (Holder and Anderson 1989). Given that 75 per cent of the BPD population is female, the element of immaturity which mental health professionals tend to associate with BPD clients could well have something to do with the overall devaluation of women in our society.

This may in turn be related to the negative attitude of mental health professionals towards the woman diagnosed with BPD. As Goldstein notes:

> While many therapists bring a high degree of commitment, if not an almost heroic effort, to the treatment of borderline individuals, there is no other patient group, with the possible exception of those who are anti-social, about whom so many negatively tinged terms are used. Among these are manipulative, demanding, sadistic, controlling, infantile, and provocative.[16]

That a pejorative attitude towards BPD clients exists was clearly indicated in a study by Gallop *et al.* (1989). Gallop *et al.* compared empathic responses of nursing staff to BPD patients and schizophrenic patients and found that nursing staff were considerably less empathic and used more pejorative language with BPD patients than with schizophrenic patients.

As well, in focusing in a collective, pejorative manner on the negative behavioural characteristics of BPD clients, mental health professionals may contribute to the burdensome sense of shame victims of sexual abuse carry. Nathanson (1989) discusses the centrality of shame in the victim's psychology and the need for therapists to be sensitive to this. He notes that ridicule, contempt, disdain and cruelty can reactivate feelings of shame around sexual abuse, negate the client's sense of reality, and further encourage her to keep the shameful secret to herself.

With the aetiological focus on separation–individuation issues, it followed that treatment for BPD focused on helping the client to achieve separation–individuation. In her review of ten of the major BPD theorists' literature, Campbell notes that all ten theorists were in agreement as to the outcome of therapy: 'All of the theorists state or at least indicate that the goal of therapy with borderline disorders is separation individuation.'[17]

In many treatment programmes, such a goal for therapy is a tall order because of time constraints and practical considerations. Feeling incapable of such a goal, it is understandable that mental health professionals would begin to view BPD clients as 'impossible' and, instead, work only at developing ways to 'cope' or 'deal' with the behaviours of these clients rather than developing an individual plan of treatment based on each client's needs. A feeling of not being able to be effective in their work as mental health professionals could lead to feelings of helplessness and inadequacy. And, as we all learn in our clinical training, feelings of helplessness soon lead to feelings of resentment and frustration. Given this situation, as well as the ongoing societal denial of sexual abuse, it is easier to understand the contemptuous reactions of mental health professionals to BPD clients. However, clearly this does not promote the healing of BPD clients who have a history of childhood sexual abuse.

RETHINKING FEMALE DEVELOPMENTAL MODELS: THE RELATIONAL MODEL

The aetiology of BPD is based on a number of assumptions about human development. In clinical practice work with female survivors of sexual abuse, these assumptions are not valid.

Ultimately, it is in the premises and assumptions about human development, upon which the aetiology of BPD is based, that this diagnostic category begins to lose meaning in clinical practice with female survivors of sexual abuse. As I have pointed out, diagnostic categories pathologise normal female tendencies and hold male development as the norm. Therefore, women's development is seen as less advanced rather than as different. Feminist theorists, notably Gilligan (1982) and the Stone Centre writers, have pointed out the need for a reworking of female developmental models.

Erickson (1950) viewed development as a process of a constant evolving of the self, moving away from dependency and symbiosis towards independence and separateness. As Miller (1991) points out, this theory serves neither gender effectively, for it is difficult to see how an individual is suddenly to reach Erickson's stage of 'intimacy', in which the individual is now capable of having mature, intimate relationships with others, after spending a lifetime separating, individuating, and developing a sense of self apart from others.

Nowhere in any of the prevailing models has there been an understanding of the interrelation and connection between the developing child and its care-givers and the role this plays in development. Even the object-relations theorists using Winnicott's concept of the 'good enough mother' stress the quality of the interaction between mother and child as it affects the child's evolution towards a separate sense of self.[18] This emphasis maintains the goal of development to be separateness. Feminist theorists are beginning to view the process of development as something other than moving from symbiosis to a separate self. They are redefining the separation–individuation process within the context of the relationship between child and care-giver. Instead of viewing the infant as experiencing greater degrees of separateness, Jordan *et al.* (1991) see the child as engaged in attending to and responding to an other (the parent). The developmental process the child is engaged in is the result of greater degrees of self-knowledge developed by relating to the parent. Miller uses the term 'a being-in-relationship' to describe the infant's early notion of self, distinguishing it from those which describe the infant's sense of self as experienced strictly as separate or in the process of separating from others.[19] This is an important distinction, carrying many implications which it is beyond the scope of this chapter to elucidate fully. Particularly relevant here and, as an example of the changes these theorists are creating in our understanding of female development, Miller notes:

Certain events in later life that other models see as detracting from the self are instead seen as satisfying, motivating, and empowering. For example, to feel 'more related to another person' means to feel one's self enhanced, not threatened. It does not feel like a loss of a part of one's self; instead it becomes a step toward more pleasure and effectiveness ... Being in relationship, picking up the feelings of the other and attending to the 'interaction between' becomes an accepted, 'natural seeming' way of being and acting. It is learned and assumed; not alien or threatening. Most important, it is desired; it is a goal, not a detraction or means to some other end, such as one's own self-development. Thus, it forms a *motivation*.[20]

The existence of another model of development more empowering to women has greatly influenced my conceptualisation of my clinical work with BPD female clients who are survivors of sexual abuse. Separation–individuation issues of BPD clients can be seen less as a causative factor and more as indicative of the deficits in our understanding of human development. This gives the issue of sexual abuse greater significance in the development of pathology.

THE RELATIONAL MODEL AND POSTMODERN FEMINISM

Another recent significant stream of thought-enriching feminist therapy is that of feminist postmodernism as discussed in the work of Spellman (1988), Collins (1990), Harding (1991) and Hare-Mustin and Marecek (1990). These theorists contribute to our understanding of gender by raising the issue of cultural and racial differences between women. Their work points to the need for feminist therapists to acknowledge the differences between the meaning of feminism in different races and cultures due to their different social, political, and economic realities. Spellman (1988), a postmodern feminist, examines the paradox at the core of feminism:

> Any attempt to talk about all women in terms of something we have in common undermines attempts to talk about the differences among us. Is it possible to give the things women have in common their full significance without thereby implying that the differences among us are less important? How can we describe those things that differentiate women without eclipsing what we share in common?[21]

While the relational model has been criticised for claiming to be able to speak for all women when it was conceptualised by a group of white, heterosexual, privileged women, the central premise 'that the goal of development is to participate in increasingly empowering relationships' does not deny differences within groups of women. The relational model can incorporate differences in race, culture, and sexuality by promoting the role of relationship in development.

> In an empathically grounded relational process, difference becomes a source of enlargement if each person can expand the boundaries of her experiences and if each can speak where she might otherwise have been silenced by shame or uncertainty. In a Western culture which, despite many changes, still operates in hierarchies of power and control, one may well hesitate to engage with full honesty, or reveal aspects of oneself that may not coincide with the experience of the other. It is hard to openly and honestly engage if one has been taught to fear or dismiss the other.[22]

CONCLUSION

As feminist theorists and clinicians continue to develop a model of psychological development which conceptualises female development, art therapists can begin to explore new ways to conceptualise their work with women. As we are no longer confined within a patriarchal paradigm, our theory, practice and research can begin to reflect this. Mutuality in relationships and the ability to interrelate are the goals of healthy development and the road to healing. In the words of Isabella, a participant in my doctoral research study:

> Sometimes the images are just too scary to do by myself. . . . I've always had this longing for other people. But now, once I've really experienced it, there's more of me so I can live my separate life too, so there isn't this need to cling. It's like the closer I get the more I can be apart. . . . [23]

ACKNOWLEDGEMENTS

The author wishes to thank 'Isabella' for sharing her experience of the recovery process and Brenda Bettridge, a friend and mentor, who introduced me to the relational theory.

NOTES

1 Burt 1995.
2 Cammaert and Larsen 1988: 16.
3 Cammaert and Larsen 1988: 17.
4 Cammaert and Larsen 1988.
5 Freud 1949: 45.
6 Birns 1985: 5.
7 Lewis 1986: 229.
8 Masterson and Rinsley 1975: 163.
9 Frank and Paris 1991: 648–651.

10 Schatzow and Herman 1989: 337.
11 Weller 1992: 34.
12 Kernberg 1975: 5–6.
13 Obernbreit 1985: 12.
14 Cantor 1989: 195–209.
15 Cantor 1989: 197.
16 Goldstein 1990: 6–7.
17 Campbell 1982: 181.
18 Winnicott 1971: 44.
19 Miller 1991: 13.
20 Miller 1991: 15.
21 Spellman 1988: 3.
22 Miller 1991: 7.
23 Burt 1995.

BIBLIOGRAPHY

Adler, G. 1985. *Borderline Psychopathology And Its Treatment*. New Jersey: Jason Aronson, Inc.

Alpert, J. L. 1991. 'Retrospective Treatment of Incest Victims'. *Psychoanalytic Review*, vol. 78, no. 3: 425–435.

American Psychiatric Association. 1994. *Diagnostic and Statistical Manual of Mental Disorders – IV*. Washington, DC: American Psychiatric Association.

American Psychiatric Association. 1987. *Diagnostic and Statistical Manual of Mental Disorders* 3rd edn – revised. Washington, DC: American Psychiatric Association.

Birns, B. 1985. *The Mother–Infant Tie: Fifty Years of Theory, Science, and Science Fiction*. (Tech. Rep. no. 21). Wellesley, MA: Wellesley College. The Stone Center.

Blos, P. 1962. *On Adolescence*. New York: The Free Press.

Bowlby, J. 1958. 'The Nature of the Child's Tie to his Mother'. *International Journal of Psychoanalysis*, vol. 39: 350–373.

Broverman, I., Broverman, D., Clarkson, F., Rosenkrantz, P., and Vogel, S. 1970. 'Sex-Role Stereotypes and Clinical Judgements of Mental Health'. *Journal of Consulting and Clinical Psychology*, vol. 34, no. 1: 1–7.

Burt, H. 1995. *The Experience of Self During the Recovery Process of a Small Number of Women with a History of Child Sexual Abuse Who Are Currently in Art Therapy*. Unpublished raw data.

Cammaert, L. P. and Larsen, C. C. 1988. 'Feminist Frameworks of Psychotherapy'. In M. Dutton-Douglas, and L. E. Walker (eds) *Feminist Psychotherapies: Integration of Therapeutic and Feminist Systems*. New Jersey: Ablex Publishing Corporation.

Campbell, K. 1982. 'The Psychotherapy Relationship with Borderline Personality Disorders'. *Psychotherapy: Theory, Research, and Practice*, vol. 19, no. 2: 166–193.

Cantor, D. 1989. 'Marriage and Divorce: The Search for Adult Identity'. In T. Bernay, and D. Cantor (eds), *The Psychology of Today's Woman/New Psychoanalytic Visions*. Cambridge, MA: Harvard University Press.

Collins, P. H. 1991. *Black Feminist Thought: Knowledge, Consciousness, and the Politics of Empowerment*. New York: Routledge.

Dutton-Douglas, M. and Walker, L. E. 1988. *Feminist Psychotherapies: Integration of Therapeutic and Feminist Systems*. New Jersey: Ablex Publishing Corporation.

Erickson, E. 1950, 1963. *Childhood and Society*. New York: W. W. Norton.

Faller, K. C. 1988. *Child Sexual Abuse: An Interdisciplinary Manual for Diagnosis, Case Management, and Treatment*. New York: Columbia University Press.

Finkelhor, D. 1986. *A Sourcebook on Child Sexual Abuse*. Newbury Park: Sage Publications.

Frank, H., and Paris, J. 1991. 'Parents' Emotional Neglect and Overprotection according to the Recollections of Patients with Borderline Personality Disorder'. *American Journal of Psychiatry*, vol. 148, no. 5: 648–651.

Freud, S. 1949. *An Outline of Psycho-Analysis*. New York: W.W. Norton.

Gallop, R., Lancee, W., and Garfinkel, P. 1989. 'How Nursing Staff Respond to the Label "Borderline Personality Disorder"'. *Hospital and Community Psychiatry*, vol. 40, no. 8: 815–819.

Gilligan, C. 1982. *In a Different Voice*. Cambridge, MA: Harvard University Press.

Goldberg, R., Mann, L., Wise, T., and Segall, E. 1985. 'Parental Qualities as Perceived by Borderline Personality Disorders, *Hillside Journal of Clinical Psychiatry*, 7, (2) 134–40.

Goldenson, R. M. (ed.) 1984. *Longman Dictionary of Psychology and Psychiatry*. New York and London: Longman.

Goldstein, E. G. 1990. *Borderline Disorders: Clinical Models and Techniques*. New York: The Guilford Press.

Gordon, R. A. and Manning, T. 1991. '1990–1991 Membership Survey Report'. *Art Therapy: Journal of the American Art Therapy Association*, vol. 8, no. 2: 20–29.

Harding, S. 1991. *Whose Science? Whose Knowledge?* Ithaca: Cornell University Press.

Hare-Mustin, R. T. and Maracek, J., 1990. 'Gender and the Meaning of Difference: Postmodernism and Psychology'. In, R. T. Hare-Mustin and J. Maracek (eds), *Making a Difference: Psychology and the Construction of Gender*. New Haven CT: Yale University Press.

Herman, J. L. 1992. *Trauma and Recovery*. New York: Basic Books.

Holder, D. and Anderson, C. 1989. 'Women, Work, and the Family'. In M. McGoldrick, (ed.), *Women in Families*. New York: W. W. Norton.

Jordan, J., Kaplan, A., Miller, J., Stiver, I., and Surrey, J. 1991. *Women's Growth In Connection*. New York, London: The Guilford Press.

Kaschak, E. 1992. *Engendered Lives*. New York: Basic Books.

Kernberg, O. 1972. 'Early Ego Integration and Object Relations'. *Annals of the New York Academy of Science*, vol. 233–247.

Kernberg, O. 1975. *Borderline Conditions and Pathological Narcissism*. New York: Jason Aronson, Inc.

La Brie, G. and Rosa, C. 1994. 'American Art Therapy Association, inc. 1992–93 Membership Survey Report'. *Art Therapy: Journal of the American Art Therapy Association*. vol. 11, no. 3: 206–213.

Lanktree, C., Briere, J., and Zaidi, L. 1991. 'Incidence and Impact of Sexual Abuse in a Child Outpatient Sample: The Role of Direct Inquiry. *Child Abuse and Neglect*. vol. 15: 447–453.

Lewis, C. 1986. 'The Role of the Father in the Human Family'. In W. Slucken and M. Herbert (eds), *Parental Behaviour*. Oxford: Basil Blackwell.

Mahler, M. 1971. 'A Study of the Separation–Individuation Process and its Possible Application to Borderline Phenomena in the Psychoanalytic Situation'. *Psychoanalytic Study of the Child*, vol. 26: 403–424.

Masson, J. M. 1984. *The Assault on Truth. Freud's Suppression of the Seduction Theory*. New York: Farrar, Strauss and Giroux.

Masterson, J., and Rinsley., D. 1975. 'The Borderline Syndrome: The Role of the

Genesis and Psychic Structure of the Borderline Personality'. *International Journal of Psycho-Analysis*, vol. 56: 163–177.

Miller, J. 1991. 'The Development of Women's Sense of Self'. In J. Jordan, A. Kaplan, J. Miller, I. Stiver, and J. Surrey (eds), *Women's Growth In Connection*. New York: The Guilford Press.

Nathanson, D. 1989. 'Understanding What Is Hidden/Shame in Sexual Abuse'. *Psychiatric Clinics of North America*, vol. 12, no. 2: 381–389.

Obernbreit, R. 1985. 'Object Relations Theory and the Language of Art/Tools for the Treatment of the Borderline Patient'. *Art Therapy: Journal of the American Art Therapy Association*, vol. 2: 11–18.

Ogata, S., Silk, K., and Goodrich, S. 1990. 'The Childhood Experience of the Borderline Patient'. In P. Links (ed.), *Family Environment and Borderline Personality Disorder*. Washington, DC: American Psychiatric Press.

Psychological Abstracts [CD ROM] '1/87–6/94'. Washington, DC; American Psychological Association: 'Producer'. Available: Silver Platter.

Rothblum, E. and Franks, V. 1987. 'Custom-fitted Straight Jackets: Perspectives on Women's Mental Health'. In J. Figueira-Mcdonough and R. Sarri (eds), *The Trapped Woman: Catch-22 in Deviance and Control*. Newbury Park: Sage Publishers.

Saunders, E., and Arnold, F. 1991. *Borderline Personality Disorder and Childhood Abuse: Revisions in Clinical Thinking and Treatment Approach* (Tech. Rep. no. 51). Wellesley, MA: Wellesley College. The Stone Center.

Schatzow, E., and Herman, J. 1989. 'Breaking Secrecy/Adult Survivors Disclose to their Families'. *Psychiatric Clinics of North America*, vol. 12, no. 2: 337-349.

Silverstein, L. 1991. 'Transforming the Debate about Child Care and Maternal Employment'. *American Psychologist*, vol. 46, no. 10: 1025-1032.

Spellman, E. V. 1988. *Inessential Woman: Problems of Exclusion in Feminist Thought*. Boston: Beacon Press.

Stone, M. H. 1989. 'Individual Psychotherapy with Victims of Incest'. *Psychiatric Clinics of North America*, vol. 12: 237–255.

Sturdivant, S. 1980. *Therapy with Women: A Feminist Philosophy of Treatment*. New York: Springer.

United States of America Bureau of Labor Statistics. 1992. *Employment and Earnings*, vol. 39, no. 1. Washington, DC: Office of Employment and Unemployment Statistics in Collaboration with the Office of Publication.

Weller, S. 1992. 'Abused by the Courts', *The Village Voice*, vol. 31–32: 25 November–1 December, 34–38.

Winnicott, D. W. 1971. *Playing and Reality*. New York: Basic Books.

Winnicott, D. W., Shepherd, R., and Davis, M. (eds) 1989. *Psychoanalytic Explorations: D. W. Winnicott*. Cambridge, MA: Harvard University Press.

Wylie, M. S. 1993. 'The Shadow of a Doubt'. *The Family Therapy Networker*, September/October, vol. 18–29: 70–73.

Chapter 6

Liberation and the art of embodiment

Miche Fabre-Lewin

The arts and therapy have a powerful role to play in exploring the relationships between concepts of self, culture and nature. However, without integrating advances in the sciences and taking account of cultural theory on the nature of oppression, Western models of psychotherapy will perpetuate practices which reinforce outdated and misconceived ideas of human nature. Within cultural theory, the concept of the 'personal is political' refers to the interrelationship between personal, individual experiences and legislative and political structures. Feminism emphasises that a woman's self-image, as well as her economic position, is profoundly shaped by the social oppression of sex discrimination. Feminist therapy then, based on the 'personal is political', accounts for the psychological damage suffered through sexism and aims to provide a space where women can rediscover their personal power and regain a healthy emotional sense of self. In ecology, Gaia theory emphasises the interdependence of the part to the whole, and that between humans and the environment, an idea which has its antecedents in the Renaissance.

The study of self in psychotherapy focuses its enquiry on the psyche, its unconscious dynamics and motivations, and the personality complexes arising from childhood ruptures. I want to address this preoccupation with the personal interior to discover how art therapy might shift our attention towards the outer landscapes of self and the environment in an attempt to reflect back an understanding of the inner world. Art therapy introduces into the therapeutic process experiential interactions with paint, paper and drawing materials from which the client creates pictures and objects. As distinct from verbal therapies, in art therapy words are a companion in the therapeutic journey, rather than the primary vehicle for the client's self-exploration. The images made by clients offer many channels for personal explorations within art therapy. They can be visual stories expressing personal relationships, have symbolic references, highlight the transference feelings between client and therapist, as well as being depictions of emerging unconscious material.

This chapter explores the potential of image-making in therapy as a medium for cultural and political change for women as well as a means for personal transformation. My focus is on the physicality of the image-making and how this can engage the client more profoundly in her path towards self-empowerment. For in art therapy the arts process introduces conscious action, physical movement, bodily gestures as the client works with and through her body. In using art materials she is interacting with and moulding her own environment. I will be exploring some of the elements in the processes and products of art therapy to illustrate how the making of images and objects within therapeutic practice offers a space for women to reconnect with their minds as well as their bodies in the journey to their liberation.

ILLNESS OR DIS-EASE

> The aura of legitimacy given to the diagnosis of madness by the profes-sionalisation of treatment is seen to obscure the reality of oppression.
>
> (Ussher 1991:134)

The new professions of psychotherapy vie for recognition as carers of people's psychological well-being. There is an ever-increasing complexity of diagnoses for dysfunctional behaviour as well as interventions and inter-pretations for curing and controlling so-called mental health problems. We hear definitions which name alienation as being the consequence of defences, drives, distortions, obsessive beliefs, neurotic symptoms, unconscious conflict, or faulty information processing. The anti-psychiatry movement rejected genetic and biological views of madness. Psychiatrist Thomas Szasz reframed mental illness as 'problems in living' and argued that people diagnosed as mentally ill were in fact scapegoats of an oppres-sive society. To support this view, psychologist Dorothy Rowe suggests that the current belief in mental illness as an organic dysfunction relieves us from taking responsibility against oppression. Kovel (1982) affirms that: 'the ultimate impact of the mental health industry is to increase alienation and false consciousness . . . by the myth of individual psychology and cure in the midst of a diseased society' (quoted in Ussher 1991: 129).

Kovel speaks of how therapy has been more successful than religion in displacing energy needed for radical social change (Kovel 1988: 121). Models of feminist therapy regard the impact of oppression on a women's life is a major cause of the 'dis-ease' which brings them into therapy. Ussher's research on the relationship between women's mental health and oppression proposes that defining women as mad acts as a form of social regulation:

> Yet wherever we turn women are controlled very effectively, so that they never gain the status of being the One. And madness, as a

description of our fears, a category for our pain, or label for our anger, both marks us as the Other, and prevents us from challenging the One.

(Ussher 1991: 14)

The medicalisation of deviance as a form of social control is not confined to women, and there are repercussions for other oppressed groups. Black psychiatrist Fernando challenges the white perspective on mental illness, highlighting issues of power, control and colonisation within Western mental health practice. On the subject of transcultural psychiatry Sashidharan writes that

transculturalism . . . has provided a safe, easy opportunity for mental health professionals to conceptualise and deal with major social and political issues like institutionalised racism and inequality in supposedly neutral terms.

(Sashidharan 1986: 174, in Cox 1986)

Having gained some insight into how mental health models inform the profession of psychotherapy, it seems that within our Western cultures, psychiatry may collude and reinforce institutionalised discrimination by defining the suffering caused by oppression as an illness of the mind requiring specialist treatment. Here then is evidence of how oppression becomes institutionalised through external social forces. However, another factor keeps oppression in place – internalised oppression. Freire's work highlights the effects class oppression has on the literacy skills of peasant workers in Brazil. He refers to the effect of a 'colonized mentality' whereby the victims of oppression take on the devalued opinion imposed upon them by the dominant group. Thus the oppressed groups internalise the negative self-images and come to believe they are of less value, and so undermine their own intelligence and worth.

Self-depreciation is another characteristic of the oppressed which derives from their internalization of the opinion the oppressors hold of them.

(Freire 1972: 38)

For women to be free of the 'colonised mentality' imposed by patriarchal structures, we need to acknowledge that we are oppressed, identify how the oppression continues to be enforced on us legally and psychologically, as well as challenge the conditioning in all its forms. So as women, a significant part of our liberation lies in recognising how we collude with sexism by accepting the role of victim. Feminist models of therapy can offer a space for female clients to shed the internalised, negative messages and attitudes imposed on us by male power structures and values. And as feminist art therapists, we are in a powerful position to reorientate the therapeutic alliance so as to avoid perpetuating or colluding with the oppression.

IN OUR OWN IMAGE

Freire defines further the dynamics of liberation and writes of speaking the world in one's own language, that is to say naming the oppression (Freire 1972: 61). I want to delve a little deeper into the 'talking cure', where through the medium of verbal language therapeutic transformation is seen to occur. In the traditional psychoanalytically informed therapies, verbal descriptions of past traumatic events are seen as the agency for catharsis, the discharge of repressed emotion. The mental awareness (or 'insight') which follows the discharge (or 'abreaction') gives way to an understanding of the causes for the distress and thereby enables changes in mental and physical behaviour. The emphasis is on engaging mental capacities via verbal recollection to enable a catharsis of unconscious conflicts. However, the focus on the mind seems to deny the body a more active and expressive role in the process of psychological resolution.

Alice Miller, a psychoanalyst of twenty years' standing, writes of her disillusion with the talking cure. Her own experiences as an analyst (and an analysand having undertaken two complete analyses) point to the inadequacy of words alone in recovering from psychic damage. Miller questions whether the constructs of psychoanalysis are creating obstacles to the healing process. Indeed, she argues that the basis of psychoanalysis, 'free association' of words to address early trauma, may be insufficient as a vehicle for addressing these experiences as it 'reinforces intellectual resistance to feelings and reality; for as long as feelings can be talked about they cannot really be felt. And as long as feelings cannot be felt, the self-damaging blockages remain' (Miller 1991: 183). Language, it would seem, is invested with the capacity to offer us intellectual insight but may be depriving us of an embodied catharsis enabling a more active and visible relationship to the world. Furthermore, feminist Spender writes of the way in which language colludes with the oppression of women:

> Language is our means of classifying and ordering the world: our means of manipulating reality. In its structure and in its use we bring our world into realization, and if it is inherently inaccurate, then we are misled. If the rules which underlie our language system, our symbolic order, are invalid, then we are daily deceived.
>
> (Spender 1982: 2)

As Freire points out, acknowledgement and descriptions of oppression are essential to the liberation process, and certainly words can evoke and convey emotion. Yet they cannot tell the whole story, and indeed may even put up smoke-screens, thereby preventing us from getting in touch with the personal and cultural violation we have experienced as women. To emerge from being victims of oppression and regain trust in our minds we will need to describe and name the world in our own language. We need to risk feeling our pain through our bodily consciousness in order to heal from the psychological wounds as well as physical damage to our bodies. In rediscovering physical sensations, intuitive impulses and the physical processes, we can reclaim the capacity to heal naturally from suffering via the emotions. I want to explore how the therapeutic space, in combination with the use of art materials, can provide the context for a liberating practice that can offer a challenge to our false, conditioned consciousness. What is it about the creation of visual images as distinct from verbal language which enables women as clients to regain a sense of their own power, and reclaim possession of their bodies?

LIBERATION THROUGH THE BODY

Sickness is not just an isolated event, nor an unfortunate brush with nature. It is a form of communication – the language of the organs – through which nature, society and culture speak simultaneously. The individual body should be seen as the most immediate, the proximate terrain where social truths and social contradictions are played out, as well as the locus of personal and social resistance, creativity, and struggle.

(Lock and Scheper-Hughes 1987: 31)

Patriarchy shames women. It silences us and renders us culturally unequal and invisible, depriving us of fulfilling our expansive potential as human beings. The oppression has repercussions not only in our psychological states but takes its toll on our physical bodies as well. Rather than being viewed as evidence of our susceptibility to mental illness, cultural theorists (Fernando 1995; Fulani 1987; Showalter 1987) view addictive behaviours, emotional and obsessional disturbances as reactions and symptoms to the dehumanising practices of patriarchal and imperialist power structures. Our body reflects the impact of oppression, and therefore it is the locus of resistance, the site from which we struggle to be free. Freire writes that for true liberation to take place, 'praxis' is necessary. Praxis involves reflection on, as well as action against, the oppression. Merleau-Ponty reminds us that our cognition of the world is more than purely mental or intellectual. Belonging to the sentient world requires making sense of our existence phenomenologically by involving the whole of our physical body with its sensory, motor and affective capacities. Through our bodies we experience the world. It follows that our body's interrelationship with the world is essential to becoming conscious, and that we cannot think ourselves into liberation alone, we need to enact our way to freedom through the body.

Psychotherapists McDougall's and Orbach's focus on the body offers direction for the personal and cultural healing work that can be done within a therapeutic context. Orbach's experience of women with addictive behaviour around food has led her to conceptualise the 'false body'

(Orbach in Erskine and Judd 1994). She writes of women having no sense of themselves inhabiting a stable, authentic and reliable physical basis of self. Instead we experience our bodies as a thing to be manipulated, done to, or displayed. Orbach refers to McDougall's view of the body as an expressive mode of expression where the earliest pre-verbal distress manifests in physical symptoms. The body is the site of 'the load of unthinkable or uncontainable feelings and conflicts.' Here we have reference to the emotional memories contained within the body which require release. For the emergence of a 'true body' a psychological birth·necessarily entails the physical and corporeal expression of emotion.

Thomas Scheff (1979: 59) argues that for true insight to occur, more than words are necessary. The client needs to experience a physical catharsis. In understanding how our bodies as well as our minds might be more profoundly engaged in therapeutic catharsis, it is useful to draw on Scheff's discussion of 'aesthetic distance' as a pre-condition for catharsis. He suggests that in working solely through language to recover from trauma, the attention is 'overdistanced' and the client remains in the role of observer. To enable the discharge of emotion, the client needs to be both participant and observer in the therapy. Expressive therapies which engage the client in physical and bodily interactions can provide the conditions and materials which support an embodied, self-directed resolution of conflict and pain.

EMBODIED IMAGES

Art has the capacity to heal psychological wounds and scars. Jungian analyst Moore writes about the languages within which the soul's mysteries are revealed and contained – mythology, the fine arts, poetry and dreams (Moore 1992). Hillman sees artists as the best example of people who turn their imagination to the raw material of suffering. For the therapeutic activity to give expression to the 'real life of the psyche' rather than adjusting a person to a dysfunctional society, Hillman speaks of an aesthetic activity which de-anaesthetises and re-enlivens the 'ore' of memories and events (Hillman 1992: 30). Pleasure in beauty, he feels, is essential to a sense of wholeness and he writes of 'aesthetic therapeutics' as a way of keeping ourselves in tune with the health of the soul. However, therapy which nourishes the soul through accepting the natural forces of the psyche, will be opening up the imagination not only to beauty, but to 'sublime terror'.

Merleau-Ponty writes that the 'painting celebrates no other enigma but that of visibility' (quoted in Crowther 1993: 112). Making marks to create images with art materials is a 'mute' expression of the body/world relationship. Pictorial images are seen as the manifestation of a person's self-realisation. And yet, the urge to make form, to reflect our relationship to the world, within the arts process is more than a matter of visibility. In Renaissance therapies of the imagination, there was an emphasis on changing the images in the psyche rather than treating the biological conditions of the mind. Artist/art therapist, Mcniff (1992: 107) writes that the material processes at work in the act of creating have greater potential for transformation than the notion of 'changing the intangible idea of the self'. We do not live independently of things, we are shaped by the dialogues between ourselves and the images and objects around us. In this way the pictures become the agencies which assist in restructuring consciousness. McNiff writes:

> Art can once again operate as a 'primary' therapeutic method in which the creative process restructures the images and interactive process that shape consciousness.

> (McNiff 1992: 107)

The artistic process and product act as a metaphor of mediation between our inner lives and the outer world. This mirroring of our psycho-physical existence through the arts process involves the body in an interactive relationship with other concrete, material objects in the world. Feminist art therapist Ellis refers to the metaphoric potential of the images created in art therapy where the tactile properties and formal qualities inherent in the media expand its capacity for enabling self-awareness:

> Traces and marks, layers and shapes reflecting a woman's conscious and unconscious bodily gestures hold meaning that is often untranslatable but that mirror back the texture and complexity, the substance and movement of a woman's experience. Women can discover a new active experience of their bodies that counter those images in our culture that . . . are based on manipulations of the female body.

> (Ellis 1989: 267)

The physical process of bodily movement, gesture and mark interacting with the matter, colour, form, line and volume embodies the experience of a woman directing and interacting in her environment with conscious intention. Her body is active in its movement of making marks and fashioning objects. Arms, hands, feet can be engaged in a range of visual and tactile expressions using art materials to scribble, stab, stamp, tear, feather, rub and cover over. Here in the therapeutic arena is the safe territory to engage the body in rigorous, noisy and violent gestures which will encourage an embodied cathartic discharge of emotion.

It is this interactive relationship with the materials and process of making objects, as well as the image's capacity for making visible the invisible which has far-reaching implications for psychological and embodied liberation. Art therapy, with its process of mark-making and modelling, and in its creation of visible, material images and objects offers a powerful medium for reconnecting ourselves with physical objects and consequently with our own bodies. In art therapy as a form of cultural action, making images and objects within the safety of the therapeutic environment can play a significant part in shedding the false internalised images we have acquired of ourselves. Women have the chance to make their mark, release painful emotion, exercise their imaginations, and re-vision themselves in the creative struggle to be free from the paralysing effects of institution-alised and internalised sexism.

THERAPIST AS WITNESS

That the therapist is viewed as interpreter of a woman's psychological experiences is according to Miller another form of control and power over women's lives, where the client is seen as uninformed and needs the analyst to interpret unconscious desires, thoughts and impulses (Miller 1991: 183). The role of the therapist as cultural activist in the therapeutic setting with women should be to recreate conditions whereby clients are able to counter the negative messages of sexism.

With this manifesto for women's liberation within the art therapy setting, a redefinition of the relationship between the client and the therapist is therefore essential. How might the therapeutic relationship foster what Freire calls a 'dialogue' between people which is an act of creation rather than one of domination? For love to be an act of freedom, he writes, it must not serve as a pretext for manipulation. The role of image-making within therapy goes some way to providing a channel for a dialogue which is an act of creation between two people. Ellis, in her work with women, gives measure of this potential. She highlights the significance of image-making in shifting the balance of power whereby the client relates to herself as a woman as well as being in the presence of therapist. In art therapy the sheet of paper can be seen as the territory within which the woman-as-client takes total control, and where the act of drawing and painting 'reinforces her awareness of her power to create and give shape to herself and her life' (Ellis 1989: 270).

The creation of an image within the presence of therapist offers great scope for a cathartic healing from the psychological bonds of oppression. Through art and its non-verbal processes women can move beyond the definitions of themselves and out of the descriptions of their suffering. Via the material, and corporeal expressions of their conflicts, women actively participate in their liberation. As well as being a space for action and enact-ment, the art-making process offers time for reverie, reflection and musing. Alone and yet witnessed, and in charge of the pace of our healing.

Bearing witness and giving space for enacting our movement towards freedom is fundamental to a therapeutic process which is to be a cultural practice in personal and social liberation. The acknowledgment that sexism affects not only our inner landscapes but deeply distorts our attitudes towards our bodies has implications for us as female therapists. We need to make a commitment to our own process of liberation if we are to offer the space and be the guides for women in their healing from cultural conditioning. This involves acknowledging the effects oppression has had on our own bodily consciousness and the limits we put on our capacity to release strong and uncomfortable emotions. We will need to risk feeling the terror at the betrayal of our souls and humanity, and only when this healing work is done, can we fully take our own bodies and hearts into our practice without pretence or domination.

CONCLUSION

Through the arts in therapy we have channels for resolution and revolution. The art process and product can provide the interactive environment for the client to recreate and to enact the conditions within which she can reclaim a powerful, visible and active relationship to her own being and her right to be in the world. If art therapy is to be reinvested with an authentic healing power and to contribute meaningfully to fundamental questions on the nature of knowing and the process of liberation, we as art therapists need to inform our practice with models of human nature which challenge the legacy of patriarchal and Eurocentric ideologies which permeate the field of psychiatry.

We are living in dynamic and expansive times and we need new languages and new maps to convey the true nature of our beings. The physical, psychological and spiritual effect of social oppressions damages the well-being of the individual and the community, as well as our planet. It is our responsibility to be aware of new research, thinking and developments in such diverse spheres as the sciences, medicine, anthropology, ecology, economics, philosophy and cultural politics. Without turning to these models we risk perpetuating dualistic and conservative concepts of identity and human nature. It would seem that there is a profound exchange to be nourished in the alliance between art and psychotherapy. In this alliance, the therapy setting offers women a physical sanctuary for naming the oppression, shedding negative self-images, and re-empowering our relationship to each other, men and the environment. Working with the arts process provides a safe territory to explore and experience strong emotion through the interaction of our bodies with art materials.

In our work with groups and individuals on innermost feelings, concepts of self and identity, relationships within communities and across cultures, art therapists are in a powerful position to effect cultural change and offer hope and vision within and outside our professional practice. To re-animate our healing practices with passion and hope, to rediscover collective rites of passage which are embodied and meaningful, we need to return to the non-verbal arts. These have always distilled raw and rupturing suffering into powerful collective visions of ennobling beauty and offered new directions and perspectives.

ACKNOWLEDGEMENT

This chapter is dedicated to my mother, Cecile.

BIBLIOGRAPHY

Cox, J. L. (ed.) 1986. *Transcultural Psychiatry*. London: Croom Helm.
Crowther, P. 1993. *Art and Embodiment*. Oxford: Oxford University Press.
Ellis, M. L. 1989. 'Women: The Mirage of the Perfect Image'. *The Arts in Psychotherapy*, vol. 16, 263–76.
Fernando, S. 1995. *Mental Health in a Multi-Ethnic Society*. London: Routledge.
Freire, P. 1972. *Pedagogy of the Oppressed*. Harmondsworth: Penguin.
Fulani, L. (ed) 1987. *The Psychopathology of Everyday Racism*. NY: Harrington Park Press.
Gablik, S. 1991. *The ReEnchantment of Art*. London: Thames & Hudson.
Hillman, J. 1992. *A Hundred Years of Psychotherapy*. New York: HarperCollins.
Kovel, J. 1982. 'The American health industry,' in Ingleby, D. (ed.) *Critical Psychology: Politics of Mental Health*. Harmondsworth: Penguin.
Kovel, J. 1988. *White Racism: A Psychohistory*. London: Free Association Books.
McNiff, S. 1992. *Art as Medicine*. Boston: Shambhala.
Macy, J. 1991. *World as Lover, World as Self*. Berkeley: Parallax Press.
Miller, A. 1991. *Banished Knowledge*. London: Virago.
Miller, A. 1995. *Pictures of a Childhood*. London: Virago.
Mindell, A. 1990. *Dreambody*. London: Arkana.
Moore, T. 1992. *Care of the Soul*. London: Piatkus.
Pinkola E. 1993. *Women who Run with the Wolves*. London: Rider.
Sashidharan, S. P. 1986. 'Politics and Ideology in Transcultural Psychiatry'. In Cox, J. L. (ed.) *Transcultural Psychiatry*. London: Croom Helm.
Scheff, T. J. 1979. *Catharsis in Healing, Ritual and Drama*. Berkeley, CA: University of California Press.
Scheper-Hughes, and Lock. 1987. 'The Mindful Body: A Prolegomenon to Future Work in Medical Anthropology'. *Medical Anthropology Quarterly*, N.S., vol. 1, no. 1, 6–41.
Schumacher, E. F. 1995. *A Guide for the Perplexed*. London: Vintage.
Sheldrake, R. 1990. *The Rebirth of Nature*. London: Rider.
Showalter, E. 1987. *The Female Malady*. London: Virago.
Spender, D. 1982. *Man Made Language*, London: Routledge and Kegan Paul.
Ussher, J. 1991. *Women's Madness. Misogyny or Mental Illness*. Hemel Hempstead: Harvester Wheatsheaf.
Weber, R. (ed.) 1986. *Dialogues with Scientists and Sages*. Harmondsworth: Penguin.

Chapter 7

Ageing: another tyranny?
Art therapy with older women

Val Huet

For nearly two years, I conducted an art therapy group with older women in a community setting. The group had been intended for men and women who needed help to avoid admission to a psychiatric hospital, or wanted art therapy on their discharge from acute services. Purely by chance, all suitable referrals were for older women. All had used psychiatric services during their lives, although not all had been in-patients. Most had been on medication for a long time, but were all able to have stable lifestyles with a varying degree of support from day centres, social workers and so on. They were all of menopausal or post-menopausal age and this turned out to be of significance as the group developed.

This unplanned situation opened up unexpectedly powerful issues such as mortality, self-image, sexuality and ageing which, or so I thought, might not have concerned me until I became older myself. I found, of course, that this was not so and that what happens to older women in our society is but the open manifestation of prejudices present throughout our lives, some sort of 'logical' conclusion.

In the first part of this chapter, I address the issue of ageing, the denial of which I perceive as a new tyranny particularly affecting women who are under increasing pressure to remain youthful-looking. I discuss how this is particularly evident in the material concerning menopause, which highlights many socio-cultural prejudices against women. The women in the group often encountered prejudice on account of their age, gender and mental health problems. In the second section, I describe how art provided a language for women who seemed to have been silenced by their experiences. The images enabled the introduction of difficult issues, such as anger, and helped the enactment and resolution of conflict. In the third section, I write about the different themes which surfaced throughout the group, such as sexuality, age, loss, and how some of these have provoked difficult countertransference feelings in me. I discuss further transference and countertransference issues in the fourth section, and reflect on how the experience of conducting this group initiated some important personal changes.

I hope I have managed to represent in this chapter the courage that most women showed in fighting against helplessness and in trying to regain some sense of their integrity and of direction in their lives.

AGEING – THE NEW TYRANNY

Western society seems to become increasingly intolerant of the ageing process: advertising urges women to buy expensive cosmetic products to delay the appearance of wrinkles, and pseudo-scientific terms are used to convince them that ageing can be kept at bay through the use of lotions and creams. Young women are promised virtually everlasting youth if they 'work hard' enough throughout their lives at keeping in shape through exercise, diets and, of course, regular use of skin products. The use of plastic surgery seems to be increasing and older actresses or celebrities often appear on television with unnaturally taut facial skin, promoting the illusion that youth can and should be kept. It is as though ageing has become a symbol of personal sloth, an outward manifestation of some moral failure. Women have never been under so much pressure to remain youthful and active, and this is much in evidence with material on the menopause.

Posner writes:

> If it is true, as Simone de Beauvoir (1973) suggests, that 'society looks upon old age as a kind of shameful secret that is unseemly to mention' (p. 1) then it is also true that menopause epitomises the stigma for women in North American society. This fact alone may best explain the scarcity of literature on the topic. Menopause not only reflects the theme of old age and desexualisation, but it specifically focuses on the aging female, a status which seems ambiguous, if not internally contradictory in many societies.[1]

Posner's statement is, I feel, also valid in our north European society as are the findings of research done by Mitteness (1983) which show a marked difference in the coverage of menopause in the American popular press through the twentieth century. Prior to the 1950s, articles addressed health improvement during menopause which was often described as marking a new and contented phase in a woman's life. Publications during the 1950s and 1960s heralded, with Estrogen Replacement Therapy (ERT), a new focus on youth preserving, and denoted a higher incidence of medical intervention. (In the UK, ERT is known as HRT, Hormone Replacement Therapy.) Mitteness also found that 'forty-seven percent of the articles published in the 1960's used a single gynaecologist, R. A. Wilson, as their primary or only source of information'.[2] Wilson was the author of the influential book *Feminine Forever* (1966) in which he argued that menopause was a disease easily cured by ERT. Mitteness writes:

He [R. A. Wilson] seems to have had an ability to articulate the cultural 'symbols' of womanhood that were prevalent then. His work captures the essence of the problem with women: they get old. Medical technology, in his view, should be marshalled to preserve youth. The only acceptable women are young, 'sexually competent' women.[3]

Ageing in a climate so hostile to old women is made no easier by a common experience of multiple losses at the time of menopause, such as children leaving home, parents dying or marriage break-up. O'Toole and O'Toole describe this as the 'empty nest syndrome' and point out that it is often a time when women are called upon to look after an elderly parent and re-enter a demanding primary care role.[4] All these factors might take the menopause an emotionally stressful time. However, the biological roots of the menopause must not be overlooked.

When seeking help for physiological complaints, older women often encounter a less than sympathetic response from the medical profession which tends to regard menopausal symptoms either as 'mainly in the head', or, as easily treatable with anti-depressants and HRT. Posner and McCrea compare medical and feminist attitudes towards the menopause. Posner finds them 'strange bedfellows' since they both assume that menopausal problems are largely 'all in the head'.[5] Similarly, McCrea (1983) discusses the 'discovery' of a 'deficiency disease' which is how the menopause was viewed after synthetic oestrogen became available. This heralded a routine use of ERT, despite research findings pointing to a link with cancer. McCrea also urges feminists not to ignore the physiological aspects of the menopause in their effort to show that it does not affect negatively a woman's physical and emotional functioning.

As O'Toole and O'Toole point out,

menopause is the final menstrual period (Utian, 1977). But like many biological events, its psychological meaning to the individual and its sociological meanings have implications far beyond biological change.[6]

No woman can be exactly sure which of her periods will be the last. It is a process which takes a while and will not be completed by the manifestation of something new, as is the case with menarche or pregnancy, but by an absence, a non-happening. Greer points out that there are no rites of passage to mark the completion of the menopause, and talks of the 'social invisibility of the menopause'.[7] She also calls the menopause the 'undescribed experience' and notes that much of the literature on the subject has been published by men, not by women who have remained silent on the subject.[8]

Perhaps one reason for this silence may be attributed to fears of loss of status: in a society which mainly values women for their youth and reproductive functions, there may not be much to be gained by declaring openly that one has ceased to be fertile as this is often equated with becoming sexually inactive, unattractive and old. Steuer writes:

> Stripped of sexuality, older women become either invisible or a nuisance. Sexiness, in a perverse fashion, means status. And status in turn means visibility and utility in our society. Thus older women are doubly undervalued, once for age and once for sexlessness.[9]

Faced by a wall of silence and by social invisibility, older women are often in a difficult position if needing help; the experience might be no more positive than with the medical approach, as older women seem to have been equally badly served by psychotherapy.

A review of feminist literature on psychoanalysis will not be undertaken here, and the works of de Beauvoir (1949), Firestone (1970), Chesler (1972) and Eichenbaum and Orbach (1982) provide a thorough appraisal of sexism and psychoanalytic theory. From its beginning, psychoanalysis seems to have found women rather problematic and Freud himself admitted to being perplexed by them, stating that 'the sexual life of adult women is "a dark continent" for psychology'.[10] Steuer (1982) sees psychoanalytic theory as not only being sexist, but also ageist. She calls for a greater awareness of the influence of the therapist's own value system on the process of therapy, particularly when younger therapists are working with older women.

Working with older women certainly highlighted issues which I found uncomfortable and which put into question my own values and beliefs, and I shall address these later on. Initially, however, art therapy seemed to provide a much-needed language for the women in the group.

'I SHOUT BUT NO SOUND COMES OUT': OLDER WOMEN USING ART THERAPY TO FIND A VOICE

Being very influenced by Foulkes's work, I value a mainly non-directive approach to groups. McNeilly (1983, 1987) and Skaife (1990) have written eloquently on the merits of non-directive art therapy. Although I find these concepts useful when working with trainees and people with no history of psychiatric illness, I feel that most clients with mental health problems would find the level of anxiety raised by such an approach quite intolerable and probably persecutory. I therefore provided some basic structure to the group by sharing the time equally between the making of images and the group discussion. The art-making process was to be non-directive, and the themes or suggestions on what to make would not be given. The ensuing talk would be 'free-floating' and group members could decide whether or not to talk about their work. Following one early drop-out, the group settled to a membership of five women: Veronica, Sarah, Penny, Iris and Lynn.

Skultans (1976) describes how menopausal women lack a language for voicing their protest at being undervalued. For most of the women who attended the art therapy group, being undervalued had been an issue encountered through their experience of living with mental illness. When assessed for the group, several women had talked of 'not being heard', of being unable to 'find the words to say it', and of fears of being 'on the scrap heap'.

In the group, art seemed to provide a language for issues which had been long repressed: initially, feelings manifested themselves through the images rather than verbally. A theme of fear of anger and conflict recurred throughout the first three months.

In the second session, an image of seven 'devouring piranhas' was made by Iris who explained that the net at the background was flimsy and might not be able to hold the piranhas. When I pointed out that their number was the same as the number of people in the room, she looked startled but reticent to talk further. Earlier on, the group had experienced a 'near conflict', when a member had described the neighbourhood as 'filthy'. This had offended another woman who said pointedly that she lived and worked nearby, and the ensuing tension had been broken up by hurriedly placatory remarks from other group members. The image of the devouring piranhas seems to symbolise the group's fear of being swallowed up by anger and conflict.

Confrontations continued to be carefully avoided for a while, although I was struck by how angry many images seemed to be. This was the case in the eighth session which followed a short break, and when four members were present. Veronica painted a house on fire, Iris drew an erupting volcano and Sarah represented a man crawling on his knees. The images were talked about as referring to angry feelings outside of the group, and regarded respectively the Social Services which Veronica wanted to burn down, Iris's feelings of 'boiling over' after receiving shoddy treatment from a psychiatrist, and Sarah's anger towards an ex-boyfriend. A fourth drawing by Lynn of a suitcase which was obviously too small to contain all the piles of clothes and presents she wanted to take with her when visiting relatives was also about angry feelings: she related it to emotional baggage and anger which might burst out of her and spill over when she is with her family.

The need to allocate angry feelings to outside issues seemed to indicate a strong resistance to addressing those inside the group. When I suggested that some material might relate to the group itself, some members responded by stating they had found coming back after the break very difficult. Sarah added that it was hard to think of something to draw, and was disappointed that no themes were set for the group. I wondered whether the need for given themes was about avoiding the themes in the group at present. I also questioned whether some of the anger was coming my way because of the break. She replied, with a smile:

Perhaps it would be easier if you gave us themes: it would give us something concrete to rebel against!

She was hiding her image with her arms, and said she was scared of the
feelings expressed in it.

The need for themes was also related to a wish for safety and containment. Lynn's image of a suitcase which could not possibly hold all the
luggage and which would burst and spill out was an appropriate symbol
for the fear of being overwhelmed by one's own emotional baggage.

The group was frightened that if the anger was expressed, the ensuing
conflict would open the floodgate to overwhelming and long-suppressed
feelings. Concerns about being 'mad' and of being swamped by the
strength of the issues were expressed. This is not unusual in many verbal
and art psychotherapy groups: Yalom (1970) describes how new group
psychotherapy clients often express fears of being made to confess awful
secrets, of being shunned, ridiculed, or 'contaminated' by others. They also
fear their own rage will annihilate the group, or that they will themselves
be destroyed by the group's anger.[11] However, what became evident was
that it was not only fear of consequences which held back some of the
women, but a lack of experience at giving voice to their feelings in the first
place. A poignant image symbolised this: Iris had represented one of her
recurring nightmares. She has fallen to the bottom of a dark pit and she
tries to scream, but no sound comes out of her mouth. Above ground, a
crowd of indifferent people look on, but make no attempt to rescue her.
She became both upset and angry when talking about her work.

The fear of being overwhelmed by anger lessened after the thirteenth
session, when the group experienced and survived a conflict during which
Penny became very angry with me, and accused me of infantilising them
by asking them to engage in child-like activities like art. She attacked me
as being incompetent and derided the purpose of art-making as a waste
of time. Her own images were mostly diagrammatic and hence tightly
controlled. Her attack on me stemmed partly from rage at parental control
(she had been left by her family to care for an elderly and demanding
mother); I shall address later on issues of transference and countertransference more fully. Her attack on the art-making process seemed to be an
attempt to halt the expression of uncomfortable feelings and it was as
though she wanted to silence these by stopping the making of art. The
group responded by stating how important art was to them, and by working
with her on the roots of her rage. This session was a significant one in the
life of the group, as there followed a sense that the group had experienced
and survived its first enactment of conflict.

This felt like an important development, as it seemed to enable most
women to deal with material in the 'here and now' and to verbalise their
feelings more easily. This helped the group address difficult issues which
are usually kept silent, such as sexuality when older and mortality.

BLOSSOMS IN WINTER: SEXUALITY, AGE, LOSS AND POWER

Steuer (1982) writes about the desexualisation of older women who, having lost their status as young, fertile women, become seen as 'sexless'. She thinks that the therapists' attitude might be affected by this and that they might find the older women's need for warmth, love and sex difficult to address.[12]

Similarly, many psychiatric patients describe experiencing a process of desexualisation: physically, the side-effects of drugs such as permanently dry mouth, general shakiness and excessive weight gain can be disturbing, and these, as well as the drugs themselves, often affect the libido. Furthermore, women patients are often told that the drugs might affect their menstrual cycle.

In the art therapy group, sexuality was addressed at first timidly, and was often connected to issues regarding age, loss and mortality. In an early session, Penny had drawn the image of a man whom she said represented all the relationships she could have had but never did. This had introduced issues of loss and a need to mourn missed opportunities. Some women had talked about how different life might have been 'if . . . '. It was as though they were all at a time of life when they were reassessing the past, and ancient pains were coming back to the fore. Lynn later disclosed that she had found her first sexual encounter with a man twenty-five years ago so traumatic that it had been her last.

In another session, Lynn had represented herself as a fat baby: she said she was fearing becoming fat again (she was in reality quite skinny) and was now beginning to develop breasts 'when it was too late'. When I encouraged her to explore the too-late feeling, she related it to the fact that her mother had died when she was her age and that she thought this would be when she would die too. The group discussed and shared her fear of death, but this also seemed linked to a fear of becoming sexually attractive by gaining weight, and sex had been a fearful experience for her. Her comments denoted ambivalence towards sexuality and fertility: sexual desires do not die when a woman is no longer fertile, and although the breasts might have appeared 'too late' to suckle a baby, they might still be viewed as sexually arousing.

Themes of sexuality, fertility and loss became stronger in the group as time went on. In the nineteenth session, Sarah had drawn two images: one she described as the branch of a prune tree, the other as womb-like. She said that in Japan, it is a beautiful symbol, because it blooms in winter. She added that she felt like a 'dried up old twig' which sparked off laughter and shared self-derogatory jokes by other women who identified with this feeling. I commented on a sense of hope and renewal symbolised by the appearance of blooms in the dead of winter. However, I failed to recognise the link between the womb and the dried, old twig in bloom, which retrospectively evokes material on loss of fertility at menopause. I also did not link this with the previous material from Lynn on 'too late' to develop breasts and did not explore the potential sexual symbol of sensuous blossoms of an old twig. I cannot help feeling that this denotes some of the difficulties described above by Steuer (1982), and that I was unconsciously avoiding areas which were creating uncomfortable feelings in me. I shall discuss this more fully further on.

Menopause was discussed directly later on, when Sarah said that her HRT treatment had made her feel terrible. Penny said she was still menstruating and could still have children, but that she found looking after her mother hard enough, although she feared her death. The women then all shared painful experiences of bereavement, although one mourned a beloved and protective mother, whilst the others needed to mourn for the good parenting they had not had.

As illustrated above, themes of sexuality, ageing and loss echoed throughout the sessions. I found the way these issues intertwined some-times confusing, and I often felt that something important was escaping me. Although I did fail to take into account the impact of menopause on the women, and issues of age and sexuality, I wondered if this reflected the women's feelings of having missed out on life, and to a certain degree, it probably did. I was sometimes aware of a countertransference feeling of helplessness, when I felt weighed down and paralysed by the level of neediness of the group. This brought up ambivalent feelings in me towards the group, as I was aware that an important process was taking place, but found it a challenge.

However, it became clear that the group members were working on ambivalence towards their own neediness, and on their wish to be more powerful. In the twenty-seventh session, Iris had drawn a bunch of balloons, some round and some square. She started the discussion by saying the square ones were probably lead balloons, as she felt picked on by a friend and wondered what was wrong with her which made people pick on her so easily. Sarah replied that it was probably because she was too nice and would not bite back, and that this echoed something brought up in her own images: her first painting of washes of colours had reminded her of being stopped one night by the spectacle of a blaze of colours coming from an illuminated old garage door. This had led to a second image, which was a child's windmill stuck to a fence, swirling in the wind. She recalled how, as a child, she had seen this beautiful windmill stuck in the fence, and had tiptoed across the garden to touch it. She was just about to reach it, when the booming voice of an adult shouted at her to get off the flower bed. Sarah described a feeling of being kicked in the stomach, and related it to her life pattern, when, every time she is close to getting what she wants, she becomes scared of being punished and having it taken away. The group shared this feeling, and talked about how difficult they found expressing needs, or having them in the first place.

As the group progressed, images and discussion seemed to echo a continuing concern with a shared inability to express needs and a sense of rage at feeling helpless. These two issues became clearly connected in a session when Sarah had painted 'symbols of power' which represented a policeman's helmet, a Mercedes car emblem, stripes, a big wheel and a pilot's helmet. On another image, she had started to paint watercolours, but had stopped to add a helicopter and a fat-looking baby with a crown in black paint. She said the symbols were very male, and made her feel powerless. She then recalled how, when her son was a baby, his first words had been 'more food' accompanied with a movement of the hands reaching out and grabbing the air. She had felt speechless and angry at the time, and now realised that she had envied her son's ability to state his needs so clearly, in a way she was unable to do. This put her in touch with her powerlessness. Penny intervened to say that having such a nice face and figure, Sarah 'could wield a lot of power over men'. This seemed to anger Sarah, who replied that this was no asset as she did not know how to use it. The group then shared a common experience of feeling that any attempt at saying 'I want' or 'I need' in such a direct way made them feel 'ugly, gluttonous babies'.

Issues of gender and power were clearly being raised. The image of an insatiable and horrible, needy baby illustrates the way little girls learn very early in their lives that their prime role is as a carer and giver, and that having needs is unfeminine. Eichenbaum and Orbach (1982) discuss how this negatively affects woman's ego development and her sense of identity. Furthermore Penny's remark highlighted the way women have traditionally had vicarious access to power, through their looks and attraction, and that this power was firmly in the hands of men. Interestingly, the theme of powerless men appeared three sessions later during a tearful thirty-first meeting.

Sarah drew an image representing two male relatives' emaciated faces and torsos, as well as their full and strong figures (they had both died of cancer), and she described how she had finally been able to feel close to them in their dying days. They no longer were the threatening, square figures she had also represented, but had become frail people who did show emotions. The group discussed how extreme circumstances sometimes bring people together, and expressed a longing for closeness in ordinary relationships. Problems seem to arise with issues of power and control. Lynn referred to her authoritarian father and invalid, but controlling, mother: as a child she felt that wherever she was, they knew what she was doing, thinking or feeling. She felt so powerless that she had reacted by burying her feelings deeply inside her, and withdrawn in a rigid shell which made close relationships impossible. Lynn acknowledged that she had internalised an image of judgemental parents, whom she constantly and unsuccessfully tried to please. Her wish to gain a sense of her identity made her fight against this, but she found it hard to gain access to her inner feelings and to connect these to her actions.

The group had been striving to address very difficult subjects, which are usually kept silenced, such as sexuality, ageing and loss. All echoed concerns with the women's needs to affirm their identity and their struggle against the paralysing feelings of powerlessness. Most talked of the group as being the only place where they could look after themselves, and art-making was seen as a very important part of this process. Retrospectively, it is clear that the group was also important for me, as it helped me to acknowledge my own ambivalent feelings towards the difficult issues brought to the group, and it also furthered my understanding of older women's conditions in this culture. As this experience also challenged how my own prejudices affected my practice, I shall now discuss more deeply issues of transference and countertransference.

MY MOTHER'S DAUGHTER: TRANSFERENCE AND COUNTERTRANSFERENCE ISSUES

Eichenbaum and Orbach (1982) describe women's psychological development from a feminist perspective and stress that the construction of the personality is linked to gender identity which reflects the prevailing culture: in this patriarchal culture, women feel like second-class citizens. As a result, issues such as negative self-image are at the core of the mother–daughter relationship. They think that ambivalent feelings towards needs, dependency and individuation are also present and play a significant part in the little girl's ego development. Eichenbaum and Orbach stress the effect of identification and projection in the mother–daughter relationship: a mother will tend to bring up a little boy seeing him as 'other' to her, whereas she will tend to see the little girl as another 'self' and it will be easier to project her own feelings onto her daughter. Eichenbaum and Orbach write,

> From our perspective the most critical relationship that is going to come up in the transference is that between the mother and the daughter. Uncovering the dynamics of the mother daughter relationship within the therapy provides an understanding of the steps of feminine personality development.[13]

Steuer (1982) describes how younger therapists working with older women may find unresolved conflicts with their own mothers surfacing and that this may interfere negatively in the process of the therapy.

As a younger female therapist, I was inviting a twin transference of feelings regarding mothers, and of those concerning children or younger siblings. This created a powerful dynamic of being perceived either as controlling and judgemental, or as helpless and ineffectual. This was well illustrated in the session where Penny attacked me for being simultaneously infantilising and incompetent. Her attack also denoted envy towards me and highlighted ambivalent feelings in the group about being in the care of a younger, professional woman: some of the women, including Penny, had given up work and careers because of their family commitments or their psychiatric problems. It was as though I painfully embodied the theme of 'if only things had gone differently . . . '

My response to this powerful 'twin' transference was to sometimes feel paralysed and ineffectual myself. Eichenbaum and Orbach (1982) describe a fear common to women's groups of 'not having enough', and I certainly was left on many occasions with the feeling that I was not providing enough, or that what was there was not good enough. This, of course, made me feel at times resentful and angry, which also brought out an unpleasant judgemental reaction. I realised that many of these feelings were linked to my own relationship with my mother, which probably was also a factor in my avoidance of issues regarding the menopause and sexuality.

The group did not, however, remain stuck and paralysed by these strong concerns, and a therapeutic alliance did develop. I feel the art medium played a central part in this process. During one session, the group discussed my non-participation in art-making, and concluded that they perceived my watchful, but non-interfering presence as making the space feel more secure. Sarah also said that since there were no images of mine to discuss she felt she did not need to look after me, and that I was there for them. Acknowledgement of a therapeutic alliance was made in the forty-first session, when Lynn had drawn one of her dreams: she had been walking in the park and had needed to get into a building to which the only access was a ladder. Being afraid of heights, she was hesitating when I appeared in her dream, and urged her to carry on, assuring her it was safe to do so. The group discussed the image, relating it to the task of therapy, how scary it sometimes was, and acknowledged that some good things were coming out of it.

On a personal level, working in this group had many positive outcomes for me: resolving negative countertransference feelings also enabled me to address painful issues regarding my own mother. Being with these women somehow helped me understand her better and helped me grow out of a mother-blaming attitude I had adopted.

DISCUSSION

As I explained at the beginning, it had not been my intention to set up an older women's art therapy group. However, as so often happens, circumstances concurred to create an enriching, if unplanned, experience.

Research on women's groups (Aries 1976) indicates that women members felt more able to disclose and that groups reach more quickly a higher degree of cohesion than the one found in mixed-gender groups. This was the case in this group from the first session, as a core of five women became quickly established, who attended quite regularly. My own experience of participating in women's groups echoes the above findings, but has made me aware that a high concern for cohesion often makes the expression and exploration of conflicts difficult. This was not the case here, and although there was an initial fear of conflict, its enactment had a liberating effect on the group. This was largely enabled by the art-making process which does not allow for as easy a censoring process as verbal interaction: the visual material, often introduced angry and painful themes, later enabling the group to explore them verbally.

Art was seen to be the central focus of the group. The individual process of art-making was particularly useful for these women who were unaccustomed to such a defined and protected personal space. All women had problems identifying and expressing their needs. Most had developed identity as carers and were at a time of life when this would inevitably be reappraised: children were leaving home, marriages had collapsed, and dependent parents were approaching death. Otway and Ellis stress the importance of the private art space in an art therapy women's group, as it offers a unique opportunity for women to explore their own issues without feeling concerned about their effects on others. They also write about women using art to 'rehearse the expression of their feelings before taking the risk of verbalising them'.[14] In this case, it seems that the images often allowed access to issues which had previously remained undefined, and for which words had been hitherto not found.

This touches on an important aspect of the art therapy group, in that all the clients were older women who were menopausal or post-menopausal. Skultans refers to a menopausal woman experiencing an exclusion from the man's world so complete 'as to deprive the women of the language in which a direct protest could be voiced'.[15]

Speechlessness and helplessness were strong topics which emerged initially through the art work. These issues had undoubtedly been long-term problems, but seemed particularly acute in this group. It seems that experiences of the psychiatric system, combined with identity developed through the care of others, had produced a general very low self-esteem. Any chance of positive identity was further threatened by a negative socio-cultural stereotyping of older women.

The shared sense of helplessness in the group initially brought up for me the strong countertransference feelings discussed earlier. Steuer writes,

If older women are to be adequately served by the mental health professionals, therapists will need to confront attitudes and behaviours which include the entire spectrum from nihilism and helplessness to overtly optimistic expectations.[16]

The process of confronting my own attitudes was certainly taking place for me as the group went on, and produced noticeable personal shifts, notably in my own personal relationship with my mother. It highlighted how mother-blaming had been an issue for me. I also became aware that much is blamed on mothers in our culture, and that psychotherapy has often reinforced this negative perception. This is well illustrated by results of research done by Caplan and Hall-McCorquodale on the incidence of mother-blaming in clinical journals in 1970, 1976 and 1982: mothers were blamed for seventy-two different kinds of psychopathology, whilst fathers were notably mentioned much less in a majority of cases. They write,

> Above all, the mothers are there. They are there for the professionals who assess and treat their children; they are there to be identified, studied and questioned by these professionals; and they are there for the general public to see, raising their children. Thus, they, more than the absent fathers, are easy targets to blame. It is easier to attribute a child's problems to the behaviour of a parent who is present than to the imagined or suspected behaviour of a parent who is no longer on the scene.[17]

One could echo Steuer's assertion on therapists having to confront their attitude towards older women with a similar one on the need to challenge mother-blaming theories. Their effect on clinical practice with women, whether mothers or not, can only be detrimental as they only reinforce an image of woman as damaging or helpless.

The group matured and grew out of the 'speechless and helpless' phase. The discussion of the pictures became very fruitful, and there often seemed to be one or more group images which embodied the group's preoccupation. This was an exciting process, where feelings which had been hidden or confusing came to the fore more clearly, enabling connections to be made between past and present, and between interactions in the room and in the women's lives.

CONCLUSION

I feel that an important process took place in this group, for the women and me. Reflecting on it, I am aware that I need to work further on these issues regarding my own ageist attitudes. As discussed in this study, I failed to realise that some of the visual and verbal material of the group related to the issues of menopause. In doing so. I sadly followed this society's attitude which does not see the menopausal process as being an important and potentially positive time.

I wholeheartedly agree with Steuer's assertion that 'Therapists need to be open to self examination and to begin to understand the source of their own ageist and sexist attitudes.'[18] This task is arduous in an environment where age has become a new taboo subject. However, the process of conducting this group did lead me to question some of my assumptions and prejudices. This art therapy group was well used by older women who, sadly, are often badly serviced by resources which treat them as if they were . . . invisible.

NOTES

1 Posner, 1979: 180.
2 Mitteness, 1983: 171.
3 Mitteness, 1983: 174.
4 O'Toole and O'Toole, 1988: 89.
5 Posner, 1979: 179.
6 O'Toole and O'Toole, 1988: 85.
7 Greer, 1991: 39.
8 Greer, 1991: 11.
9 Steuer, 1982: 432.
10 Freud, 1926/1959: 212. This negative self-image originated with Freud's notion of the 'castrated female' (editor's comment).
11 Yalom, 1970: 288.
12 Steuer, 1982: 432.
13 Eichenbaum and Orbach, 1982: 49.
14 Otway and Ellis, 1987: 16.
15 Skultans, 1976: 650.
16 Steuer, 1982: 434.
17 Caplan and McCorquodale, 1985: 352.
18 Steuer, 1982: 434.

BIBLIOGRAPHY

Aries, E. 1976. 'Interaction patterns and themes of male/female and mixed groups'. *Small Group Behaviour*, vol. 7: 7–18.
Caplan, P.J. and McCorquodale, I. (eds) 1985. 'Mother blaming in major clinical journals'. *American Journal of Orthopsychiatry*, vol. 55, no. 31: 345–353.
Chesler, P. 1972. *Women and Madness*. New York: Avon Books.
De Beauvoir, S. 1949. (1972.) *The Second Sex*. Harmondsworth: Penguin.
Eichenbaum, L. and Orbach, S. 1982. *Outside In . . . Inside Out*. Harmondsworth: Penguin.
Firestone, S. 1970. *The Dialectics of Sex: The Case for the Feminist Revolution*. New York: William Morrow.
Freud, S. 1926. 'The question of lay analysis', *SE 20, Standard Edition of the Complete Psychological Works of Sigmund Freud*, London: Hogarth Press.
Greer, G. 1991. *The Change – Women, Ageing and the Menopause*. Harmondsworth: Penguin.
McCrea, F. B. 1983. 'The politics of the menopause: the "discovery" of a deficiency disease. *Social Problems*, vol. 31, no. 1, October: 111–123.

McNeilly, G. 1983. 'Directive and non-directive approaches in art therapy.' *The Arts in Psychotherapy*, vol. 10: 211–19.

McNeilly, G. 1987. 'Further contributions to group analytic art therapy'. *Inscape Journal of Art Therapy*. Summer edition: 8–11.

Mitteness, L. S. 1983. 'Historical changes in public information about the menopause'. *Urban Anthropology*, vol. 12, no. 2: 161–179.

O'Toole, R. and O'Toole, A. W. 1988. 'Menopause: analysis of a status passage'. *Free Enquiry in Creative Sociology*, vol. 16, no. 1, May: 85–91.

Otway O. and Ellis, M. A. 1987. 'Painting their way out of the blues'. *Community Care*, vol. 9, no. 4: 16–17.

Posner, J. 1979. 'It's all in your head: feminist and medical models of menopause (strange bedfellows)'. *Sex Roles*, vol. 5, no. 2: 179–190.

Schubert-Walker, L. J. 1987. 'Women's groups are different'. In C. M. Brody (ed.) *Women's Therapy Groups*. New York: Springer.

Skaife, S. 1990. 'Self-determination in group analytic art therapy'. *Group Analysis*, vol. 23: 54–60.

Skultans, V. 1976. 'The symbolic significance of menstruation and the menopause'. *Sociological Abstracts*, 639–651.

Steuer, J. L. 1982. 'Psychotherapy with older women: agism and sexism in traditional practice'. *Psychotherapy Theory, Research and Practice*, vol. 19, Winter: 429–436.

Yalom, I. D. 1970. *The Theory and Practice of Group Psychotherapy*. New York: Basic Books.

Chapter 8

Women and conflict

Carol Ross

Conflict is a part of life. It can be seen in every aspect of existence, permeating our relationships, needs and desires, internal states and the choices we make. Conflict is an essential part of growth and development – without it, there is stasis. The crucial issue about conflict is not how it can be avoided, but how it is handled.

There are certain types of conflict, however, which can arise for women in particular and be especially problematic for them to deal with. In this chapter, I will be looking at some of these areas and discussing the role of art therapy in enabling women to explore issues of conflict in relation to their gender. There are a number of ways in which gender norms and roles dictate against women confronting conflict in an assertive and forthright manner. I will be describing art therapy sessions with three different groups which highlight some of the contradictions and constraints which women must reconcile in order to negotiate conflict successfully.

Before looking at specific case studies, I want to briefly discuss and put into context some types of conflict which women may face. What are the social expectations and pressures that primarily affect women? How does social context help shape our personal experience and ways of coping? How does adopting and internalising gender stereotypes affect the way we deal with conflict?

I am using the term gender to refer to social behaviour which people are expected to adopt. It is at the very centre of our perception of ourselves and others. Whyld (1983) points out that gender is so basic to our understanding and appreciation of people that unless we have ascertained whether someone is male or female, we cannot make sense of their behaviour. Images of gender norms abound, constantly reflecting and reinforcing expected behaviour.

We are bombarded with media portrayals of femininity which emphasise selflessness, passivity, nurturing and gratifying the needs of others. Masculinity is portrayed in terms of action, power, assertiveness and self-reliance. Language itself reinforces gender expectations. Norms, roles and differences in power and control are conveyed through the language we use.[1] Even very young children are influenced by prevailing messages about gender.[2]

Specified gender characteristics are, of course, stereotypes. As such, they are not true reflections of any single individual. Nor do they allow for the complexity of the way other social factors (such as race, class, culture) mediate and modify our experience of gender. Nonetheless, gender stereotypes are very powerful. In order to appreciate their impact, it is useful to consider how and why they arise.

Like any stereotype, ascribed gender characteristics are socially constructed. Baker-Miller (1976), in her introduction to her work exploring female psychology, explains how gender expectations occur within the context of social organisation and are the framework within which the personality develops. Though written in 1976, it remains an astute analysis. She theorises that socially defined attributes arise in relation to a person's dominant position within society. She suggests that the characteristics of socially dominant groups determine the norms of society and that the acceptable roles and characteristics of subordinate groups are defined in relation to the dominant ones (and typically involve performing a service for them).

Women, says Baker-Miller, as socially subordinate to men, are encouraged to develop personal psychological characteristics which are supportive to men. They are valued and considered well adjusted if they display these characteristics, but if they display dominant characteristics they risk being viewed as deviant. These 'female qualities' are often central to a woman's identity and sense of self-worth.

Traditional female roles (both at home and in the workplace) place women in the position of being defined in relation to the support of others. The selfless, caring or nurturing behaviours which are usually part of these roles can be contradictory with the expression of anger, disagreement or self-interest. Where, then, does this leave women when their own needs conflict with others, or when the various roles in their lives come into conflict?

Orbach (1991) writes about the way a woman's identity may depend upon her capacity to be understanding, sympathetic and in tune with others. A woman may experience her own needs as threatening when they conflict with her perceptions of how she is valued and values herself. The taboo on expressing anger ('nice girls aren't angry') can act as a 'brake' on acknowledging such feelings. Rather than focusing on her own direct experiences, a woman may learn to experience herself through her impact on others, becoming 'out of touch' with her own true feelings and desires. When anger and resistance are difficult to deal with, conflict becomes extremely problematic and may be internalised, rather than expressed.

Being out of touch with herself may put a woman in conflict with her own body. In a society which systematically objectifies the female form, women can become alienated from their own physicality. This is reflected in the high incidence of eating disorders among girls and women. Images of thinness predominate, corresponding with notions of desirability, and worth. Much has now been written about the way a woman's own body can become the battleground for issues of boundaries and control.[3] Power then becomes an issue of power over oneself, as control over circumstances involving others may be perceived as impossible or unthinkable.

Physical aggression towards women is an act of overt conflict of power and control. In our society, violence against women permeates much of our everyday experience. It is a constant theme in media entertainment, as well as in the news. Violence, including sexual abuse, forces women into a position of submission and powerlessness, an extreme version of the female stereotype. In the same sense, physical and sexual aggression are extremes of the male stereotype. Benn (1985) suggests that sexual abuse and harassment is a direct result of the constructs of 'masculinity' and 'femininity'. However, challenging these constructs can be devastating to women's sense of identity.

Central to the handling of conflict are issues of 'owning' and asserting needs, expressing feelings and retaining power and control. Managing conflict in an effective way for the individual may require defying stereotypes and going against deep-rooted internal values and prohibitions. An action which is in conflict with one's self-image and sense of worth may be necessary. The feeling that conflict is irreconcilable with one's self-identity can lead to the suppression of feelings.

Art therapy can provide an opportunity to explore the conflicts inherent in social constructs of gender and their impact on women's lives. Art therapy processes can facilitate self-determination by providing women with a means of redefining ourselves.

Muller (1986) describes how

> we live in a racist, sexist class society and in no way is it possible for us individually not to take inside ourselves that which is outside of us since birth. Experiencing our self image through painting can enable us to gain a clearer picture of ourselves, an image that is more real and powerful than ideas imposed. (Muller 1986: 27)

A growing body of literature documents how focused art therapy activities and theme-centred workshops can enable women to confront conflict by becoming aware of external definitions they have internalised. Turner and Clark-Schock (1990) describe how the contradictions between images of femininity and those of power and success may prevent women from asserting themselves or advancing their careers. They describe the way they have used art therapy workshops to help women to reconcile their ambivalence towards success and move forward in the workplace. The women explored their self-image and became more aware of their strengths.

The notion of using art therapy to enable women to explore conflict in relation to their identity is a recurring theme. Ellis (1989) writes about the way disowning or repressing emotions such as anger, hate or competitiveness (which can be inconsistent with a woman's image of herself as caring, giving and gentle) distorts self-image and the way reality is experienced. She describes her work with women from varied class and ethnic backgrounds, using spontaneous art-making as a 'mirror reflection' which allows the individual to reflect back a balanced self-image and thereby recreate her life.

Art therapy has been useful in helping women understand the conflicts they are struggling with in their relationship to food and their bodies. Rust (1987), for instance, recounts the way she uses art therapy to help women confront public images that affect them, exploring the connections between the personal and political issues involved. Art therapists who work with victims of sexual abuse describe how the consequences of such events can be feelings of helplessness, repressed rage and aggression. Art therapy can provide a model for achieving a sense of control.[4]

THREE WORKSHOPS DEALING WITH CONFLICT

I want to describe art therapy workshops with three different groups of women: professionals; trainees; and clients. I have chosen these groups first, because the sessions illustrate areas of conflict women commonly experience; and, second, because the participants have varying degrees of power and control in relation to the context of the group. All the groups are connected in some way with speech therapy, which in itself raises issues for women of communication, including the contrast between using language for supporting others or for self-expression. I found the issues that emerged both poignant and representative of wider concerns.

Group one

The women in this group were all professionals, members of staff of a speech therapy department of an inner-city hospital. I had been told that there were tensions within the groups which concerned status and authority and commitments outside the workplace. We decided to explore some of these issues.

I asked the group to consider the various roles they had in their lives. For example, they were all professional therapists, but they were also partners, lovers, mothers, daughters, friends. They may have other professional or non-vocational roles. Within their professional roles, they were senior or junior in relation to each other. How did they see themselves within their different roles? Did they experience conflict within or between their roles? I asked them to create images which reflected their experience, using materials of their choice.

At the end of an hour and a half, I invited participants to reflect on their images in pairs, before coming back as a whole group. Because of the complex dynamics as well as the size of the group, I felt this would allow individuals a safer context in which to talk more openly. The members of the group had considerable facilitating skills and the 'co-counselling' format allowed them scope to enable each other to consider their images in some depth.

When the group came back together, people raised both personal and social issues. Conflicts between home and work were also raised by some of the women. The demands of the job meant a long working day and they would arrive home too tired to be very attentive to their families. They expressed feelings of guilt. Several described feeling disapproval from partners or parents. One image showed home and work colliding with each other like meteorites. Another image showed a figure stretched out in several directions at once, being pulled by different people, distended to the point of distortion. The group talked about pressures on women to be 'all things to all people'.

There was resentment around the question of who should be required to do evening clinics. Women with children felt they should be given special consideration; not to be given such special consideration they considered to be discrimination. One woman without children was quite upset and felt this meant she was being regarded as a 'second-class citizen' for being childless. She said she often encountered the attitude that she was required to 'compensate' for her childlessness. Her image showed pictures of smiling women in one corner of the paper and angry looking women in the other corner. As some of the group discussed divisions between women with families and those without, the discussion turned to look at some of the social pressures on women to have, or at least want, children or be regarded as abnormal.

Conflicts relating to seniority and status within their professional roles emerged in several pictures. One senior member expressed the real anxiety she felt when she was required to impose her authority within the staff group. She described her conflict over the desire to be 'nice' with the need to be critical of a colleague's performance occasionally. Her pictures showed herself with two faces: one pretty, one hideous. She talked about her inability to reconcile asserting authority with being a kind and caring person. She described how hard she found it to arrive at an integrated self-image that would encompass both aspects of her role.

A theme which emerged with many of the women in the group related to difficulties in establishing appropriate boundaries with clients. The desire to be supportive and nurturing, especially towards clients in distress, meant some staff found they were unable to set limits on what they should offer. Their sessions would continue beyond the set time, thereby increasing their workload. One especially vivid image depicted the smiling therapist being swallowed by the figure of the client.

As the group participants discussed their images, they became clear that some of these conflicts they were experiencing related to tensions between their own needs and the needs and expectations of others. They felt under pressure always to be available and supportive. As speech therapists, they had chosen to work in a caring profession which carried certain undefined expectations. Though many pressures came from other people, the women decided that some of the most difficult pressures to deal with were self-imposed. These internal pressures, created anxiety, guilt or stress, particularly when they attempted to put their own needs first.

Group two

The women in this group were trainees. Although already qualified as speech therapists, they were taking a further training course to specialise in working with people who stammer. As their course included an element of assertiveness training, we decided to use this art therapy session to explore the concept of assertiveness in their own lives. I asked them to create images which expressed their experiences of behaving in both assertive and unassertive ways. How did they feel when they were behaving assertively and unassertively? What enabled them to stand their ground or put their needs forward? What prevented them from doing so?

The first thing that struck the group when they had come back together to discuss their images was the contrast between images of assertiveness and lack of assertiveness. Most people had divided their paper into two separate areas. The participants said that the pictures reflected the way they felt like two different people, depending upon whether they were being assertive or not. Only two women in the group had depicted a single individual with two aspects. The rest had created two separate individuals.

This workshop turned out to be extremely emotive and powerful for many of the participants. In reflecting on their experiences of behaving assertively and unassertively, some women got in touch with very painful memories of feeling unable to act or make an impact on a situation causing them distress. Two women found themselves creating images representing childhood sexual abuse. (One of them said the memory had surfaced for the first time during the session.)

Recalling experiences of not being assertive brought up memories of feeling impotent for some of the women in the group. One woman's picture had a large empty area which represented her 'invisibility'. She talked about feeling as though she 'wasn't there' and about 'losing' herself and 'not having a voice'. She thought these feelings may have had something to do with her decision to become a speech therapist 'to help find a voice'. Another woman depicted herself as a crumpled and bent-over flower, saying sometimes she felt unable to stand upright and put herself forward. People talked about feeling 'acted upon' rather than able to act. It was observed that many women found themselves constantly in the role of responding or reacting to other people and this left them feeling overwhelmed mentally and physically.

In many of the situations or experiences depicted, the women were describing a power differential between themselves and the person they were in conflict with. Some of these pictures related to real circumstances, involving a difference of power such as relations between a child and an adult; an employee and a manager; a woman and a physically stronger male. Others seemed to involve perceptions of power differences. The group discussed the way women may be 'taught' to be helpless or feel impotent. Some women had learned to respond to even low-level conflict with passivity. For other women, fear of disapproval or reproach was the largest factor preventing them from asserting themselves (thereby investing others with inordinate power over them).

The group's images of 'feeling assertive' were also very powerful. These images were described in terms of 'really being there', 'being real' and 'feeling strong', whereas the images of being 'unassertive' tended to be fragmented, with small partially completed figures. In the pictures of assertive behaviour, the content included large, full-bodied figures. Though still depicting power differentials, these images were about 'overcoming' the powerlessness.

The women in the group agreed that being able to assert themselves strengthened their sense of identity and their ability to be themselves. But while being assertive felt good, it did not seem to come easily. They talked about why it seemed so difficult to put themselves forward and decided it was often connected with feeling 'less entitled' than the other person. They were often afraid to stand up for their own needs in case they hurt someone's feelings, or were being unfair or selfish. Behaving assertively for many seemed to be an ongoing effort, representing moments of 'achievement', rather than an aspect of their personality.

Group three

The participants of this group were clients in an ongoing group for women who stammer. We agreed to use the art therapy session to explore some of the feelings relating to a lack of control that people who stammer often express. I suggested to the group that they create two separate images: 'powerful' and 'powerless'. What did it mean to them to feel powerful? What were they doing? What did it feel like? What did it look like to feel powerless?

When the group reassembled to look at their images, it was noted that most images centred on issues of control. The most striking thing to emerge was how interpretations of being in or out of control went far beyond speech control to wider gender issues. Most of the group used magazine pictures to build up their images. Pictures of female bodies and food prevailed.

It became clear that for most of the women in the group feeling powerful related to feeling in control over themselves. Women talked about controlling their appearance, their eating and their appetites. The power struggles they described were largely expressed as internal-conflict scenarios relating to self-control and self-discipline. Feeling powerful was about 'winning' this struggle, while feeling powerless was about 'losing' their fight against themselves.

'Powerful' images were full of magazine pictures of slim women in swimming costumes or work-out clothes and of 'virtuous' foods such as salads and crispbread. One 'powerful' image showed a cut-out of a refrigerator with a chain drawn around it. In another image, pictures of 'thin' foods, thin bodies, exercise equipment, and 'home beautiful' created a circle around the figure inside.

'Powerless' images also showed food, but these were cakes, chips, pies and other 'forbidden' food items. There were also magazine pictures of overweight or dowdy women. One woman represented herself as an enormous mouth with a spiral inside. She described feeling like a 'bottomless pit of appetites'.

As the group talked about their images, they began to discuss how notions of power and control were connected with gender. It became clear that to many of the women a sense of power and control had little or nothing to do with exerting power or control over others. But when they considered public images of powerful men, this was precisely what came to mind: the more powerful the man, the further reaching his control. Yet when the group of women considered power in terms of what it meant in their own lives, they found it centred almost completely on control over themselves. This self-control was expressed as attempts to conform to stereotypes of desirable women and ideal wives and mothers.

It seemed to the group that for them as women feeling powerful and in control was inextricably bound up with suppressing their natural appetites and repressing their own needs, impulses and desires. 'Powerful' was a contractive rather than expansive state which was dependent upon 'holding back' and 'keeping in'.

In this chapter, I have been considering how gender norms and social expectations may affect the way women experience and deal with conflict. I have discussed how social pressures can create conflict within the individual, as well as the individual relationships with others. The issues raised in the three workshops highlight this, as the women in the groups expressed tensions between home and work, their needs and the needs of others, their sense of entitlement to their own appetites, and to feelings of power and helplessness.

For women to find productive ways of dealing with their conflicts, we must recognise the inter-connectedness of the inner, psychological world and the outer, social material world: the personal and the political. Art therapy can be a valuable way of enabling women to explore and 'unlearn' female stereotypes. In art therapy women can develop a greater range of emotional expression and be empowered through an increased understanding of the social context within which we operate. Through greater appreciation of social causation, women can be encouraged to express, rather than repress, aspects of ourselves which do not fit social expectation and learn to validate ourselves for who we are rather than deny aspects of ourselves and deny our bodies and learn to assert ourselves and say 'no' to abuse. Though a greater apprehension of gender norms, women can be envisaged to assert aspects of ourselves which do not meet present social expectations.

NOTES

1 Dale Spender (1980), in her book, *Man Made Language*, gives numerous examples to illustrate the 'semantic derogation' of women and the way language, far from being neutral, shapes ideas and beliefs and reinforces social status. Even very young children are aware of and influenced by prevailing messages about gender characteristics.
2 In our interviews with children in nursery and infant classes, we found that they held strong convictions about appropriate gender behaviour and roles and that these beliefs influenced their own behaviour and play choices. (Browne and Ross, 1991)
3 Pennycock (1987), for example, writes about the way young women learn to experience their own needs as excessive and then 'act out' denying their needs through becoming anorexic.
4 Spring (1985), Peacock (1991), and Serraro (1989) write about art therapy sessions with victims of sexual abuse, including incest. They describe the feeling of powerlessness and sense of emotional fragmentation that can result from experiencing violence, and how they use art therapy to help clients clarify and integrate their experiences to regain a sense of control and identity.

BIBLIOGRAPHY

Baker-Miller, J. 1976. *Toward a New Psychology of Women*. Harmondsworth: Pelican Books.
Benn, M. 1985. 'Isn't Sexual Harassment Really about Masculinity?' *Spare Rib*, no. 156, July.
Browne, N. and Ross, C. 1991. 'Girls' Stuff, Boys' Stuff – Young Children Talking'. In *Science and Technology in the Early Years*, ed. N. Browne. Open University.
Ellis, M. L. 1989. 'Women: The Mirage of the Perfect Image'. *The Arts in Psychotherapy*, vol. 16, no. 4.
Muller, G. 1986. 'On the Way to Self-Determination'. In Partington, A. *Women's Work*. Fly Press.
Orbach, S. 1991. 'Anger's Furious Shield.' *Weekend Guardian*, 28 December.
Peacock, M. 1991. 'A Personal Construct Approach to Art Therapy in Treatment

of Post-Sexual Abuse Trauma'. *The American Journal of Art Therapy*, vol. 29, no. 4.

Pennycock, W. 1987. 'Anorexia and Adolescence'. In *Fed up and Hungry*, ed. M. Lawrence. London: Women's Press.

Rust, M. J. 1987. 'Image and Eating Problems'. In *Fed up and Hungry*, ed. M. Lawrence.

Serraro, J. S. 1989. 'The Arts in Therapy with Survivors of Incest'. In *Advances in Art Therapy*, ed. H. Wadeson *et al.* John Wiley and Son: Chichester.

Spender, D. 1980. *Man Made Language*. London: Routledge & Kegan Paul.

Spring, D. 1985. 'Symbolic Language of Sexually Abused, Chemically Dependant Women'. *The American Journal of Art Therapy*, vol. 24, no. 1.

Turner, G. and Clark-Schock, K. 1990. 'Dynamic Corporate Training for Women: A Creative Arts Therapies Approach'. *The Arts in Psychotherapy*, vol. 17, no. 4.

Whyld, J. 1983. *Sexism in the Secondary Curriculum*. Harper & Row: London.

Chapter 9

Looking and reflecting: returning the gaze, re-enacting memories and imagining the future through phototherapy

Rosy Martin

WHO'S LOOKING?

How can an individual take back the power of the look, the act of looking? How can individuals look back over their life history to begin to tell their own story from their own point of view?

How do I look? What image do I present to the world? How do I activate the power of the look and with what preconceptions? How do I find myself reflected in the images that surround me, or not? How do I mediate and interrelate those pre-existing images with my ever-changing self-image?

We are constantly bombarded with reproduced images, in television, films, newspapers, magazines and advertisements which act to produce meanings and images of the world for us, shape our sense of reality and even our sense of our own identities. There is no essential self which precedes the social construction of the self through the agency of representation.

Feminist film theorists in the 1970s analysed mainstream Hollywood cinema, using the tools of psychoanalytic theory:

> In a world of sexual imbalance, pleasure in looking has been split between active/male and passive/female. The determining male gaze projects its phantasy on to the female figure which is styled accordingly. In their traditional exhibitionist role women are simultaneously looked at and displayed, with their appearance coded for strong visual and erotic impact ... they connote 'to-be-looked-at-ness' ... The male protagonist is free to command the stage in which he articulates the look and creates the action.[1]

Theories on the male gaze have been extended to include all visual media, and have analysed how, in patriarchal society, it is the gaze of power which denotes the ability to control, classify, define and objectify. This is not a question of biological innateness, but rather of the dominant cultural representations and how these function in the constructions of meaning. This act of definition is linked to social control. This power position, which claims both gender and racial superiority, assumes a belief of centrality, from which all differences are seen as 'other'. In the claim of universality lies the effect of marginalisation of women, black people, people of different ethnicity, gays and lesbians.

More recent work in cultural studies on the role of the audience in the creation of meaning, as well as dissonant readings, appropriation and the polysemic possibilities of texts, have highlighted how meanings are contested, never simply fixed.[2] Oppositional work in photography and art practice has attempted to deconstruct, exposing how meanings are constructed through representation, and from this process aims to try and make new meanings and new readings possible.

Work on identities, which problematises and helps to redefine those aspects constructed or labelled as other *vis-à-vis* gender, race, ethnicity, class, sexuality, age or disability and in receipt of the negative projections of those with power, is part of naming and reclaiming the complexities of occupying a marginalised position. Far from being externally fixed in some essentialist past, identities are subject to the continuous play of history, culture and power. For an individual, identity cannot be encompassed in some simplistic ID-checklist; there is a complex interplay amongst these different aspects of subjectivity and the conscious and unconscious processes by which they are culturally reproduced.

'Gender is a construction that regularly conceals its genesis; the tacit collective agreement to perform, produce and sustain discrete and polar genders as cultural fictions is obscured by the credibility of those productions; the construction compels our belief in its necessity and naturalness.'[3]

However, disputing the giveness of social categories gives no exemption from the necessity of negotiating their social meanings in everyday life. Whilst knowing intellectually that femininity is a construct, I am still a woman and have to deal with the very real consequences and cultural baggage that comes along with it.

MIRROR, MIRROR ON THE WALL ...

The notion of the gaze has been discussed by such differing theoreticians as Winnicott, Lacan and Foucault, in their explorations of how identities are formed through mirroring. Sometimes these gazes are loving or benevolent, but often they are more intrusive and surveilling. Out of the myriad fragments thus mirrored to us, first unconsciously as babies, then as we are growing into language and culture and are subject to the various discourses of society, aspects of our identities are constructed.

The 'good enough mother', in Winnicott's model, offers her face to the baby's gaze, and mirrors back the baby's reflection.

> When I look I am seen, so I exist. I can now afford to look and see. I now look creatively and what I appercieve I also perceive.[4]

But if the mother is caught up in her own projective identification, reflecting back her own feelings of despair, hopelessness and rage about the inadequate mothering which she herself had received, the baby finds not herself, but her mother reflected back. She then has to learn to predict and respond to her mother's moods and feelings, instead of focusing on her own.

Lacan theorised the 'mirror phase' which begins a process in which the child will acquire a gendered subjectivity and a place in the symbolic order.[5] The child gazing into a mirror misrecognises itself as the 'gestalt', the totalised, complete external image of the subject. The discordance of the visual gestalt with the subject's perceived reality means that the image remains both a literal image of itself and an idealised representation, since it prefigures a unity and mastery that the child still lacks. The mirror stage initiates the child into identification with and dependence on representations for its own form.

THE APPEARANCE OF HYSTERIA

Charcot, at the Salpêtrière Clinic in Paris in 1877–80, used the objectifying eye of the camera to make visible different stages of hysteria. Yet the women patients he photographed were acting out the different roles which he prescribed to them, and which he named: 'Threat, Appeal, Supplication, Eroticism and Ecstasy'.

Did he chose particular photographs to illustrate his theories, unaware that he was busily constructing his own version of reality, rather than simply reflecting it, as the belief in the link between scientific objectivity and photography then held to be true? The belief that physiognomy gave information directly about the character of the person portrayed, and that symptoms could be directly read off the body, was paralleled by the realist ideology that the photograph functions to confirm the premise of a simply observed truth. The control was totally held by the photographer/doctor, his patients were under his care and authority, incarcerated in the hospital for the insane, the objects of pathological scrutiny. It was not the psychic lives of his patients that he portrayed, but rather his own theories as to what these might be. He did not give voice to his patients, but spoke for them.

Freud began *Studies on Hysteria* when working with Charcot, and shifted attention to the act of listening. He discovered that 'hysterics suffer mainly from reminiscences' and that the symptoms could be relieved when the memory of the event which had provoked the symptom was brought to light and described in the greatest detail, when the affect had been put into words.[6]

A PHOTOGRAPHIC MEMORY?

> Recovering memories in therapy significantly helps a person to develop
> a sense of identity, individuality, uniqueness and meaning – all of which
> may add up to a sense of self.[7]

But what of the photographic memory? The existing documentation lies
in the family album, but that itself is an ideological construct, carefully
framed and edited to maintain the mythology of the happy family. It
functions as a public relations document that mediates between the
members of the family themselves, providing a united front to the world, an
affirmation of successes, celebrations, domestic harmony and togetherness.
The conventions of picture-making that we absorb through popular culture,
and the multi-national corporations such as Kodak are occluded, as are
the questions: who took the picture, for what reason, and in what context?
Viewing the 'family album' often activates a response of nostalgia – the
return 'home' to an idealised golden past, an imaginative past, free of
conflict, where each had a place, everyone knew their place and 'reality'
was 'real'. Yet these photographs can provide a shiny surface of slippery
meanings upon which to reflect and project, and contain a myriad of latent
narratives.

In the 1970s in USA and Canada therapists started to use photographs
as counselling tools.[8] Working from differing theoretical frameworks,
they investigated the use of the photograph as metaphor as a route to the
unconscious. The personal meanings that an individual identifies and
uncovers in a photograph are a projective process, and will mirror the inner
map she is using unconsciously. A therapist, using a non-judgemental
approach with skilful listening and open-ended questions, can enable the
client to make conscious her value systems and belief structures and then
reflect upon them using photographs as the catalyst. Family albums have
provided a rich resource for autobiographical story-telling and an exploration of family systems, how it was to be part of this family and how these
early experiences continue to affect the individual.

But what if we had more photographic 'evidence'? What if the pages of
the family album suddenly parted to show the power dynamics, conflicts,
traumas and pains that lie masked within?

RE-ENACTMENT PHOTOTHERAPY: EVOLVING THE PRACTICE

Since 1983, working collaboratively with the late Jo Spence, I evolved and
developed a new photographic practice, which we called re-enactment
phototherapy. Having become aware of the structured absences within the
visual representations of our lives, we began the task of reconstructing and
creating images of the multiplicity of our identities. Our work came out

of photographic discourses, cultural theory, the links between images and image-making, and notions of conscious and unconscious identities, to which we added therapeutic skills.

Looking behind the 'screen memories', the simplifications and myths of others we had for too long accepted as our histories, we began to tell and make visible our own stories, from our points of view. One reason why we chose to use photography was the paucity of representations on offer to us at that time, as middle-aged working-class women dealing with our own specific life crises. Moving beyond the always already impossible notion of finding any 'ideal' or 'positive' image, an idea which ignores how meanings are constructed or subjectivity produced, we sought to make visible to ourselves the very complexity and contradiction inherent within the existential questions: 'Who am I? How did I get to be who I am? Who might I become? How am I both subject of and subjected to the discourses within society?'

Our approach in evolving the practice was experimental and integrative. We drew upon a range of techniques which we had learnt from attending courses including: co-counselling, gestalt, visualisation, psychosynthesis and psychodrama.

Assagioli developed the notion of sub-personalities, in which we come to group our experiences in constellations of behaviour, as we learn to play out different roles in different circumstances for differing audiences.[9] These roles could be, for example, 'the frightened child', 'the teacher', 'the judge', 'the parent', or the 'hedonist'. This model provides a way in which we can map internal conflicts and motivations. Acting-into these various roles in psychodrama can recapture the spontaneity of fantasy play in childhood. In phototherapy, we synthesised postmodern theories on the construction of a fragmented subjectivity with techniques for exploring and making visible our multifaceted identities, moving through transformations to acknowledge a myriad of selves.

Since photographs are mimetic, clothes, props and hair styles all contribute to re-creating a sense of time and place. There is a performative aspect to phototherapy, but the drama replayed is one's own. The photography sessions are not about 'capturing' the image, but rather seeking to make it happen, to 'take place'. The body as the scene of cultural inscriptions may then be seen as performing rather than essentially containing those meanings.

Working from the specificities of our own personal histories – our location in time, place and culture – we foregrounded the social construction of identities within the drama of the everyday. By mapping out class pain and shame, how we both learnt from and rejected our mothers gender-role models, the history of our sexualities, and our relationship to the discourses of medicine, education, law and the media, we made visible links between the personal, the social and the political. In my practice I recognise and respect both the outer and inner realities of my clients.

Jo Spence and I had worked together as co-counselling partners and our work developed as a collaboration between equals, in which we took turns to be client and phototherapist. Having created a deep sense of safety and trust through co-counselling, we built upon this and continued to incorporate the support, challenge and opportunity for re-framing of our therapeutic exchange. This offered many advantages in developing the practice, since there was an exchange of power relationships and we each knew how it felt to be in front of the camera, subject to and of the gaze. There is both a joy and a fear in being thus seen; the pleasure in being the centre of attention, the fear of being exposed and found out.

My experiences, as client, of the intensity and the power of this way of working has enabled me to be more empathetic to the range and depth of feelings that the client may go through in this process. I am able to speak about this work from both standpoints, that of the phototherapist and that of the client. I learnt, too, from the mistakes that we made and the limitations of the co-counselling approach. In my work as a phototherapist now I am much more formal about contracts and boundaries, so that the client feels adequately held and contained. I work as a counsellor to develop a therapeutic relationship with each client before moving to use photography. I am much more aware of how I work with the transference and countertransference, which is always present and often actively played out in the photography session.

EMBODIMENT AND OWNERSHIP

Embodiment and ownership are fundamental to re-enactment phototherapy. The aim is for the clients eventually to own their own histories, their past, their pains, distresses and traumas, previously denied and disavowed. The work is rooted in and contained by counselling. It is through the counselling process that the issues and patterns surface, are identified and traced back through the client's life, and transformative goals are imagined. Clients embody the issues they wish to work on, by entering into them through re-enactment, in front of the camera. By putting themselves in the place of re-experiencing that pain in the here and now, and moving into a transformative goal, clients experience a cathartic release. Through working, in counselling sessions, with the photographic record produced as 'objective' evidence, clients move to seeing for themselves, recognising themselves, tolerating themselves. Ultimately they move towards accepting themselves and re-integrating the denied, disavowed parts of themselves, thereby acknowledging the depth and range of who they are. It is an act of disclosure, within the therapeutic relationship, of not only telling the 'secrets' believed too shameful to tell, or so repressed that they are 'secret' to the client; but also seeing them, facing up to them, and thereby defusing their power. It is about saying the unsayable, seeing the unseeable, facing the unfaceable, confronting shame and by so doing releasing and letting go of the power those 'secrets' held. By taking the risk to explore the dynamics, for example of power and powerlessness, and taking up the different positions within the polarity a greater range of 'selves' is made known to the client. It is a way of making the 'shadow-side' visible. No longer is the 'other' the depository of all that is split off and disavowed, aspects of the 'other' are recognised as within.

MY WORKING METHODOLOGY

All the clients I have worked with using re-enactment phototherapy techniques are self-selected and self-referred. I think it is very important that the client makes the active choice to work in this way. It appeals to clients who have an interest in working with images, be it through photographs, art, drama, therapy or creative writing, and who think symbolically and metaphorically. It is particularly useful for those who over-intellectualise their psychic distress, since it offers an unfiltered connection with the unconscious. I am well aware that this modality would not be appropriate for any client whose current grasp on reality was small, or who lacked any solid sense of their own personal identity. The danger is the risk of stirring up too much material from the unconscious when the personality is incapable of integrating it.

When starting, I stress that the work is confidential between the two of us, with the proviso that I will want to take the counselling work to supervision. This is a particularly sensitive area when working with photographs, since the client is identifiable. I always carefully negotiate any use of any photograph and wait until the client has integrated the emotional work and separated from the images themselves before making any request about any possible usages of the images. I spell this out in detail in my contract.

I draw upon a number of different theoretical models – client-centred, gestalt, psychodrama and art therapy – whilst working with and embodying transference and countertransference, projection and projective identification within the therapeutic relationship. I incorporate ideas of the mirroring offered by the 'good enough mother', the photograph as the transitional object and the model of the therapist as witness, advocate and nurturer moving the client towards becoming aware of their own inner nurturing self.[10]

I recognise the importance of a respect for both outer reality *and* inner reality. Drawing from my own personal experiences as a client in long-term therapy, I know that unless my conflicts within external reality are truly recognised, reflected and respected, I feel unheard, resentful and resistant to taking in the learning and seeing the parallels and amplifications that my internal realities are giving to external events and how this is affecting my emotions and thoughts. Once I know that my pain has been respected in external reality, I can move to unpick and explore my psychic reactions to it. Because I use an integrative approach, I ensure when I am working with clients that they know that I have heard the depths of their emotional responses to both external *and* internal reality.

> Empathy is not only about feelings. It is about feelings in relationship to knowledge. In order to respond empathetically the counsellor needs not only to experience the other's emotional world in the 'here-and-now' but to understand the personal and social history of that world, locating it in the 'there-and-then' of society and culture.[11]

Each phototherapy cycle has clearly defined stages:

- Counselling to enable the client to identify what she or he wants to work on and how.
- Counselling to explore how the client wants to make the 'issue' visible.
- Counselling to enable the client to identify their transformative goals.
- The phototherapy session.
- Seeing the photographs produced, within the 'holding' of counselling.
- Counselling using the photographs, as aspects of the 'self' out-there, objectified, worked with in a psychosynthesis/gestalt way.
- Counselling to integrate the insights and aspects of the self.

The nuances and subtleties that are part of a therapeutic relationship cannot be represented by such a simple schema. The rapport, mirroring and reflection, the noticing of repeated themes and tracing these back into childhood, sitting with resistances and challenging, clearly and appropriately, the uncovering of unconscious processes and patterns all form part of the client's journey of discovery.

I see my role as being there for the client and offering active listening to the story as it unfolds, being empathetic. (I see this as a skill I will spend my life developing.) I am acting as a sounding-board and bringing into conscious awareness, for example, when a theme is repeating in the telling of their story, reflecting it back, and going with a hunch, expressed as 'I was wondering if . . . ' I also work to encourage the clients to be more concrete and specific about their feelings and the underlying source: for example, in noticing when phrases sound as if they come from an internalised voice from the past. In exploring that time, I may suggest that the client speaks in the present tense, or role-plays/speaks as the other. If the client wants to, she may get into a dialogue with the other: the two-cushion gestalt technique.[12] This makes it both more vivid for the client and helps me to learn the words and the way of being of the other, that I will need to use, later, in the phototherapy session. I am careful to remember the exact phrases, it is always more powerful to repeat the client's exact recalled words, her way of telling. It is a process of focusing in to identify a key incident or moment that sums up and brings together all the themes that she is working on and to find a transformative goal.

In working to make the ideas and feelings visible, it is important that the images come from the clients: it is their symbols, with their meaning, their history. My task is to draw it out, through the counselling. I also offer up possible ideas as to how to make the concepts visible, to be used or discarded. It is a collaborative process. I ask the clients to provide the props and clothes, and I also offer things from my extensive personal store, when they seem appropriate. I am working to facilitate and I do ask the clients to take responsibility. This is important: it demonstrates their commitment and gives me a sense of when they are ready to move to the photography stage. Finding the props and clothes brings up a lot of feelings and I invite the clients to bring what they have found to work with in the counselling.

THE THERAPEUTIC GAZE?

The phototherapist's gaze does not attempt to control, nor to objectify, but rather to enable meanings and memories to be unpicked within a context of nurturance, safety and acceptance. The phototherapist occupies the gaze of the 'good enough mother', who mirrors back the reflection of the other but without projecting her own distresses. The client is offered the possibility of her own direction and control of this non-judgemental mirroring, encouragement and permission-giving so that she can explore aspects of herself and her feelings which she had learnt, through her psychic development within the family, to hide and block.

> Psychotherapy is not making clever and apt interpretations, by and large it is giving the patient back what the patient brings . . . It is a complex derivative of the face that reflects what is there to be seen . . . if I do this well enough the patient will find his or her own self, and will be able to exist and be real . . . This task of reflection is not easy and is emotionally exhausting . . . [13]

The giving back of the look is made manifest through the photographs which show what was there to be seen.

The containment offered by the phototherapist enables resistances to be overcome. Whilst holding this gaze and being sensitive to the client's needs, the phototherapist may be required to play the role of the other, in direct relation to the client's enactment, to enable the client to more fully inhabit the role she has chosen to explore. These roles arise out of the counselling process, and I may also use gestalt or psychodramatic techniques to clarify and give life to these images. For example, if the client is working on a specific moment in her childhood in relation to her mother I may play the role of the 'bad' or 'surveilling mother' who aims to control or punish in her attempts to socialise the child; or the 'disapproving', rejecting, judgemental mother, to prompt the client's feelings, which may be anger, fear, stubbornness, resentment, grief or abandonment. This is 'being with' at a complex level, within the therapeutic dynamic.

Within the preceding counselling I do subtly suggest that it would be valuable to explore both sides of any polarity and wait for the client to suggest it, as their own idea. I have noticed that by enacting both sides of a power inequality, the clients find within themselves their own personal power, which was previously experienced, and then later in their life projected, as being outside. A catharsis, a release of anger or grief often happens.

Through re-enacting and mapping out being the object of various familial and institutional gazes, a complex network of fragmented selves, constructed out of the needs, views, projections and attributions of others, can be made visible. The anger and grief at the overwhelming impossibility of meeting all these outside, contradictory demands is validated. From recognition it is possible to move to mourning the losses that have been experienced and reach compassion.

THE IMPORTANCE OF THE TRANSFORMATIVE

Whilst I was developing this modality, it became apparent that what was needed for the client – and I did start by alternating between both client and phototherapist, so I know at a deep level, not just a theoretical one – is a transformation. Being or doing something different. Not just to replay old pains, distresses, traumas, but to make them have a different outcome in the here and now. For example. if the work is about powerlessness – to take power, to be powerful, to see how that feels, to say what was never said at the time, to do it differently.

Now, I stress this aspect, and ensure that in the counselling the client identifies what that transformation would be for them, so we have a plan from which to work. Then in the here-and-now moment of the session, to let it unfold; permission is given to say and do that which was not said and done; for the client to be in some other, new and different way, to map a change. This is the moment of freedom, from all those old injunctions and patterns, 'all the old shit'. It is vital to the process, to have a transformation, a way of being that is healing to the client, represented out there, on those external, little pieces of paper that are the photographs, to be integrated back within the personality in the counselling sessions that follow the photo-session. Often it is about becoming angry, if pent up anger was the issue, 'letting rip' – literally. It is also important for the client to find from within themselves their inner nurturer, an aspect lost or hidden, a part of the self that would have been a good ally, yet was too dormant at the historical time we are looking at. This then gives the client a sense of her own resources, to make use of in ordinary reality. Integrated into psychic reality, this is finally the healing process: to have been witnessed and to have the evidence of that witnessing – in the photos as evidence; to have an advocate, the phototherapist who is on their side, saying 'go for it', the permission-giver. To have made an image and, within the counselling process that follows, internalised that part of the self that can act as the inner nurturer, the supporter within, the self that is capable of self-love.

PLAY

This way of working is intuitive and playful; play in its complex and contradictory form. I draw upon my experience from many years of working with children at play, designing toys and play equipment, studying and observing child development and play. A re-enactment phototherapy session can be seen to have parallells to the way children use fantasy play to re-enact frightening, troubling scenarios, or to try out different roles, gathering 'dressing-up' clothes and a variety of objects as props, to give form to their desires and fears. In play the child is the active agent, controlling and transforming the outcome. By working through deep feelings, from the position of power, as opposed to being acted upon, a child can resolve the conflicts of powerlessness within the family.

> Playing implies trust, and belongs to the potential space between (what was at first) baby and mother figure . . . Play is essentially satisfying. This is true even when it leads to a high degree of anxiety . . . is inherently exciting and precarious . . . (because of) the interplay between that which is subjective and that which is objectively perceived . . . It is in playing, and only in playing, that the individual child or adult is able to be creative and to use the whole personality, and it is only in being creative that the individual discovers the self.[14]

WHY USE PHOTOGRAPHS AS THERAPEUTIC TOOLS?

Photographs are paradoxical: both real – they have that physicality as bits of paper – and not real. Photographs are constructed, framed, chosen moments, over-determined, pulled out of a continuum of possibilities. Yet we invest them with meaning, with notions of representing the 'truth', the photographic record is treated as evidence, even proof. With the advent of digitised imagery and the myriad possibilities for manipulation, this old belief has almost completely collapsed . . . and yet, we hand round our holiday snaps or photographs from a party as if to show we really were there. So, the photograph which provides this objectivity, this view from outside, can be embraced, with the new wisdom that comes from taking a different perspective. It can be discounted and torn up, if what it shows is too hard for the client to engage with.

The objectifying eye of the camera, which is merely a piece of technical apparatus, can offer a blank screen and the necessary distance to see from a different point of view.

The pleasure and excitement of having so many images offers the sense of having been seen, which for many clients is itself therapeutic.

Photographs produced in re-enactment phototherapy provide an unfiltered connection with the unconscious since what takes place within the phototherapy session is rooted in unconscious processes. Although there are intentions or plans, the session itself grows out of the therapeutic relationship, flowing in the here and now.

The photographs provide a mapping of the session. Often there is surprise expressed when the pictures themselves are seen, as aspects of what happened within the session can so easily slip back into the unconscious and be repressed again. Yet here they are, markers, that offer up the possibility to reconstruct and recall what happened within the session itself.

Maintaining life-long patterns of shame, secrecy and denial is contested by these photographs which mirror back and give form, size, weight and colour to psychic pain and to its history, its source. Externalised and made visible, these aspects can be worked with and reflected upon in the counselling relationship. The photographs may then be seen as transitional objects between inner and outer reality.[15] The phototherapist bears witness to these previously hidden aspects of the selves. Offering a nonjudgemental positive regard, the phototherapist enables the client to work towards integration of all these parts.

Taking up the role of significant others within the client's life, especially that of parental figures, can be very personally challenging. Introjections may be confronted, projections and projective identifications are suddenly seen for what they are, in a flash of recognition. The split off, disowned parts of the self may be acknowledged as such and accepted back within the self.

As Assagioli (1975) has said of psychosynthesis, symbols are seen as 'accumulators', in the electrical sense, as containers and preservers of a dynamic psychological charge.[16] This 'charge' can be transformed by the use of the symbol, channelled by it, or integrated by it. The use of symbolic representations are especially powerful for connecting with and transforming unconscious belief systems, since the unconscious does not operate with the language of logic, but with images – as in dreams.

The photographs produced can be re-ordered at will, giving the possibility of telling so many new stories, making new outcomes. In creating new narratives it becomes possible to disrupt any sense of closure, endless new stories can be created by juxtapositions that suggest new versions of old realities, linkages and the possibility of transformations.

A dialogue between individual photographs, which represent different parts of the self, or significant others, can be facilitated by the therapist as an externalised gestalt.

Fixity is challenged by making visible and mapping out the complex interweaving of the multiplicities of identities that any one individual inhabits simultaneously, parts of subjectivity which may often be in conflict or contradiction, for example how we may each occupy positions of both victim and persecutor in different contexts.

Photographs can also provide a slippery surface of meaning. The original intentional meaning of a photograph can be overlaid with other associations, especially when one image is contextualised by others. This moving and altering of signification can reflect the changes within the therapeutic process.

Looking at the range of photographs produced and witnessing the mutability of the images enables the client to see how identity is fragmented across many 'truths'. This understanding frees up the client from the search for the 'ideal' self and allows the self as process and becoming to be understood.

RE-ENACTMENT PHOTOTHERAPY AND ART THERAPY: SIMILARITIES AND DIFFERENCES

Both modalities use images, so the connections that symbolic representations have with the unconscious is common to both.

They both work as ways of giving visual form to feelings and making the invisible more visible – a kind of 'unconsciousness raising'.

Symbolic representation is the only language we will ever have for expressing and communicating thoughts, feelings, memories and other inner experiences, even though it necessarily mediates and filters those experiences in the process of describing them. All art therapy is based on the idea that visual symbolic representation is far less likely to interrupt and distort than verbal translations of sensory-based experience, and that we not only frequently project unconscious meaning through such metaphoric communication from deep inside, but also tap into those areas while simply reacting or responding to symbolic imagery produced by others. Non-verbal, personal symbols are immensely powerful because they arise from the unconscious. When we look at the art or phototherapy work which we produce, and while we explore the themes and patterns that emerge, we are able to learn about our own unconscious.

However, these images are generated in very different ways. In art therapy, clients produce their images spontaneously. Working outwards from the feeling, the body is used to express a visual mark, as a process offering unmediated contact with the unconscious. There are particular techniques, such as painting with blind eyes, or using the non-dominant hand, which over-ride conscious control.

Art therapy relies on the client's internal concerns to arise from the unconscious through the process of art/mark-making, whereas photographs require something to have been there to photograph. Art therapy is dependent on externalised internal subjects, while phototherapy is dependent on internalised external subjects.

Re-enactment phototherapy is about embodiment, how an individual is seen, how she presents and how she is represented. Like finding oneself in a 'hall of mirrors' at the fair, a range of reflections is offered back to the client. The counselling work, starting from a memory or a feeling, focuses the client on an issue of enquiry, a series of stories to re-tell. Clothes and props are found from outer reality, to represent inner reality. What is seen and felt is shown in the body of the client, within the photo-session, as it would be in gestalt or psychodrama. It is made visible to the client through the photographs.

In art therapy transference occurs not only with the therapist, as in 'talking counselling', but also with the object produced, so there is greater autonomy from the therapist. In re-enactment phototherapy the transference onto the photograph may be very direct, for example when a client is 'becoming' her mother or father.

A particular advantage of phototherapy is the ubiquity of the camera and the photograph. They are seen as ordinary, everyday objects, not given the cultural baggage of art. 'Just press the button and we'll do the rest', as Kodak's adverts used to say. Individuals do not feel hampered by 'not being artists', which can block some people when confronted by paints and paper, especially if their creative spontaneity was measured as not good enough in school, an all too common experience.

In both art therapy and re-enactment phototherapy the reintegration of that which has been made visible is achieved through the counselling.

PROCESS TO PRODUCT: MOVING FROM AN INDIVIDUALISED TO A PUBLIC SPHERE

When Jo Spence and I were evolving re-enactment phototherapy we decided to make the work public, through articles and exhibitions, as a way of sharing our ideas and practice. In re-enacting distresses from the past and working with the images produced it became possible to move beyond resistance to engage with painful memories and find new ways of creating an inner dialogue. As this process continued a complex, interweaving matrix of narratives was generated, old simplistic belief systems could be gradually put aside as the contradictions within a fragmented subjectivity were made manifest and self-healing proceeded. It is only when the images no longer hold the individual's pain, only when the trauma has been sufficiently worked through, that the images can become potential raw material to be extracted from to create art works. It is totally inappropriate for any work to be exhibited until this process has been completed, to do so before would be a form of exploitation. All phototherapy work is done respecting the confidentiality of the sitter/director. No images are made public unless permission is granted. The vast majority of phototherapy images remain private. Almost all the phototherapy work that has been shown has either Jo or I as the subject, since we were willing to use ourselves as 'case histories' to explore the modality. As practising artists we used the images from phototherapy sessions as clues and traces in an archaeology of the self, making the links between personal experiences and a critique of the socio-cultural context in a politicised remembering.

> The task of an alternative photography is to incorporate photography into social and political memory, instead of using it as a substitute which encourages the atrophy of any such memory . . . Very frequently photo-graphs are used tautologically so that the photograph merely repeats what is being said in words . . . (but) memory is not unilinear at all. Memory works radially, with an enormous number of associations all leading to the same event . . . A radial system has to be constructed around the photograph so that it may be seen in terms which are simultaneously personal, political, economic, dramatic, every-day and historic.[17]

In moving the work from the private to the public domain the question is no longer one of individual therapeutic resolution, but rather whether the images, selected out from the hundreds created in the process, have the power to communicate to a broad audience. This is achieved when they speak to the social, cultural and political formations of subjectivities and, by activating a personal or collective memory, produce a resonance of recognition in the spectator.

Issues, concerns and critiques are rooted in and addressed through personal experience. Through a process of unravelling different kinds of knowledge, reflecting and representing the work becomes an act of communication. Since quotation is unavoidable, the question becomes who or what are the chosen source, which voices are given credence. The work is informed by discursive struggle, engaged with the politics of represen-tation and the creation of identities through history, culture, memory and the everyday, filtered through the complexities of psychic formation. It is presented as a complex interweaving of fragments of narratives, which rather than offering any closure opens up questions and debates, and leaves space for the spectator to engage with the work.

Each exhibition is thematic. For example: Jo's experience of having breast cancer in *The Picture of Health?*, health, smoking and the relation-ship to my father in *I Pose a Paradox: a Discourse on Smoking*, the mother–daughter relationship in *Libido Uprising* and *A Daughter's View*, childhood, conflicting family histories and the construction of heterosexuality in *Minefield of Memory*, and exploring my lesbian identity in *Don't say cheese, say lesbian*.

THE PICTURE OF HEALTH?

In 1982 Jo was diagnosed as having breast cancer. She wrote:

> I realized with horror that my body was not made of photographic paper, nor was it an image, or an idea, or a psychic structure . . . it was made of blood, bones and tissue.[18]

She took her camera with her into the hospital, to document what was happening to her.

> My body was completely out of my control. Photographing gave me a kind of power – the power of the observer in her own history.[19]

She refused traditional allopathic medical treatment – mastectomy and radiotherapy – chose to have a lumpectomy and to follow an alternative holistic regime using traditional Chinese medicine. To confirm for herself that she had made the right choice, she asked Maggie Murray to document her healing strategies.

Using phototherapy Jo and I worked collaboratively to make visible her mind/body split, by going beyond the documentation of physical progress to explore her experience of illness. In one series she re-enacted her feelings of powerlessness, depersonalisation and victimisation as a patient at the hands of the medical profession, manifested in the moment when the doctor came and marked up her breast saying, 'This is the one that's coming off'.

To fully appreciate how pioneering the *Picture of Health?* was, it is necessary to see it in its historical context. At that time issue-based work that aimed to be educational used social documentary photographs with sociological texts, made by 'experts' about someone else's 'problems', not by those directly involved. Jo's work offered a subjective view. She inhabited the issue, and used her theoretical knowledge to ask questions: of the medical discourse, of representation, and about how her identity had been re-constructed at the point of the doctor's pen.

I POSE A PARADOX: A DISCOURSE ON SMOKING

In generating this art work, I had to face my own resistances. I explored the contradictions of knowledge versus desire.

I chose to draw upon images from a range of different genres to contextualise the phototherapy work. Like a detective, I searched for traces and clues, making linkages between my own smoking history and that of my father. I juxtaposed pages from the family album, of my father as a young man, with his carefully studied resemblance to current matinée idols, always posing, cigarette in hand, with contemporary popular culture, film stills, film scripts and music scores which encapsulated the notions of smoking as glamour and sophistication.

Using phototherapy, I explored the anxieties and discontents which lay behind these constructed desires. I took up the role of my 'dapper daddy', and then my memories of his asthma, emphysema and dependency upon medications. My experiences of class shame form part of this history. My feelings of being silenced were embodied in my stuttering, in response to the multiple humiliations I received as a working-class scholarship girl in a middle-class school. I took refuge in becoming a rebel, and adopted the social prop of sophistication and bravado, and found along with that a group I could belong to – 'You're never alone with a Strand'.[20] The cigarette as comforter, to replace sweets and chocolates and to silence the hunger pangs resulting from the rigours of teenage dieting formed part of the impossible longing for an idealised thin femininity. Gleefully burning money, and set historically against the changing mode of address of cigarette advertising, which becomes more obscure and subtly more seductive, my response moves from pleasure to fear.

In the final section, I selected images from my 'alternative photographic diary', that I had made at the time of my father's death, to mark my sense of grief and loss. A series of triptychs of hands: my father's in the coffin which I had carefully staged holding objects which symbolised different aspects of him as part of a ritual of separation and reparation, my mother's shucking peas, which evoked a vivid memory from childhood, and my own, dealing with the materiality of death and the feelings that engulfed me. Images within images refer back to the earlier sections, reaffirming linkages and challenging the taboos that surround public and private representations.[21]

Such a close exploration of feelings and facts is no instant cure, rather a recognition of contradictions. These photographs offer a means of thinking through feelings, feeling through thoughts.

SOME NARRATIVE FRAGMENTS EXTRACTED FROM THE PROCESS AS EXAMPLES

In selecting individual images to be read with this article, I have included narrative textural fragments, highlighted how each epitomises aspects of the methodology and the therapeutic significance. These then are offered as extracts from the case histories in which the client's voice is privileged.

Great Expectations (Figure 9.1) came out of co-counselling sessions exchanged between Jo and myself in which we both explored our complex reactions as little girls to the icon of the fairy. In costume I re-enacted a memory of pleasing Daddy as the 'good' yet mischievous fairy. I revelled in the desire to be the centre of attention riven with the recollection of failure, of being the first to be rejected for the role of fairy in the primary school play.

After making this image, I found within the family album a snapshot of myself aged six, in the self-same pose: in contacting a childhood role I

Figure 9.1 Great Expectations, circa 1952 (original in colour)

had touched a somatic memory. I had actively taken up this stereotypical feminised role, since it was a highly rewarded activity. 'Isn't she cute?' I reflect now that one of the tasks I unconsciously took on, as the youngest child and only girl, was to mediate and intervene in family disputes. I used my 'charms' – my transforming powers, in my attempts to try and keep everyone 'happy'. As a strategy for survival as a child, within the context of my dependency upon my parents I learnt to become the go-between, the peacemaker.

Figure 9.2 Poor Relations?
circa 1954 (originals in colour)

My starting point for *Poor Relations?* (see Figure 9.2) was a memory from my childhood holidays in Cornwall, when we stayed with my uncle's family. My cousins seemed to me to have everything they wanted, whereas I had to be aware that my parents were scrimping and saving. For my special treat I had to chose between an ice-cream and a fizzy drink. But I wanted both. So I re-enacted my greedy child self, a fantasy of having it all, enjoying and luxuriating in the indulgence. I also re-enacted my mother's gaze of restriction and admonishment, with the almost empty purse, saying we can't afford it.

This mother–daughter exchange seems now to me to represent the task of learning not to ask for too much. I reflect now that this has become an inner dialogue, between the part of myself that desires and my internalised mother who rebukes me saying that to have what I want is to be selfish. Externalising this inner polarity has helped me to become more aware in my current decision making processes.

I worked with Sue Isherwood tracing the psychic histories of six generations of women in her family. Sue worked by inhabiting each woman in turn to explore the legacy of family mythology, history, and each woman's collusion in passing on patriarchal values. She re-enacted how she 'saw' each woman and their interrelationships. In so doing, it became clear in the counselling that followed how each manifested parts of herself, some of which she had repressed up until then, or chosen not to acknowledge.

We traced how, down the generations, a love of books, fictions and the imagination, co-existed with an overwhelming respect for authority, embodied in 'holy writ'. For Sue, who prioritised her intellect, writing was 'word made flesh'. But these were the words of others, defining and confining this 'flesh', which within patriarchy she found both seductive and oppressive. In a move to affirm her own voice, her right to write, I suggested that we celebrate her ability to speak articulately. She chose the word 'prestidigitator', and I made the image of her as a magician, conjuring up a profuse flow of words, in joyous command and reclamation of the Bible/dictionary (see Figure 9.3). This validatory image of her own skills could then act as a talisman, a way for her to reconnect with that aspect of herself.

Double Talk – Double Bind (Figure 9.4) emerged from my work with Lynn Harvey in which she explored how her experiences at art school had blocked rather than expanded her own creativity.

An extract from Lynn's feedback:

I came to the first session with photos of myself around the time of art college (the late 1960s). I talked to Rosy about my feelings and experiences. Through this councelling process I regained some self-respect, and confirmation that in my own terms I had experienced and witnessed 'abuse'. By pointing out the language I used, Rosy helped me

Figure 9.3 The Prestidigitator, circa 1990 (original in colour)

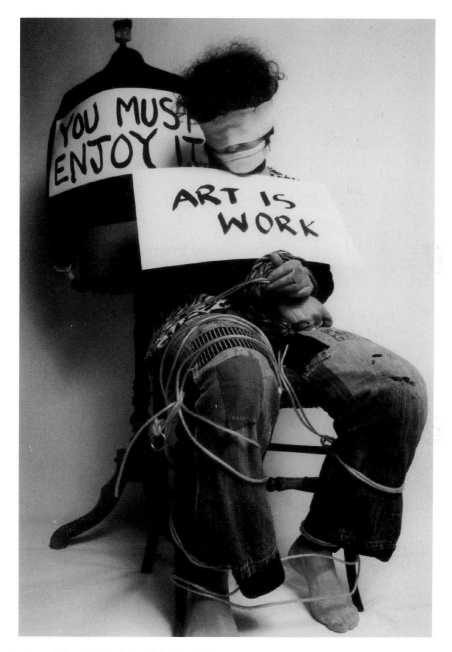

Figure 9.4 Double Talk – Double Bind, circa 1967 (original in colour)

to pinpoint the conflict as I experienced it, of 'guts versus hat'. The 'guts' were that part of me that intuitively perceived the manipulation and power being played out by the tutors, together with my own reactive anger. The 'hat' was the reasoning and conditioning that told me I was there to learn from people, they 'knew better', and I must suppress my anger and disbelieve my perceptions. I realised that the message shouted by the tutors was 'do your own thing', but their reactions and power games said, equally loudly 'do what we tell you'. They shouted 'express yourself', then, through reaction and manipulation, 'this is what I want you to express'. My emotional experience of the onset of depression was one of 'disintegration' under this onslaught.

Rosy suggested ways of making these two contradictory sets of messages visible, using placards. I was to be myself, as a student, and a tailor's dummy, dressed in a leather jacket (which was the ubiquitous uniform), was to stand in for the tutors. This felt right, whilst I am angry with them, I am also aware that I was projecting power onto them.

In the phototherapy session I dressed in my clothes from that time, and was struck by the look of separation of my head from my body that the choker I always wore created. Together with Rosy, we selected the most contradictory quotes. I re-enacted my feelings at that time, in response to these double messages. We tried to resolve some of the conflicts during the session, by releasing the feelings. One of the most healing resolutions was with the 'work hard/I am lazy' injunctions. Owning the 'I am lazy' placard, by wearing it like a hat and luxuriating in it . . . like a cat – I am saying 'I am lazy when I choose to be, lazy is appropriate at the times I choose'.

When I viewed the photographs, with Rosy there as counsellor, I noticed that some showed me to myself as a child/woman. I felt compassion for the child, and fondness for her child-like look, it helped remove the guilt and self-consciousness of the label 'naive'. I had never before experienced the luxury of seeing so many different photos of myself, it helped correct my self-image. This woman looked expressive, vital and warm; she had wit and I liked her.

On reflecting on these multiple images I realised that it was not the anger that had done the damage . . . it was my own collusion through fear of disagreement with those around me that made me ill. The surrender of my 'authority of response'. The disempowerment of myself made me 'sick'.

In *New Mournings?* (Figure 9.5) I used self-portraiture and multiple exposure to make visible my process of bereavement and mourning: moving from grief and despair, through self-nurturance to an openness to new possibilities. Using the dying flowers to represent those whose deaths had shaken me to the core, I reconnected with my grieving process as a way of authenticating my journey.

Figure 9.5 New Mournings? 1994 (original in colour)

Facing death's finality, in grief and loss my abandoned child-self returns, takes centre stage in her terror, desolation and powerlessness. Her cry 'take care of me, love me whatever, accept me as I am, don't leave me'. My despair: that there is no return to my imagined Eden, to my sweet illusions. Lost. In the pain of loss I find what it was I truly valued in each unique, specific loss. I inhabit again and again that child-part who never grows, and learn more each time I touch my vulnerability. It is as if to change we must keep in touch with the changeless.

There is, too, a nurturing, caring part of me, so ready to listen to the pain of others. My needy helper, she gives what she needs to receive. She hears the cry, can she learn to respond? Slowly and unsure at first she contains and holds; I am learning to take care of my own needy child-self.

Embrace life. The part of me who reaches out for new possibilities, brave and courageous in the face of loss and rejection. Learning to let go, she finds the strength to begin to move old obstacles, to recognise new blooms. The phoenix, with singed wings, must learn to fly again. Coming out of the shadow, yet part of the shadow: in death, life; in life, death.

CONCLUSION

Phototherapy practice bridges art, photography and therapy, and sits across defined boundaries of knowledge. I believe that it is only by synthesis, experiment and risk-taking that new ways of imagining can be developed.

Phototherapy is a means of re-claiming the power of the look for oneself, by making visible the multiple strands that have contributed to the construction of the self through mirroring. Acting into roles which represent one's own cultural and historical formation, recording and re-viewing the photographs produced offer a form of active looking, in which new meanings can be made, new stories told and new narrative fragments constructed. This act of making concrete, making visible a fragment, a moment in one's own history, a tiny detail which encompasses a range of meanings offers a glimpse at psychic reality. Who we are looking for is who is looking.

NOTES

1 Mulvey, 1975: 11.
2 Gamman and Marshment, Bad Object Choices, 1988, 1991.
3 Butler, 1990: 140.
4 Winnicott 1971: 134.
5 Lacan, 1977.
6 Freud, 1976–85.
7 Jansen, quoted in Dowrick 1992: 22.
8 Fryear and Krauss, 1983; Weiser, 1993.
9 Assagioli, 1975: 74–7.
10 Winnicott, 1971; Miller, 1981.
11 Waterhouse, 1993: 67.
12 The two-cushioned technique is intended to be used as a method for bridging splits within oneself. For example, in giving expression to two opposing voices. The client is encouraged to act out both sides of the polarity, by taking one side, when seated on one cushion and the other when seated on the second. A dialogue is conducted between these two positions, in the here and now. The technique is direct and immediate and encourages the expression of feelings.

13 Winnicott, 1971: 137.
14 Winnicott, 1971: 60–1, 63.
15 Transitional object is a term theorised by Winnicott to designate a material object with a special significance for the sulking or young child. Reliance on such objects allows the child to make the transition from the first oral relationship with the mother to the true object-relationship. 'The term "transitional object" gives room for the process of becoming able to accept difference and similarity . . . for the root of symbolism in time, a term which describes the infant's journey from the purely subjective to objectivity . . . The task of reality acceptance is never completed, no human being is free from the strain of relating inner and outer reality, and that relief from this strain is provided by an intermediate area of experience, which is not challenged (arts, religion etc.) This intermediate area is in direct continuity with the play area of the small child who is 'lost' in play.' (Winnicott, 1971: 7, 15).
16 Assagioli, 1975.
17 Berger, 1980: 58, 60, 63.
18 Spence, 1980: 151.
19 Spence, 1992: 11.
20 Late 1950s advertisement for cigarettes.
21 Martin, 1995: 67–74.

BIBLIOGRAPHY

Assagioli, R. 1975. *Psychosynthesis*. London: Turnstone Books.
Bad Object Choices. 1991. *How do I look?* Seattle: Bay Press.
Berger, J. 1980. *About Looking*. London: Writers and Readers.
Butler, J. 1990. *Gender Trouble: Feminism and the Subversion of Identity*. London: Routledge.
Dowrick, S. 1992. *Intimacy and Solitude*. London: The Women's Press.
Freud, S. (with J. Breuer) 1976–85. *Studies on Hysteria*. Harmondsworth: Pelican Freud Library.
Fryear, J. and Krauss, D. (eds) 1983. *Phototherapy in Mental Health*. Springfield, IL: Thomas.
Gamman, L. and Marshment, M. (eds) 1988. *The Female Gaze: Women as Viewers of Popular Culture*. London: The Women's Press.
Lacan, J. 1977. 'The mirror stage as formative of the function of the I', *Écrits*. London: Tavistock Publications.
Miller, A. 1981. *The Drama of Being a Child*. New York: Basic Books.
Mulvey, L. 1975. 'Visual pleasure and narrative cinema', *Screen*, vol. 16, no 3.
Riviere, J. 1929. 'Womanliness as a masquerade', *International Journal of Psycho-Analysis*, vol. 10.
Spence, J. 1986. *Putting Myself in the Picture*. London: Camden Press.
Spence, J. 1992. 'The Artist and Illness', *Artpaper*. January.
Waterhouse, R. 1993. 'Wild women don't have the blues'. *Feminism and Psychology*. London: Sage.
Weiser, J. 1993. *Phototherapeutic Techniques: Exploring the Secrets of Personal Snapshots and Family Albums*. San Francisco: Jossey-Bass.
Winnicott, D. W. 1971. *Playing and Reality*. London: Tavistock Publications.

SUGGESTED FURTHER READING ON PHOTOTHERAPY

Martin, R. and Spence, J. 1985. 'New portraits for old: the use of the camera in therapy', *Feminist Review*, 19, March. Reprinted in Betterton, R. (ed.) *Looking On – Images of Femininity in the Visual Arts Media*. London: Pandora.

Martin, R. and Spence, J. 1988. 'Phototherapy – Psychic Realism as a Healing Art?', *Ten:8*, no. 30, October.

Martin, R. 1991a. 'Dirty Linen', *Ten:8*, vol. 2, no. 1, Spring.

Martin, R. 1991b 'Don't Say Cheese, Say Lesbian', in Fraser, J. and Boffin, T. (eds) *Stolen Glances – Lesbians Take Photographs*. London: Pandora.

Martin, R. 1991c. 'Unwind the ties that bind', in P. Holland and J. Spence (eds) *Family Snaps: The Meanings of Domestic Photography*. London: Virago.

Martin, R. 1993. 'Home truths? Phototherapy, memory and identity', *Artpaper*, March.

Martin R. 1995. 'Memento mori manifest: a rite of inheritance', in J. Soloman and J. Spence (eds) *What Can a Woman Do with a Camera*. London: Scarlet Press.

Spence, J. 1991a. 'Cultural Sniper', *Ten:8*,.vol. 2, no. 1, Spring.

Spence, J. 1991b. 'Soap, family album work . . . and hope' and 'Shame-work: thoughts on family snaps and fractured identities', in P. Holland and J. Spence (eds) *Family Snaps: The Meanings of Domestic Photography*. London: Virago.

Chapter 10

The pregnant art therapist's countertransference

Sally Skaife

INTRODUCTION

Pregnancy is a major life event involving profound psychological changes. When the therapist is pregnant she will be concerned about the effect these changes in herself will have on her clients, the issues her pregnancy will raise for them, and also about the effect of the interruption of the therapy. In the therapy group there will be a shift whereby the therapist will become a focus for intense feelings at a time when she is conspicuously vulnerable.

In this chapter I shall review the psychoanalytic literature on the pregnant therapist and comment specifically on changing attitudes to countertransference responses in this area. I shall then describe an art psychotherapy group conducted by myself from its inception, when I was twelve weeks pregnant, until three months after I returned from maternity leave. The focus in the case study is on how my own process affected the process of the group as a whole, the extent of which came as quite a surprise to me. What emerged was that I had struggled against the changing processes going on in me in order to present to the group a solid, consistent figure. The suppression of my own feelings in the group may have made it more difficult for group members to express theirs.

I only fully understood this after reading the very recent literature when I realised that there was a connection between my experience and current social changes. When I began my group there was only one paper (Breen 1977) that looked at the pregnant therapist in a group, and I knew of no other working, pregnant group therapists or art therapists. Very recently there has been a dramatic increase in the psychoanalytic literature about the therapist's pregnancy; this appears to be linked to the fact that professional women working up until confinement and returning to work after maternity leave are a recent phenomenon. Despite a conscious understanding of the need to review ideas about the role of the therapist, and indeed of the mother in the light of social change, the case study I will describe reveals that I was resonating to some powerful unconscious images, 'superwoman', and the 'blank screen therapist' amongst them.

Another interesting issue was the striking similarity I found between my two-and-a-half-year-old daughter's reaction to my pregnancy and the group's, which I have found useful as a means of understanding the group process.

Also discussed is the particular role art had to play in the group. The use of art allowed members to actively engage with their feelings in an arena other than the transference, perhaps allowing for an identification with the creativity of the therapist.

I shall now go on to discuss the psychoanalytic literature on the pregnant therapist before describing the case study, and discussing the material that arose in the light of the literature.

LITERATURE REVIEW: GENERAL OVERVIEW

Despite the fact that it is only recently that women are having their children later in life after they have established their careers, there has been a surprisingly small amount of literature about the pregnant therapist. At the time I conducted this research (1995) only twelve articles had been published in Britain on this topic. Of these, six had appeared in 1993 and 1994, three of which are on the pregnant therapist in individual therapy – Deben-Mager (1993), Etchegoyen (1993), and Mariotti (1993) – with three on group therapy – Anderson (1994), Gavin (1994) and Rogers (1994). This dearth of literature and the recent increase deserve some consideration.

Clemental-Jones (1985) puts forward the notion that the lack of clinical observation in this area is linked to a need to defend an outdated view of analytic neutrality and that this is connected to an underplaying of the effect of the real person of the mother on the baby. This view is in keeping with work by Alice Miller which emphasises the results of neglecting the effects of parental attitudes on children (1984).

The recent increase in the literature may be related to the advent of feminist psychoanalytic theory. The early women psychoanalysts (Horney, Deutsch, Anna Freud and Klein) drew considerably on their experiences of motherhood but did not make this explicit. One would imagine this to be due to a need to show themselves to be comparable to men. More recently feminist psychotherapists (Orbach, Maguire, Ernst, Eichenbaum) concentrated on developing a theory of female development. A number of current books look at the implications of the therapist's gender (Schaverien 1995, Maguire 1995). Schaverien (1995) cites Guttman (1984) as pointing out that women are at the vanguard in discussing counter-transference issues.

Though the papers on the pregnant therapist reflect changing attitudes to women and pregnancy, there is little sociological or cultural comment in the literature. There is a gradual development, though, towards discussing countertransference and the interrelationship of the pregnant therapist's and client's feelings, in a more personal way (Etchegoyen, 1993, Deben-Mager 1993, Mariotti 1993, Anderson 1994, Gavin 1994 and Rogers 1994).

Other themes explored in the literature (but not discussed in this chapter) are practical considerations such as when to tell the patients of the pregnancy, how long a break to take and, in the case of groups, whether or not to have a locum therapist. Alterations to the analytic role are also considered as is the outcome of the therapy.

ISSUES FOR THE PATIENT

All the writers agree that the therapist's pregnancy has a profound effect on clients, involving fears of being abandoned literally through the feared death of the therapist, the real interruption of therapy and through the therapist losing interest in them. Intense feelings about clients' own mothering are activated. Memories of the births of siblings, and sibling rivalry are often major issues. Intense envy may be experienced of both the therapist, focused on her now supposedly having everything – husband, baby and career – and of the foetus housed at one with the therapist. The therapist's intimate relationships and her active sexual relationship with the baby's father are now open material.

Lax (1969), was the first to make two important observations: that identification with the therapist was the main form of defence from facing the powerful feelings aroused, and that borderline patients may have difficulty in containing the intensity of feelings aroused and are likely to engage in acting-out behaviour such as becoming pregnant themselves or having unnecessary operations. This was also observed by later writers (Berman 1975, Bassen 1988, Anderson 1994).

Breen (1977) compared the themes that came up in individual therapy with those in groups. The themes in individual therapy were similar to those already described, but in the group which she co-ran with another woman, sexuality was a main theme and the pregnant therapist became characterised by the group as a bad sexual mother whilst the other therapist was good. This split did not get resolved in the group and Breen explores fundamental differences between individual and group therapy in working with anger. Anderson (1994) felt that group members had found it hard to express anger in her group whilst she was pregnant but were able to do so after her return. She felt that returning after the birth and being the sole therapist were important factors in enabling group members to work through their anger.

In her discussion of patients' envy towards the foetus, Deben-Mager (1993) draws attention to Fenster et al.'s research (1986) which showed that aggression towards the foetus was seldom expressed but the defence against it was. Deben-Mager explains the fact that her patient was able to express aggression directly towards the foetus as related to the therapy being psychoanalysis as opposed to analytic psychotherapy,[1] Rogers (1994) says that much of the aggression towards the therapist is felt as projective identification, and she speaks of the power of the group's murderous fantasies and the importance of the conductor keeping a hold on reality. However, she describes as an important mutative process the transforming of envy into desire. I understand this as the patient moving from a position of envious aggression through to acknowledgement of envy, to desiring to be creative like the therapist.

Rogers (1994) compares the group's response to the pregnancy with what happens in a family. In comparison with the first child's insistence that it is still a baby, her group tended to regress, becoming more dependent on her and denying work achieved. She talks about the importance of the special time with the first child before the second comes along and parallels this with the need for the conductor to make contact with each member before the break.

One-to-one therapists focus on the individual nature of the degree to which any of the issues described above are prominent, dependent on the patient's early conflicts (Lax 1969, Clemental-Jones 1985, Fenster et al. 1986, Penn 1986). However, in all cases they point to the intensification of transference and countertransference, the 'transference neurosis' being shaped by the response to the therapist's pregnancy. Group therapists found that identification with the creativity of the therapist was an important spur to self-development.

ISSUES FOR THE THERAPIST

Pregnancy involves a major psychic upheaval for the prospective mother. Clemental-Jones (1985) suggests that there is a psychic withdrawal of the pregnant therapist into her inner world, a lessening of her logical ability and theoretical interests which is balanced by increased intuitive and empathetic capacity. She appears more in touch with the irrational and the unconscious. This all happens at a time when she can be a recipient of projected, intense feelings aroused in her clients in response to the pregnancy.

Several writers describe the different countertransferential issues that arise in the three trimesters of pregnancy (Balsam 1974, Penn 1986, Fenster et al. 1986, Deben-Mager 1993). In the first trimester self-absorption, nausea and tiredness may make the pregnant therapist feel vulnerable. She may feel anxious that patients guess she is pregnant while she feels reluctant to tell them because of fear of miscarriage. The second trimester brings anxiety about telling the patients, but at this stage the boost that the pregnancy gives may lead to a feeling of inner calm and increased sensitivity to patients' feelings. In the third trimester she fantasises about the baby, and increasingly withdraws. Winnicott has termed this 'the maternal preoccupation'. Anxieties about death may surface at this time. Raphael-Leff (1980: 189) suggests that the 'fear of death during or following delivery is very common among contemporary women despite the advances in medicine and the infrequency of complications.' Throughout the pregnancy there may be concern that complications of the pregnancy demand an unexpected change in the plans for the group.

Reflecting her time, Lax (1969), rather than talking about her own countertransference reactions to the patients' transferences she has just been describing, looks at the countertransference reactions of her colleagues and relates these to their own infantile conflicts. For example, therapists may deflect attention away from the pregnancy because of a fear of being attacked, which unconsciously stemmed from their own unresolved childhood rage at the birth of a sibling. Lax found that some therapists believed their patients did not notice they were pregnant as their laps were hidden by embroidery! (Coltart, 1993, reports that therapists doing needle work or knitting were apparently quite common in the past.)

Nadelson et al. (1974) are amongst the few writers to address issues of sexual politics on this subject; they talk of therapists overworking to compensate in a need to prove themselves as competent as men. They explore colleagues' attitudes to the pregnant therapist in her place of work and her responses to these. Some staff may encourage a heroic attitude in the therapist and give little support when it comes to reducing workload. Some therapists may feel that if they admit to special needs they may be seen as weak, or as inferior in their ability to do their job in comparison to their male or non-pregnant female colleagues. If they are uncomfortable with their increased emotional lability and personal needs, Nadelson et al. say, they may blame themselves for what they see as self-indulgence, deny their needs and take on even more work. Anderson (1994) and Gavin (1994) suggest that therapists may find their patients' kindness and concern more difficult to deal with than aggression because of it threatening their omnipotent defence, that is, of denying their own increasing physical and psychological vulnerability.

Lax (1969), Nadelson et al. (1974), Penn (1986), Fenster et al. (1986) and Deben-Mager (1993) advise that therapists beware of denying or minimising the pregnancy or giving interpretations too soon out of guilt. Another danger is that the therapist concerns herself only with feelings about the break and gives little attention to other responses to the pregnancy. She must guard against identifying with patients' transference of the idealised mother, acting out by missing appointments because of feeling angry in response to patients' anger, and unconsciously colluding with patients dropping out of treatment, particularly if they are difficult.

Recent writers explore the interrelationship of transference and countertransference in greater depth. Etchegoyen (1993) looks particularly at issues that come up for the therapist about her pregnancy which may influence the therapy, and she gives some personal vignettes. She describes, for example, becoming aware of her envy of her client's youth and omnipotence as she feels old and powerless. Another example is a feeling of triumph she experiences in relation to her colleagues which was preventing her from organising her client's future treatment. Gavin (1994), also talking openly about countertransference feelings, describes experiencing distressing feelings about her ability to mother, in response to her group's intense transference reactions to her pregnancy which strongly echoed feelings she had experienced in childhood. Mariotti (1993) and Deben-Mager (1993) both mention ways in which their technique was effected by countertransference feelings. Mariotti discusses when and how to tell patients of the pregnancy. She describes a situation where a patient asked if she was pregnant when she was only six weeks pregnant. She deflected attention away from the subject, inhibiting her patient's free association. She explores her feeling that if the patient knew and she had a miscarriage or was carrying a malformed foetus she would not be able to hold herself sufficiently together to work. However, knowing but not knowing set up an enormous amount of tension and fear. She links this to the small child's fantasies about where babies come from and their fear and dread of being replaced by another. Deben-Mager (1993) talks about actions she took which she regretted. One was working right up to her confinement without giving a finishing date, and the other was showing her baby to the patient. In both cases it seemed she was acting out of terrible feelings of guilt perhaps in response to her patient's envious aggression.

Having looked at the discussion of countertransference in the literature, I will now look at how the issues so far discussed in this literature review tallied with my own experience.

Discussion of how best the expression of the intense feelings aroused by the therapist's pregnancy can be facilitated forms a central part of the material. Breen (1977) felt that group therapy posed particular difficulties for working with anger, whereas Anderson (1994) found that if there was only one therapist who returned after her maternity leave, anger could be worked through after the pregnancy was over. Like Anderson, I was a sole therapist and returned after the break to find, as she did, that anger became more fully expressed and worked through after the birth. Deben-Mager (1993), unlike Fenster *et al.* (1986), concluded that her patient could express anger towards the foetus because the therapy was psychoanalysis as opposed to psychotherapy. In my art psychotherapy group I found that anger was expressed towards the foetus quite explicitly in the images, but that this was not verbalised. However, held in the image, it was part of the group material.

I found a striking similarity between many of the issues raised in the literature and my own experience. Roger's (1994) comparison of the group with a family expecting a new baby was similar to what I had observed in my group, Mariotti's (1993) discussion of countertransference issues involved in when to tell the patient related to my own thoughts, and I was particularly struck by Nadelson *et al.*'s (1974) comments on the pregnant therapist's omnipotent defence as I felt that this was a defence I had employed myself.

I have discussed the literature on the pregnant therapist on transference and countertransference issues illustrating with the latter the increasing depth and openness of discussion. I will now go on to describe an art psychotherapy group I ran whilst pregnant, looking at the ways in which my countertransference influenced the process of the group.

CASE MATERIAL: THE GROUP

The group comprised six women. All the members were self-referred, all of childbearing age, five with professional careers, only one with children. None of them had suffered mental health problems needing intervention. There was a professional interest in art therapy in the group as well as a self-help interest.

The period of time discussed is from the group's onset when I was twelve weeks pregnant until nine months into the group, three months after my return from maternity leave.

The first three months of the group

I became unexpectedly pregnant when the group was in preparation. It was a welcome, though unplanned second pregnancy. I was presented, though, with an immediate dilemma and cause for guilt. I was raising clients' expectations of a safe and consistent space for exploring difficulties whilst knowing all the while that this would be disrupted by my pregnancy.

However, an awareness of my pregnancy was in the group even before it started. In a preliminary interview with one member, she revealed that the year before she had had a late termination of pregnancy due to results following an amniocentesis which revealed that the foetus had Downs syndrome. I felt very affected by Rose's story as I was myself in the process of deciding whether or not to accept the offer of the same test. Just as I was showing her out of the door, she asked me if I was pregnant. I could not have been more taken aback as I had been careful not to reveal my own feelings. I told her to raise the question again in the group if she so wished. Once the group was started I was concerned that if my pregnancy became known it would affect the developing cohesion. Rose did not mention it again, but this also made me feel rather uncomfortable, as though knowing my secret gave her power over me.

The group established a cohesive feel. Negative feelings were projected onto absent men, but Fiona's start in the fourth week brought up feelings about sibling rivalry and some of these feelings began to be owned. Her arrival sparked off associations to new babies and was a forerunner of material to come. They talked about themselves as a group of women with the underlying theme, I felt, of whether or not they could create something new without being fertilised, as it were, by men. Was the group doomed to be sterile without men? Other themes were about sharing space and needing mother's love. Perhaps these themes were affected by an awareness at some level of my pregnancy.

In the first three months I felt uncomfortable and deceitful trying to hide my pregnancy under loose clothing. I was strongly aware of my daughter's need, and that of other family members, for a developing process parallel to my own, which would allow them to accommodate a change in their own position. However, I was also concerned about the developing group cohesion and my ability to cope with the group's projections were they to know and I miscarried.

Telling the group

I will describe the session in which I told the group. This followed a Christmas break and I was by now twenty-five weeks pregnant. Their first response was to discuss whether or not they welcomed knowing more about me; some did not, whilst others were angry that I was so opaque (a theme which was often to recur). They expressed anxiety about what would happen to the group. I tried to reassure them by saying that there would only be a slightly longer Easter break than usual. I think this was rather prohibitive to eliciting their feelings and associations, and was said out of guilt. Fiona said that her last therapist had had a baby during the therapy and had subsequently died. The therapist, like me, had said there would be a shortish break, in fact it was very long as there had been complications. She reassured me, though, that these two events, the therapist's death and the long break because of complications, were actually unconnected.

They settled down to painting. When they laid out the pictures on the floor, which was the custom of the group, I was powerfully affected by Fiona's (Figure 10.1). Once I had seen the juxtaposition of the foetus and the coffin I wished I could somehow take the baby out of the group. It was as if I too could share the magical belief that their bad feelings could harm my baby. I was concerned that my silence might show I was afraid of the power of the image and so asked Fiona if she could say more about it. She talked about her fear that her anger could destroy relationships and mentioned a recent row with a friend. I suggested that she might fear that in some magical way her anger with me might harm the baby. She asserted

Figure 10.1 Fiona's picture

that she was unaware of feeling anger towards me. My interjection was probably hasty, but it helped dispel my fears.

Heather said she felt very shaken by my saying 'my baby' during this interpretation. It sounded intimate and made her feel envious. After this a lot of sadness was expressed about a longing for intimate relationships but a fear about never achieving them. Rose talked about her termination now and cried.

It was interesting that the group verbally expressed sadness and longing, but the images expressed something different. Two of them depicted red water, a reference to miscarriage? One had the paint scraped off, which had an echo in a reported dream by another member of plaque being scraped off her teeth. Was this a reference to a Dilation and Curettage, an operation that follows a miscarriage? One person had painted a faceless head. This made me think of a small child's feelings of annihilation at the appearance of a sibling.

Something held inside

In the following three weeks I felt that there was a definite shift away from the more dependent position of the group in relation to me during the first three months. In fact I often felt that I was being excluded. Some of them talked about a wish to train as therapists (another form of identification with me?) whilst others expressed feelings of emptiness and depression because this did not interest them. They put me into the role of the assessor for student admission (I am a tutor on an art therapy training course) which effectively excluded me from the group.

They discussed sister transferences which led on to a discussion about what would happen if people became angry in the group. When I suggested that they might feel angry with me as my pregnancy would disrupt the group, it was brushed off. They made it clear that their interest was with each other and not with me, and I began to feel rather stupid for drawing attention to myself. They became concerned with Fiona who had a secret she was afraid to tell the group. The group pushed and pushed her to tell, but still she would not. Meanwhile a number of the images made in one session depicted something 'held' inside, a knotty scribble in one, an enormous belly in another, a knot of anger in another, and a deformed baby in a birth canal in a fourth. There seemed to be no conscious recognition of this material relating to my pregnancy. A metaphor was being acted out and painted that synthesised holding onto rage, holding babies inside and keeping secrets. When I related this material to my pregnancy the following week, they at last began to talk about it. What would happen to them when I had the baby? The birth would really interrupt the process of the group. I responded to all this rather defensively, again saying that it would only be a short break. Stories of abandoned babies followed this. Then Fiona disclosed her secret: she believed she had been sexually abused by her father when a child. The group responded supportively to her, but I felt there was a challenge from her to me to disbelieve her. This made me wonder about the timing of her disclosure and whether it related in some way to my pregnancy.

On looking back on these sessions I see that I give double messages. On the one hand, I try to draw the group's attention to their concern with my pregnancy, yet as soon as their attention is turned on me and the effect of the pregnancy on the group, I require them to be rational. I think that they were feeling excluded and abandoned and I was feeling guilty in response. Also, in trying to reassure them that I would not be away for long, I was also showing myself to be a neglectful mother to my real baby soon to be born. What sort of a mother was I? This episode illustrates something of the conflict between the therapist's feelings and the group members'. In a sense the group was my baby and I felt upset that it had to be affected by this rival. I felt guilty that I wanted to have my cake and eat it too. This had a clear parallel with feelings about my first child in relation to the new pregnancy. I expected she might feel outraged that I could be so greedy as to want another baby. Was she not enough for me? I was struck by the metaphor of 'things held inside' in this group as at the time my daughter believed she had a baby inside her which she talked about endlessly. This seemed to be her way of dealing with feelings about my pregnancy.

Birth and death

Leading up to the birth, I found it increasingly difficult to carry on working, not particularly with this group but with all my work. I felt very tired and could feel myself withdrawing. There were problems with the pregnancy, I was worried about the baby's survival. I felt intensely aware of death and of the extraordinariness of my being two people in one, and a sort of existential terror of the event that would make me one person again. I felt that at some level the group must be affected by my preoccupations with life and death. Meanwhile I was concerned that plans for the group went as smoothly as possible and that I enabled the group to survive the break. I was not worried about any individual members as they all had sufficient personal strength, I felt. I was, though, worried about the survival of the group.

A lot of powerful emotions were expressed at this time. Hannah declared she was thinking about leaving the group. Heather said she was starting individual therapy. Lesley said she took more to her individual therapy and found it hard to be involved in the group. Meanwhile the pictures were at one time very sad and at another very angry. One week they were nearly all in tears, and spoke of experiences that had made them sad and feelings that came upon them without their understanding why. Heather interpreted that they all longed for the loving closeness that I was going to have with my baby. Whilst these sorts of feelings were being expressed I felt very in tune with the group, in a more intense way than before I was pregnant. However, when angry feelings were expressed about my competence as a therapist, when I was not as careful as I might have been over a practical arrangement for the group, I found myself annoyed. I was aware of a strong split between what I was saying to the group and what I was feeling. On the one hand, I was encouraging them to express feelings of anger, in fact attempting to flush these out before the break in case they should prevent people returning. On the other, I felt resentful and the thought kept going through my mind that they ought to be behaving better!

They were very involved with their art work at this time, though they did not want to explore the images in any depth. Many of the pictures made obvious reference to pregnancy and babies. Some were about death. Hannah painted a picture which she said was about her father's illness from cancer, something she had not told the group about before. It occurred to me that the different phases of my pregnancy and after brought up new personal material which the group worked on. It was though they were in a sort of parallel process to my own.

The last planned session for the group had to be cancelled as I had to go into hospital early for delivery of the baby. The members were informed that all was well.

Adults or babies

The break was eight weeks long. In the first weeks after the group reconvened attendance was sporadic. It was not until the fourth week that the group was whole.

There were only three members in the first group back which I shall now describe. They talked about how they had received news about the birth but asked few questions, and moved quickly away from it to talk about applying for courses and group interviews. Fiona described an interview in which the group had been asked to find a subject they felt comfortable with. The group had chosen the abortion act.

For the first time Fiona and Lesley worked with clay, and both made babies. Fiona's baby was herself and she was concerned whether I would have time for them now that I had a baby. Lesley felt similarly anxious about my availability for the group. She described her model as a monstrous mother-figure with an underdeveloped baby, herself not yet ready to be born. She was beginning to shed her child-like self, though, and assert her adult self. She revealed for the first time that she had had an abortion this time last year; it had felt too painful to mention this before. She was aware of feeling very envious of me as I had everything she wanted, a baby, though she did not want one yet, and a job as a therapist. Fiona also felt she had progressed in the interval; now she felt really part of the group. Heather said that she had a new job and felt more optimistic. They all declared that they had not missed the group.

I found it difficult to return to the group, firstly because of leaving the baby. I also found switching from the kind of attention given to infants – total involvement at an intuitive level – to the thoughtful attention necessary for patients, difficult. At a conscious level I was interested in the members of the group; however, I found that despite my efforts I could not summon up the sort of interest I usually had. My constant thought was, I do not have space for any more at the moment.

I wonder if the group's leap into self-sufficiency was a response to my feelings picked up at an unconscious level, as well as a reaction to the knowledge that I now had a real baby to look after? There seemed to be a combination of angry attacks on the baby and myself expressed through the discussion of the abortion act and the 'monstrous mother', but also feelings of sadness and loss in the material.

I felt strongly reminded of my daughter after the birth. I felt they did not want to be vulnerable in my presence, but at the same time, wanted me to 'come and get them' and show I still cared.

The following session Hannah returned. She seemed rather distant and aloof and expressed ambivalent feelings about coming back to the group. After they had finished painting, Rose arrived forty-five minutes late and immediately asked me several questions about the baby, which showed up

Hannah's reticence. I answered most of these, but declined to give the name.

This made Hannah angry; she said that we were about the same age and therefore equals, why should she not know more about me? But she was unsure if she wanted to know. This was the first time she had openly challenged me.

Fiona described the picture she had made this week as a disguise of her feelings. She was blocking out the images of babies that came to her. Hannah related to this, and said she did not want to be introspective, she had just wanted to lay on paint. Heather expressed similar feelings; she had tried not to make the image she had made of a foetus. The group all felt the foetus looked sad, and looking at it I was reminded of my now lost, imagined baby of pregnancy. I had not as yet thought of this outside of the group. The group seemed very sad, and I was aware that if the baby had ever belonged to the group, it now no longer did.

They moved on to a discussion about breast-feeding from suggestions of breasts in the imagery. Heather said I was her idol and she kept wondering if I was breast-feeding. If I was, was I not neglecting the baby through being with the group? If I was not, was this also not neglect? They talked about memories of their younger siblings being breast-fed, and I was reminded how my daughter finds my breast-feeding the baby difficult to tolerate. There was talk about my coming to feed them, leaving the baby to do so. So, said Hannah, they were strongly connected to the baby but did I have enough milk?

Intimacy and anger

In the third session after the break Hannah talked of her difficulty with forming intimate relationships. She wondered whether individual therapy might be better for working with this problem. Was this an attack on me or envy of Heather? She went on to describe fears of being engulfed in other people's personalities if she got too close to them. She was afraid she was someone who only took and never gave, because of a fear of being 'used up'. She described her picture (Figure 10.2) as a big earth mother with big breasts. The mother was bound to nature and therefore right about everything. Hannah was unsure whether she wanted to be this mother or have this mother. Fiona felt it was the all-loving, nurturing mother that we all long for. I said that I felt that the other side of it was rather stifling. If the mother was always right how could one grow up and be different, and I linked this to Hannah's fear of being engulfed. In retrospect I see the image, and my response to it, as a powerful symbol of the whole process of the group at this time. It represented their uncertainty about wanting to identify with me or with the foetus, and my own unconscious countertransference response of wanting them to grow up a bit.

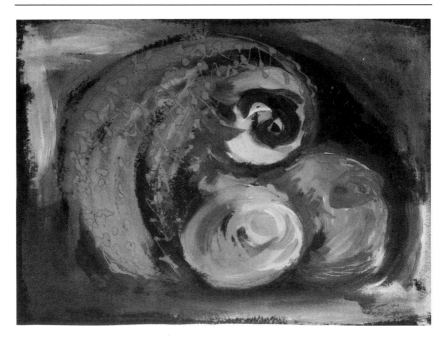

Figure 10.2 Hannah's picture

The next period in the group seemed to be very dense and stormy; feelings of sadness and need began to slip away. Chris said she was 'off' therapy. A previous group she had been in was much better as the therapist had answered questions. The talk was of intimacy but the feeling was of anger, and some members were staying away, without messages, for odd sessions. There was a lot of talk about the superiority of individual therapy and attempts, I felt, to make me feel useless and envious of their individual therapists. This seemed to relate to feelings of envy and exclusion in response to my relationship with my baby. Comments were also made about my being a sham, hiding feelings of inadequacy and pretending to know what I was doing. Angry fights broke out in the group between members.

There were ambivalent feelings about this new stormy atmosphere in the group. Some felt it was good to get things out in the open but others felt afraid for the survival of the group. I felt accused of not protecting the group from the rage that had been released within it and threatened to destroy it, and also of the group not working, not being 'deep or intense' enough. I too felt afraid for its survival with so many absences and so much disenchantment. One picture from this period, of a little baby cuddled by a stormy sea seems to sum it all up (Figure 10.3). I found myself feeling wobbly and uncertain at times. An overpowering rage took me over at one point where I felt furious that I was having to look after so many people,

Figure 10.3 Anonymous picture

and who was there to look after me? This feeling was not entirely related to this group, but afterwards I realised it to be in part a projective identification of Rose's.

Sexuality

A new theme emerged in the group of sexuality. The sexual images and the discussion that followed seemed to link sex with violence and there was discussion again about feeling they might have been sexually abused. This also became linked with mother being absent. I was not sure how to understand this material, and how far the theme of sexual abuse was a metaphor, or lost memories evoked by my pregnancy.

The group had a different feel now and one member talked movingly and at length about her mother's death. I was concerned that with all the recent conflict in the group, Heather might not get the support she clearly needed. However the group responded as a nurturing mother. I had a strong realisation that the power of the group is in its capacity to hold all that is brought to it, and, in this dual function of holding and hearing what is brought as well as contributing to its dynamic, the group creates itself and provides its own mothering. I said something like this and I felt a new shift had been made away from myself as the primary stimulus.

I have described an art psychotherapy group from its start when I was twelve weeks pregnant until three months after I returned from maternity leave. With the exception of one member, Rose, who left eight months after the birth, all the members continued in the group for some time after and continued to work on relationships. It seemed that for Rose my pregnancy was an impossible stimulus coming so soon after her own termination. She felt that the group was not a safe enough place for her to explore her feelings. It seems likely that her feelings about this were a response to my pregnancy.

DISCUSSION

I shall now discuss the transference and countertransference aspects of this group experience in relation to the psychoanalytic literature and to thoughts about the effects of social change on the role of the therapist.

Transference themes

In common with other pregnant therapists, I found the main issues in the group to be identification with the pregnant therapist, envy, sibling rivalry, loss and sexuality. The main dynamic in the group was one where members evaluated themselves in relation to me, feeling at one time empty and needy and at another angry, distant and competitive with one another. My pregnancy seemed to give them the impetus to strive for their own fulfilment through intimate relationships and satisfying work. Rogers' description of the process of the group as transforming envy into positive identification seems highly relevant (1994).

Unlike Rogers' groups in which her patients became more dependent in response to the pregnancy, and unlike Gavin's (1994) where there was a focus on pre-oedipal material, denial of dependency needs and focus on three-person relationships were more apparent in my group. Although this difference could be understood by differing styles of conducting, or the particular client group, I think that the use of art was the major factor. In making art the members actively engaged with their feelings, the creativity involved enabling identification with the pregnant therapist rather than temptation to regress.

The making of art also altered the transference, so, whereas in verbal therapy feelings were expressed and worked through in the transference, feelings in this group were expressed as much in the art work. This gave a more neutral arena, enabling strong feelings to be expressed, such as the attack on the foetus in Fiona's picture in the first week.

There is little in the literature to show that patients were as preoccupied with therapist transparency as they were in my group. I think this may have been to do with the group being all women. McWilliams and

Stein (1987) talk of the tendency in women's groups for women to make the therapist one of them, projecting their feelings of inadequacy on her by devaluing her. With my pregnancy the group were given an opportunity to know more about me. They responded with anxiety, unsure whether or not they welcomed it. They did not use it to attack me, perhaps because the group were less inclined to project feelings because they could express them in their art work. This phenomenon, though, could explain their preoccupation with knowing too much, or not enough about the therapist.

Perhaps another feature of the group being all women was that sexuality was a less important theme than it was in Breen's (1977). When it did emerge as a theme it was manifest in dreams and paintings associated to sexual violence. I wonder if there was a group fantasy that my pregnancy was a result of sexual violence, that is, not of my intending? This might explain the preoccupation with abortion that came up repeatedly.

Countertransference

In looking back at the group, I am aware that my response to the members' increased focus on myself was to withdraw and to try to take attention away from myself by regarding the pregnancy only as an interruption to therapy. I was also requiring the patients to be 'grown up' about it! I was not consciously aware of this at the time and recognised the value for them in exploring the feelings that it evoked. I think now that, like Anderson (1994) and Gavin (1994), I found attention to myself at this time very uncomfortable as it threatened my omnipotent defence, which was to deny my physical and emotional changes. As a result of this denial I found myself feeling resentful of their demands and aggression. I feared they would recognise that I was actually feeling out of control and very tired both before and after the birth, and because of their anger and envy feared they would take advantage of my vulnerability. I also instinctively wanted to protect the baby from attack. As a result of this I made myself rather inaccessible and was not able to process the material of the group in an effective way.

I feel, though, that as well as having a personal nature – that is, the pregnancy posed a threat to my identity as a competent professional – there is also a more socio-cultural aspect to it, which relates, I think, to the recent increase of interest in this subject. I felt I had been resonating to some powerful images at an unconscious level. One was the image of a superwoman who could manage home, children, career without any difficulty at all. The other was the ever-constant therapist, ever available to her clients during therapy time. Although at a conscious level I was quite aware of the impossibility of attaining either of these, my interventions seem to have been influenced by an attempt! Both these images are about women trying to be the same as men in the professional world. The fact that it is only very recently that the implications of the therapist's gender, including her pregnancy, have begun to receive significant attention suggests that there is some catching up to do in an integration of new ideas about therapeutic technique.

Comparing the therapist's feelings towards the group with the mother's towards her first child can help illustrate the importance of the therapist's acknowledgement and acceptance of her feelings. In my experience mothers pregnant with second children often fear that they cannot love two equally; there seems some impossibility about it. The special relationship with the first one before the birth that Rogers (1994) refers to is the shared awareness of an impending loss in that relationship. For a time after the birth, there is a period of adaptation which involves an inevitable change in the mother's feelings towards her first child. If the mother can acknowledge this quite natural process of adjustment, then I believe she can better enable the child to cope with her or his justified jealousy. It seems to me that if the therapist is able to acknowledge the fact that her feelings towards the group do change and not feel guilty about it, the clients will be able to better accept the validity of their own feelings.

CONCLUSION

The recent dramatic increase of literature about the pregnant therapist illustrates the fact that we are in a time of change. Professional women becoming pregnant are a relatively new phenomenon and there are rapid changes in thinking about working mothers. Transference and counter-transference feelings in therapy are thus influenced by social change. I have described an art psychotherapy group before and after my pregnancy to explore the complexity of the interrelationships at this particular time in the context of social change.

The use of art in the group allowed split-off feelings to be expressed and held in the images and later returned to. It also allowed members of the group the opportunity to experience their own creativity in parallel with the therapist's. It is possible that this helped in the containment of destructive and envious feelings.

ACKNOWLEDGEMENTS

I would like to thank Dr Diane Waller who supervised my MA thesis from which this chapter is derived and Dr Andrea Gilroy who read and commented on the draft. I would also like to thank the members of the group without whom this chapter could not have been written.

NOTE

1 Psychoanalysis is based around three main concepts: free association, interpretation and transference. If other techniques are used it is more correctly termed analytically orientated psychotherapy (Rycroft 1968).

BIBLIOGRAPHY

Anderson, L. 1994. 'The Experience of Being a Pregnant Group Therapist'. *Group Analysis*, vol. 27, no. 1, pp. 75–85.

Balsam, R. M. 1974. 'The Pregnant Therapist', in *On Becoming a Psychotherapist*. Boston MA: Little Brown.

Barbanel, L. 1980. 'The Therapist's Pregnancy', in Blum, B. L. (ed.) *Psychological Aspects of Pregnancy, Birthing and Bonding*. New York: Human Science Press.

Bassen, C. E. 1988. 'The Impact of the Analyst's Pregnancy on the Course of Analysis'. *Psychoanalytic Inquiry*, vol. 8, pp. 280–298.

Berman, E. 1975. 'Acting Out as a Response to the Psychiatrist's Pregnancy'. *Journal of the American Medical Women's Association*, vol. 30, pp. 456–458.

Bibring, G. L. 1950. 'Some Considerations of the Psychological Processes in Pregnancy'. *Psychoanalytic Study of the Child*, vol. 14, pp. 115–121.

Breen, D. 1977. 'Some Differences between Group and Individual Therapy In Connection with the Therapist's Pregnancy'. *International Journal of Group Psychotherapy*, vol. 27, pp. 499–506.

Clemental-Jones, C. 1985. 'The Pregnant Psychotherapist's Experience: Colleagues' and Patients' Reactions to the Author's First Pregnancy'. *British Journal of Psychotherapy*, vol. 2.

Cole, D. S. 1980. 'Therapeutic Issues Arising From the Pregnancy of the Therapist'. *Psychotherapy: Theory: Research and Practice*, vol. 17, pp. 210–213.

Coltart, N. 1993. *How to Survive as a Psychotherapist*, London: Sheldon Press.

Deben-Mager, M. 1993. 'Acting Out Transference Themes Induced by Successive Pregnancies of the Analyst'. *International Journal of Psychoanalysis*, vol. 4. p. 129.

Etchegoyen, A. 1993. 'The Analyst's Pregnancy and its Consequences on Her Work'. *International Journal of Psychoanalysis*, vol. 74, p. 141.

Fenster, S., Phillips, S. and Rapoport, E. 1986. *The Therapist's Pregnancy: Intrusion in the Analytic Space*. New Jersey: The Analytic Press.

Gavin, B. 1994. 'Transference and Countertransference in the Group's Response to the Therapist's Pregnancy'. *Group Analysis*, vol. 27, no. 11, pp. 63–74.

Guttman, H. A. 1984. 'Sexual issues in the transference and countertransference between female therapist and male patient'. *Journal of the American Academy of Psychoanalysis*, vol. 12, 4: 187–97.

Hannet, F. 1949. 'Transference Reactions to an Event in the Life of the Analyst. *Psychoanalytic Review*, vol. 36, pp. 69–81.

Lax, R. 1969. 'Some Considerations about Transference and Countertransference Manifestations Evoked by the Analyst's Pregnancy'. *International Journal of Psychoanalysis*, vol. 50, pp. 363–375.

McWilliams, N. and Stein, J. 1987. 'Women's Groups Led by Women: The Management of Devaluing Transference'. *International Journal of Group Psychotherapy*, vol. 37 (2). April.

Maguire, M. 1995. *Men, Women, Passion and Power*. London: Routledge.

Mariotti, P. 1993. 'The Analyst's Pregnancy: The Patient, the Analyst and the Space of the Unknown'. *International Journal of Psychoanalysis*, vol. 74, p. 151.

Miller, A. 1984. 'Art Therapy with the Elderly and Mentally Ill', in Dalley, T. (ed.) *An Introduction to the Use of Art as a Therapeutic Technique*. London: Tavistock.

Nadelson, C., Notman, M., Arons, E. and Feldman, J. 1974. 'The Pregnant Therapist'. *American Journal of Psychiatry*, vol. 131, pp. 1107–1111.

Naperstak. 1976. 'Treatment Guidelines for the Pregnant Therapist'. *Journal of Psychiatric Opinion*, vol. 13 (1), pp. 20–25.

Paluzny, M. and Poznansky, E. 1971. 'Reactions of Patients during the Pregnancy of the Psychotherapist'. *Child Psychiatry and Human Development*, vol. 1, pp. 266–274.

Penn, L. 1986. 'The Pregnant Therapist: Transference and Countertransference Issues', in J. Albent (ed.) *Psychoanalysis and Women*.

Price, J. 1988. 'Single Sex Therapy Groups', in M. Aveline and W. Dryden (eds) *Group Therapy in Britain*. Open University Press.

Raphael-Leff, J. 1980. 'Psychotherapy with Pregnant Women', in B. Blum (ed.) *Psychological Aspects of Pregnancy, Birthing and Bonding*. New York: Human Sciences Press.

Rogers, C. 1994. 'The Group and the Group Analyst's Pregnancies'. *Group Analysis*, vol. 27, no. 1, pp. 51–61.

Rycroft, C. 1968. *A Critical Dictionary of Psychoanalysis*. Harmondsworth: Penguin.

Schaverien, J. 1995. *Desire and the Female Therapist*. London: Routledge.

Chapter 11

Art therapy and empowerment in a women's self-help project

Marian Liebmann

INTRODUCTION

This chapter describes an art therapy group run for women who attend a project in Bristol, on a large, deprived housing estate on the edge of the city. It outlines the commitment of the project to empower people, and how the art therapy group fits into this project and makes its own contribution. The development of the group is described, and the art therapy work done by some of the most regular attenders. The group members themselves have taken part in the writing, and the way this happened is also documented.

THE NEWPIN PROJECT

NEWPIN stands for New Parent Infant Network. Its aims are to

- break the cyclical effect of destructive family behaviour
- prevent child abuse
- raise the self-esteem of individual parents who are suffering from depression and loss of identity
- inspire parents to recognise the value of consistent good practice in caring for children

(NEWPIN Information Pack)

NEWPIN combines self-help, support, group work, therapy and training to achieve lasting change in family behaviour. Parents (mostly women) may be referred to NEWPIN by a social work or health professional, or may come through contact with another project member, or refer themselves. Whatever the route, it must be the individual's own decision to join NEWPIN.

The programme starts with the use of the drop-in and creche, to build up a wider circle of friends and take advantage of the twenty-four-hour support network. An existing NEWPIN member is matched to the person to provide support. When the time is right, the individual enrols for the personal development course (including assertiveness, employment skills, self-assessment and much more), and works towards changes in their life. Individual and group verbal therapy is part of this process. As members become more experienced in the project, they in turn help to support new members, and also take part in the running of the project. In time, they can undertake further courses to become co-ordinators and obtain paid work with NEWPIN or in a related field.

NEWPIN began in 1980 in South London with one centre, then four more. The Bristol NEWPIN was set up in 1992, on a large, deprived housing estate on the edge of the city, about six miles south of the centre. Few people living on the estate have paid work, especially since the closure of a large tobacco factory in the area, and all the usual problems associated with poverty are in evidence: high crime rates, abuse of drugs and alcohol, mistreatment of children, overstretched agencies, and few facilities. The NEWPIN project itself has struggled to raise funds and find suitable accommodation for its activities. For the first two years it was housed in temporary buildings belonging to other projects, such as the Community Farm, and this limited the range of activities and who could attend. In April 1994 the project moved into its own building and this signalled the start of a new phase.

Although NEWPIN deliberately uses the word 'parent' in its title, and one of its publicity leaflets includes a photograph of a young man with his child, in practice almost all the members are women, and this was certainly true for the Bristol project. In the area where it is based, women are almost always the main parents, and often lone parents, and are the ones to suffer the depression and lack of identity which often result from this.

Women's oppression is mediated and perpetuated by many of the agencies of society. Often abused (both physically and sexually) by their families and 'friends', women grow up and may be forced to continue this pattern with abusive partners or husbands, suffering injury, hardship, depression and poor self-esteem. Turning to social services or psychiatry, they often find themselves in a hierarchical relationship which perpetuates their lack of self-esteem (Corob, 1987).

There is, therefore, a need to provide facilities which empower women and help them change through an equal partnership. NEWPIN was set up to try to achieve this, and the Bristol project sees itself mainly as a resource for mothers and their children.

THE ART THERAPY GROUP

The art therapy group was started for several reasons. The co-ordinator was interested in the potential of art therapy to provide a balance to the verbal therapy through non-verbal expression and creativity, and be of particular help to those finding it hard to express themselves in words. She also saw a need to provide a forum for two groups who had completed the personal development programme to come together. For a while the project was 'between therapists' for the verbal therapy component, and there was a need to provide a therapeutic input for new members to the project.

Art therapy in itself can contribute to personal empowerment through personal creativity and self-expression. Art therapy can be practised so as to emphasise the empowerment of those taking part (Dickson, 1982; Houston, 1984). In the context of the NEWPIN project, this meant sharing with the group most of the decisions about the running of the group, and being willing to be as much part of the group as is possible, while also being responsible for it (Ernst and Goodison, 1981).

The proposed art therapy group was discussed by members, and I was asked to provide an outline for further discussion as follows:

Art therapy is ...

a way of using art materials for personal self-expression. It can be fun and also serious. It can provide a space for people to play and be creative in their own way. Sometimes it helps people become more aware of their feelings, and can also provide a release for those feelings.

Art therapy is not ...

about someone else reading your mind (that is for everyone to do for themselves) or about being 'good at art' – anyone can do it.

I was keen that the art therapy group should be integrated into the rest of the project, so the co-ordinator added: 'The Art Therapist and the Co-ordinator will be talking to each other in order that members of NEWPIN will receive the support that they need, and for their mutual benefit and good.'

The group was then advertised to all NEWPIN members as a facility available to them. The group started in autumn 1993 as a weekly group on Friday mornings, and ran until January 1995. It was held in a room in the local youth club for two terms until NEWPIN's premises were ready the following April.

From the start, I wanted to create an atmosphere of safety, so that the women could develop at their own pace and in their own time. We spent most of the first session developing ground rules, a familiar concept to them as part of a therapeutic project. The list they made was:

- Confidentiality – it all stays here
- No 'rubbishing things'
- Commitment – come every week
- Be on time

- No put-downs of others
- No smoking in the room, but OK to have one outside the room
- No alcohol or drugs
- Honesty
- Tea to start with, and tea-break of 15 minutes in the middle (plus food or a smoke if wanted)
- It's OK to 'pass' on exercises or sharing if it doesn't feel right

We got these out at the beginning of every term, and checked through them, especially for new people. Over the four terms, extra ground rules were added:

- Pictures do not have to be good or 'nice'
- Prepare the room beforehand if possible
- All help clear up
- Respect for equipment
- The space is ours

The youth club room was quite suitable in many ways, being self-contained and quite cosy, though not always very clean; and it had a sink and running water. There was a locked store-room in which to keep the art materials, but the women did not feel safe leaving their work there, so everyone made a folder, and these were taken back to the project (or later to my house) for safe keeping, until the project moved to its own premises.

The pattern adopted was for each term to start with three open sessions for new people to join, and then become a closed group for the rest of the term. There were six members who became the mainstay of the group: Angie, Carol, Jean, Karen, Kim and Tanya. Others, such as Sue, came for shorter lengths of time, and were then prevented from further attendance by illness or crises, or drifted away from NEWPIN, or decided art therapy was not for them. The weekly attendance varied from two to eight with an average of four to five.

At the women's request, I either brought a theme each week, tailored to their needs, or else one was arrived at after an initial round of how they were feeling (Liebmann, 1986). However, I made it clear that, if they had something they wanted to express, the space was there for them to use how they wanted. As time went on, although they still wanted me to 'have something up my sleeve', increasingly they knew what they wanted to do, and got on with it.

At the start of the group, some women found it hard to get going, and were often exhausted after half an hour's work. Gradually the time lengthened until some of them wanted to work for over an hour, using an increasing variety of media. I always made sure we had some time for discussing the work, but this time could vary from ten minutes to three-quarters of an hour. It was part of our ground rules that anyone could say 'pass' or simply talk about their work.

I joined in with the activity, according to the participative nature of the group, but initially did not share what I had done, feeling the space was there for them rather than me. As the group progressed, the women challenged me on this, and I also talked about my work.

The group was intended to be ongoing. However, a local funding crisis in the late autumn of 1994, when expected grants from social services and mental health funding bodies were not renewed, meant that the art therapy group had to come to a fairly abrupt end just after Christmas.

THE PROCESS OF WRITING

To fit in with the ethos of the group, I did not want to write just from my perspective, but to find a way of enabling the women to put their point of view. In this way, the chapter would be part of the life of the group and the project, rather than something external to it. Of course, this was no easy task. For women who found it difficult to start art therapy, writing about it would be even more difficult.

In June 1994, NEWPIN held an open day. To my surprise (and the co-ordinator's), several of the women put up some of their pictures, and wrote about the art therapy in their annual report:

Sue: I go to art therapy which I find very helpful as I can put down on paper what I feel, take my frustration out on the paper and no one will question me or pester me for an answer or explanation.

Jean: Art therapy for me means my own space, somewhere safe to take my feelings. No one laughs at me – (I think I can't draw). It really helps me understand why I'm feeling this way. My scream on paper looked like an eye. I really needed someone to see how angry I was and support me. My wild horse, I need at times for freedom and strength to carry on. My flower that survived hell and fire. I am a survivor. I can do things on paper that I don't feel confident to do in life. I can transfer my anger, my pain and my tears to paper. I can have a swing and pick wild flowers. Art therapy is MY space where it is safe to be me.

I was also aware of the growth of 'new paradigm' research (Payne, 1993; Reason, 1988; Reason and Rowan, 1981), which acknowledges all the human factors affecting research and includes clients as participant co-researchers rather than 'subjects'. Views of client can significantly alter the course of research and its findings. I felt that writing about the group would benefit from this approach, and also be more in keeping with the philosophy of the group.

We started by brainstorming all their ideas, in any order, on to several sheets of flip chart paper.

Next we looked at *how* to actually get something down on paper, quite a formidable task! Each woman selected a personal mix of writing (by hand or on NEWPIN's word processor), dictating into a tape, and personal interview. I agreed to write up the ideas into a set of questions to act as prompts. We set deadlines, and three women produced a piece of writing. The co-ordinator, Suzi, also decided to contribute something. At the last minute, two others decided after all to add their views, by personal interview.

In putting the work together, I was faced with a dilemma: to preserve each person's work intact (and possibly lose sight of the key themes) or organise it thematically (and possibly lose track of the people and their development). After some thought, I decided the latter would be clearer, and that the group members' personalities were strong enough to shine through!

The writing is arranged in order of the themes picked out, with the women's contributions in the same order (alphabetical), to make it easier to follow the personal threads.

When we started writing, I reassured everyone that names would be changed to preserve anonymity, and the women were greatly relieved. However, by the time they had finished writing, and commenting on the succession of drafts I produced, they all decided to stay with their real names.

PERSONAL BACKGROUNDS

The women wrote about their personal backgrounds, and why they came to NEWPIN, very vividly:

Angie: I am one of five children. I didn't have a very happy childhood as my father was a very domineering man. I was quite unhappy at school and left when I was 15 with no qualifications. I worked in shops until I met my first husband and got pregnant at 19, when I moved away to Norwich. My husband was a very violent man who hospitalised and raped me throughout our seven years of marriage. In the seven years together we had three children. We split up when my youngest child, Sarah, was 7 months old. By this time we had moved back to Bristol. My ex-husband stopped seeing my children, so I was left to bring them up alone. Later I met another man and we lived together until I fell pregnant. My boy friend made me get rid of the baby, and we split up a few weeks later. I then met my present husband, and thought at last I and my children would be happy. But he had three girls from a previous marriage who were in and out of care, and soon they were creating problems, so not only did I have my own family to deal with, I had his family as well. We have been married for seven years now and our marriage is in trouble .

I heard about NEWPIN from a friend and phoned Suzi, the co-ordinator, to see if it would be beneficial to me and my family. I know

I need to change the way I relate to people. All my life I have had people criticise me and put me down. So I tend to put on this act as if nothing hurts me or worries me, but in reality I am hurt by lots of things and worry about everything especially things that affect my children. I need to be loved and needed. Through NEWPIN I think I am slowly learning to change. NEWPIN has made me look at myself in a different way, so that I understand myself better – and also the people around me, like my family.

Carol: We are a group of parents in NEWPIN, which is a project for parents who wish to relate to their past, and accept what has happened to them, and work out how their life with their family could be better. NEWPIN has been going for about three years now in Hartcliffe. The group does things to help us get in touch with our feelings. Some things run for a short time and others run for much longer. One of these is art therapy.

Jean: I am a member of NEWPIN, which is a support group for main carers and their children. It is much more beneficial to my children and myself than any other groups I have been involved with (e.g. mother and baby, mother and toddlers, playgroup). It is fairly structured: you do a 38-week personal development programme which covers all aspects of your life as a woman. Its aims are for parents and children to achieve positive changes in their lives and relationships, based on respect, empathy, confidentiality and trust. Both children's and parents' views are respected.

I came to NEWPIN about two and a half years ago, because I just felt everything was useless and hopeless. I didn't really understand why at that time. I only knew I didn't want things to be that way any more. I'd had cervical cancer and also my daughter, who was only 14, became pregnant and had a baby son. I was trying to cope with my other teenager and three younger children, who were 4, 3 and just over a year old. I was also very very tired. That was about the only feeling I knew at that time – and anger, but that was always well hidden.

STARTING ART THERAPY

There were the expected feelings of apprehension about starting art therapy, even though all the women had been involved in the decision:

Angie: When I started, I thought the art therapist would say, 'Draw a plant' and then analyse how we did it. I thought you had to be able to draw, then I realised you didn't, which is just as well because I can't. I've learnt that you've just got to let things come out without trying to control it – sort of letting go.

Carol: Art therapy started for us about one and a half years ago. There were four of us in the group to start with. Some people came and didn't like it, but new people have started and stayed. I didn't know what to expect or what I would get out of this, only time would tell me. The reason I joined this group was to help me to understand my feelings and build my confidence in myself and others.

Jean: I started the art therapy at the beginning. I wanted to belong, I didn't want to be different. I was very frightened, I felt I couldn't draw, and when I did, I felt everyone would laugh. We set ground rules, the same really as we have for NEWPIN, confidentiality and being non-judgmental, not rubbishing ourselves or each other's work, respecting each other and supporting each other. I now know I will not be laughed at. Other members of my group really do support me when I'm angry or upset.

Karen: When I first started art therapy, I thought the art therapist would analyse all my pictures and tell me I was a nutter. Now I think art therapy works like counselling – you work things out for yourself, and analyse your own pictures.

I couldn't draw before I started art therapy. Now I think – what's drawing anyway? I like making a mess!

BEING PART OF A GROUP

The group aspect was very important to the women, in building confidence and providing support. The other side of the coin was that, if the group dynamics were difficult, everyone was affected:

Angie: The group's been a support just by being there. It's important to me to know who's going to be there, and that it's the same people who keep coming – it helps to make the group feel safe.

If it's a day when hardly anyone turns up, I feel they don't value the group, and then I feel devalued as well. And if people arrive late, then I don't know whether to start or not. Also if there aren't enough people, there's nobody to share what you've done. On the other hand, if there's too many, then there's not enough room and I can't have my own space – there are physical restraints with the room.

Having other people around changes my moods too, as I empathise with them. Sometimes I look at someone else's work and it triggers something in me. It's only a painting, but it can be very powerful.

Although it's hard work it can also be a laugh sometimes. We don't always sit and paint. It's a group, so sometimes we talk and discuss, and say funny things.

Karen: The commitment of the group was important to me, the fact that it was the same people each week, and nobody laughed at me.

THE PERSONAL ART THERAPY PROCESS

All the members of the group were able to write about the process of art therapy for them:

Angie: Art therapy is one way of expressing my emotions and being accepted for who I am, and also it is a way of coming to terms with my past. In art therapy I can say things in a safe environment without feeling judged or being laughed at. Sometimes I am really surprised at a picture I paint – I look at it, and it just expresses the way I am feeling that day. But weeks later the same picture might have a different meaning. Or I can tell I have moved on from that particular problem or time in my life.

You start off with a blank piece of paper, and suddenly it's full of things, and I'm not sure how they got there! I look at these things, and often I can relate them to something in my life that's around for me that day – it's really surprising. Sometimes I see it during the session, sometimes only much later. Because you've got something physical to look back at, it's easier to recognise you've moved on from that.

Things can change even during one session. I might come in feeling really angry and choose a colour that feels right, then do an angry painting, sploshing paint about. I get it out and get rid of it, and move on to other moods. I could move through several emotions while I'm painting – and then two or three more when others are talking. It can be quite draining actually!

Carol: Art therapy gives you your own space, helps you to express yourself, and get support for yourself and others. It's a place where you can go and put on paper what you want to express but don't know how to – or you might not know what is going on inside you until you put it down on paper. It helps to build up your confidence in yourself and others. You don't have to share what is going on for you if you don't wish.

It was hard to work through the bad stuff to see what was going on for me, and to look at myself in a way I didn't before, and to talk about my work and my feelings. There were good times and bad times; there were times of sadness and times of gladness. But to look back on the work of my life in pictures helps me to see how far I have come.

Jean: If I'm angry or upset, usually by the end of a session the pain is less severe. I can get rid of a lot of it on to my paper. It feels easier for me to put it on paper than to say it out loud. It's easier now than at the beginning to get the feelings out.

Several pictures I've done, I've felt really exhausted afterwards. Most of these times are when I'm angry, and I want to get rid of some of it.

I've been surprised how things come out of me at times without me really knowing. I'm thinking of my scream that looked like an eye, I really did want someone to see how angry I was. I couldn't ask for help, but I really did need it at the time.

Karen: Art therapy has definitely helped with feelings. It's difficult to elaborate on that. I think it helps you work through them.

MATERIALS

Two of the group commented on the materials they used:

Angie: I choose paints normally, though I have used other things. I don't like using them straight from the palette, I like to mix my own colours because it's a surprise. I feel I can be more creative with paint. If I'm using felt tips or crayons and I make a mistake, I can't change it. If I paint a mistake, I can disguise it or go over it. Paints make me feel freer – I get lots of surprises.

Often it just grows. I start off with a mistake and like the effect, so experiment a bit more, until I do one I really like. I'm surprised how creative I can be, I didn't think I was any good at art at school. I think I'm not too bad now.

Jean: In the beginning I tried different materials but after a few sessions I would nearly always go for pastels. They were nice to use, they always looked good to me. I'd like things to be nice, hiding my true feelings with nice things is something I've discovered about myself.

As the sessions went on and I felt safer, it became easier for me to put my true self on paper. I went on to using paints – it was OK for me to show how messy, dirty and angry I felt. I could use a really big brush. Just trying to write this down, I can feel all the anger going from my shoulders down my arms through my brush, and pushing right across my paper in large violent strokes.

PERSONAL CHANGES

The women were able to articulate some of their personal discoveries, and changes they had noticed in themselves, which they attributed to their involvement in art therapy:

Angie: One change I've noticed is that I'm not so critical of my own work. I used to always think it was rubbish. Now I'm more tolerant of myself.

I am not sure if my pictures have changed. I think I experiment more, try out new things. I feel more able to go with my own emotions, to do what I want to do, without always thinking of others. I still feel fairly new to all this. At the beginning I thought 'It's got to be good' because I was so aware of other people. I think my pictures are better now because I'm not trying so hard. I do them to please me more than other people. They make me feel good about me.

I am also learning to come to terms with the sad parts of my life, like my first marriage and the loss of my baby. I know I can't rush the changes, but with art there is plenty of time and everyone has their own space, and I feel each picture is equally important as another. Before I came to NEWPIN, I didn't know what art therapy was, but now it is a very important part of my life.

Carol: Art therapy helped me to have time and space for myself and not just for my family. As time went on, it helped me learn to relax and have fun. My life has changed for the better, so I feel it's time for me to move on from NEWPIN. So I don't come to the art therapy group any more, I do it in my own time. I miss the people but I thank them for their support.

Jean: It's easier most weeks to start, I don't have to sit and worry about what to do. I just do it, my confidence has improved.

Before I came to art therapy, I found it really difficult to express any feelings. I just didn't understand. I could say what I felt I was expected to say. But I didn't experience any feelings at all. I now know different feelings – I think, 'Why am I crying – is it sadness, happiness or anger?' I used to try to cover up my real feelings with nice things – I now feel that I can say at times or know what I am really feeling. I have also discovered through art therapy that my anger can be controlled.

Karen: It's confidence – I can draw something now – I just go and do it.

Suzi, the co-ordinator, also noticed movement and change:

The other striking thing about the sessions, was that they became a source of inspiration and strength to the group. Members were able to realise that we can be our own best helpers. It was extremely moving to see women finding their own inner sources of power and strength, which when externalised in their work, became symbols of hope for them at difficult times. Indeed, they hung their paintings on the wall of the living room, where they became important symbols for other women, who were not themselves participants in the art therapy group.

KEY PICTURES

I asked members of the group, if they could, to select one or two pictures which stuck in their minds as particularly meaningful. Some women mentioned several pictures.

Angie: One drawing I did when I first started art therapy was of a police car with a blue flashing light, prison and a key. The police never helped me because the violence was 'domestic'. I can look at that picture now and know that I am no longer locked into that relationship; I am free and my first husband can no longer hurt me. He no longer has control over me or the children, and thankfully they are growing into good caring young adults who want to make something of their lives. I am really proud of my children.

Another one shows a shape which starts off with nice yellow stuff in the middle, when you're born, and gets worse and worse as life goes on. It even goes off into space and bits break off. I put a line round it, which is strength, to keep it together, but it doesn't work, it still all gets out.

I did a collage of Me – the things I like and the things I am – I collected pictures over quite a long time. There's a cup of Horlicks, my gran's mirror, a Christmas tree, shopping, vegetables as I'm vegetarian, sweeteners, long nails, a mother with children, a dolphin, a desert island, an ironing board (I hate ironing), and my blue car, which means a lot to me.

Carol: This black picture [Figure 11.1] is one of the first pictures I did in art therapy. It was a time when all things seemed black and black. I felt anger, bitterness and other mixed-up feelings. I painted a large piece of white paper black, then, when it dried, I stuck pictures on to it that meant different things which were bad, in and around my life. By the time I finished the picture, I felt a little better and could talk about it.

The other picture I did towards the end of my time in the art therapy group. At this time of my life, I felt I needed to get away on holiday, but for many reasons I couldn't, so this was a way I could do it, just in imagination. I was on my own little island, relaxing with one other special person. At the end I talked about what this picture meant to me, and what I had got out of doing it. It also helped others in the group to smile and laugh a little.

Jean: My first experience was a collage, which we did on the personal development programme. I found it really incredible, just cutting out pictures, then looking at them afterwards and relating them all to my life – a clock face (no time for me), a pile of dirty dishes, brothers and sisters – and the abuse I suffered. It was all there.

I remember being really angry inside at one session, and I felt I couldn't put this on paper. I wanted to use paint this session, but I felt it would just go all over the place, the walls and the ceiling as well as the

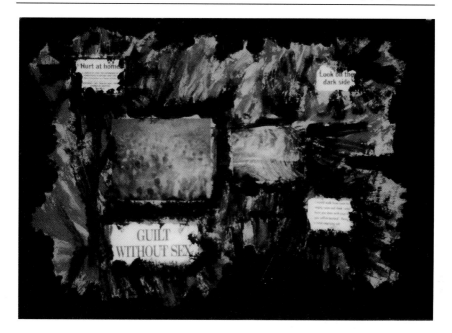

Figure 11.1 Carol's Black Picture

floor. Marian, our art therapist, suggested I try anyway, and all my anger (the paint) stayed on the paper. I felt great relief. Anger really scares me. But I felt after this session that I was able to control my anger. It doesn't have to turn into violence. Another picture that comes to mind is one I did in a session when we were asked to draw a wild animal that we would like to be. I started with a small piece of paper, but it wasn't big enough. I sellotaped four pieces of paper together and drew a large white powerful horse searching for freedom. I was frightened to show this, thinking everyone would laugh. But I felt safe enough in my group to say how I was feeling. I did show it and no one laughed. I really wanted to be strong and free. I now realise I am strong, I don't have to take everything that's thrown at me. It's easier now for me to challenge things and to be assertive – though not always, as it's hard to change, even when you realise these things. It can be really difficult for me to hold on to things that make me feel more comfortable in myself.

My 'Kindred Spirit' picture: when this collage came out, I didn't realise what it was about. I didn't understand. I didn't immediately connect with the aerial photography of patterns found in circles of corn. Other pictures have been the same for me, it can be days, weeks or even months before I can make a connection with part of (or all) of my picture. I started to cut the words 'Kindred Spirit' off my corn circles, but stopped – I didn't know why. I didn't know what 'kindred spirit' meant, I just felt it had to be part of my picture. The other smaller pictures I'd cut out and put round the outside, were all things I connected with – a dolphin, a bird, natives – simple uncomplicated normal natural things, expressing a real need to be free.

I see this picture clearly now. All these different pictures of corn circles, like all the flashbacks, memories of sexual abuse – are they real or not? I now believe these pictures in my head, they did happen, they are real.

Kim: I started another picture, not knowing what I was doing, just trying out oil pastels, in broad stripes up and down, and across the paper. Afterwards, when I looked at it, it seemed like 'life behind bars' – which was how I felt, trapped, especially by the black I felt I was inside, looking out of a window.

An important step for me came when I first realised I could make a mess. I'm such a tidy person as a rule. And I do quite like the result as well (blue, red and yellow splodges), which is surprising.

MY VIEW

Originally I had intended the women's voices to stand on their own, but as we approached the third draft, they said they felt it was incomplete, and wanted a contribution from me concerning the progress I thought they had made. So I made the attempt.

Initially Angie felt she had to keep up a bright and cheerful façade, but as time went on, she was able to express her real feelings – sometimes happy, sometimes sad, sometimes angry – and to use a greater range of colours. She showed considerable creativity in mixing colours and using paint, and came to experience a real enjoyment. As someone who was used to always thinking of others in her life, and never herself, she found a space where she could begin to develop a sense of self. While reading the pieces of writing, I also realised that the group aspect of the art therapy sessions was very important to her.

When Carol started art therapy, I often had difficulty understanding her when she was talking. Her pictures, while always colourful, were rather disjointed. As time went on, her pictures became more coherent and she could communicate better verbally too. She gained tremendous enjoyment from the materials (the messier the better on occasions!) and found a space for herself in the midst of considerable family turmoil.

At the start of the art therapy group, Jean found it very hard to put anything down on paper, and became exhausted after a short while. She seemed desperately tired and quite unwell most of the time, but insisted on doing things for others just the same. The first breakthrough came with the 'wild horse', when Jean was able to imagine herself 'strong, wild and free', and this was followed later by unleashing her anger on to huge pieces of paper on the floor. She hardly missed a single session. She changed visibly into someone who seemed altogether more solid, robust and assertive – her family circumstances remained difficult, but she had a different attitude and was no longer so ground down by them.

Karen was able to use the sessions to explore quite deep problems. She did not always want to share these explicitly with the group, but it was clear that she knew what her pictures were about. She also used paint and crayons to work through some difficult feelings which blocked communication. As time went on, she took more responsibility for her own moods and how to deal with them.

Initially very diffident and dissatisfied with herself, Kim admitted to an obsession with tidiness. She found that making a mess was possible, and could even be enjoyable. She began to express her feelings with startling honesty and freshness.

For the first ten sessions, Tanya was occupied with a series of Disney cartoons for her children's bedroom, and she was proud of the results. She seemed to find it hard to be open about her feelings. Later she went on to experiment with paint, and was able to appreciate even paintings where she was not quite sure what was going on, and talk about some of the feelings involved.

As a group, the members got on well, and this contributed to the powerful experience. They did not always agree, or even get on with each other, but found ways of relating through the painting and the images. They were often struggling against the odds – and succeeded.

We did not do much group painting, as the women mostly preferred to work individually. However, at the end of term on two occasions, we painted 'gifts' (tangible and imaginary) for each other, and I was impressed how sensitive and thoughtful they were towards each other.

The last group painting expressed the essence of the group. Tanya painted flowers for all the group members, and Karen fireworks. Jean did a sturdy tree reaching out to everyone else, and Angie unified the painting by scattering white paint carefully over the whole.

REFLECTIONS ON GENDER ISSUES

It is interesting to reflect on how far the experience of art therapy for this group reflects gender issues. The themes that arose in this group are ones that are familiar to those who run women's groups, or have been members of them, especially in areas of deprivation: low self-esteem, abuse, violence, lack of material resources and overburdening family responsibilities. However, these themes may also emerge in other contexts. It may be useful to compare experiences of this group and other client groups I have worked with, such as probation clients and mental health clients.

Some of these themes may also be features of the mixed-gender art therapy groups of mental health services. Men too can suffer from low self-esteem, poverty and violence. This may be due to personal history or structural factors such as inner-city poverty, but is rarely due to just the fact that they are men.

The extra factor in women's groups relates to the power imbalance between men and women, which makes physical and sexual abuse more likely. This destructive use of power can also be exacerbated by conditions of poverty and unemployment, where men are unable to exert traditional sources of power, such as taking pride in work and being the breadwinner.

In my experience, most members of women's groups have responsibilities for children. This is obviously true for the NEWPIN women, whose reason for attending was connected with their children, but was also true for women's groups I have run in a probation context, and for mixed groups in a mental health context.

The same has not has not been true for most men in the art therapy groups I have led. In the probation context, many were single men, and those with partners and families generally took only a small part in child-care responsibilities. In an inner-city mental health team context, although the expression of their problems was different, the picture was similar – most of the men were single or were married men with no children.

This general pattern, reinforced by cultural patterns and social arrangements, influences the concerns of women and men in art therapy groups. Women tend to worry more about others – their children, their partners and how to make ends meet for the family – and have difficulty claiming their own space. Men seem to worry about themselves and reflect on the harsh treatment they have received from others. (This is, of course, a simplification, and I can think of many examples which do not follow this pattern.) One small way in which this was expressed in the art therapy group was the women's concern about using too much paint, sometimes trying to scrape left-over paint back into the bottles at the end of a session. This concern to 'scrimp and save' also meant that the women took some time before they were able to use the materials freely.

Art therapy is often recommended to help people who experience difficulty in expressing feelings. Women and men are educated very differently with respect to feelings: women may display feelings, as long as they do not include anger, while men often do not display feelings at all. Much of the work I undertook in the probation context was concerned with helping men get in touch with feelings they often did not even realise they had – but which lay behind their violent actions. The women in the NEWPIN group knew very well what their feelings were – but needed 'permission' to express them, especially anger.

When groups start work together, it takes time for trust to build. A lack of trust can exhibit itself very differently in women's and men's groups. On the whole, women are very cautious about what they will express if they do not trust others in the group. Men may also reserve themselves in this way, but some men 'rubbish' the sessions or even damage other people's work. This may happen particularly in the probation context, but I have also witnessed it elsewhere, although not in a mental health context. I have only very rarely seen women damage each other's work.

A very important difference between women's groups, on the one hand, and mixed or men's groups on the other, is one which may never raise its head explicitly. This concerns sexual abuse. In the NEWPIN group this was not referred to directly very often, but was never far from the surface, and there was an implicit understanding that it was part of the women's experience. In a mixed group in a mental health context, one woman gave me a note to read after the session, saying that, while she enjoyed the group, she could not bring up the things that were troubling her (concerning sexual abuse) because she did not want to do this in front of men. In this respect, a women's group fulfils a function that other groups cannot.

In this connection, the gender of the art therapist can be very important. As a female art therapist (and a mother), I was aware that these facts enabled the women to feel safer expressing feelings concerning general 'women's issues' (such as childbirth, marriage, gynaecological problems, relationships with men, relationships with children) and also their allusions to sexual abuse. It could be quite difficult for a male art therapist to work with this group in this context. Many male art therapists working with women who have been sexually abused, make extra and separate provision for women clients to discuss explicit details of sexual abuse with a female colleague, to avoid unwittingly being agents of revictimisation; and they also arrange to be supervised by women colleagues.

The issues are not the same as in the 'vice versa' situation – a female therapist with a men's group – where, despite the extra authority of the therapist, there remains the possibility of the female therapist being victimised by men in traditional ways. In these situations, it can be helpful to have a male co-therapist, to notice if this happens, and to act as a role model.

On the other hand, there can also be a 'homely' dimension to such groups, as men who have suffered childhood damage often find it easier to talk to women than men, reflecting the fact that more abuse (though not all abuse) is perpetrated by men, and men often find it difficult to talk to each other about feelings.

Art therapy groups also naturally reflect, in the themes that emerge, the contexts in which they take place. In a mental health context, these may include depression, loneliness, and the perceived stigma of being a mental health patient. In a probation context, crime, poverty, unemployment, alcohol and drugs may feature. In the NEWPIN context, children, families and relationships were themes that reoccurred; and these are all associated with women's issues as described above.

This led to a consciousness-raising aspect to the project, and of the art therapy group, which provided a vehicle for expression – of being a women's group in a deprived area. They began to recognise the social factors influencing their condition, mental as well as physical. This brought the group together and gave rise to the other noticeable strand of themes – their courage, tenacity, friendship and inner resourcefulness in the face of enormous problems. It also lifted the burden of feeling isolated and personally responsible for all the bad things which happened to them, and helped them move forward.

CONCLUSION

The art therapy group in the NEWPIN project provided an opportunity for women with many problems to express themselves, gain confidence and move forward in difficult circumstances. By engaging actively in art therapy, in a women's group, the women empowered themselves to feel more in control of their lives.

Suzi, the co-ordinator, summed it up in these words,

> At NEWPIN, our belief is that everyone has the potential to give and receive love and to develop meaning and purpose in life. I feel that the art work in particular has been crucial for some women in gaining insight, and developing an inner sense of their own worth. It has been a pleasure to see how the sessions assisted in helping people become more confident and 'whole'. However, 'no gain without pain', these sessions are not for the fainthearted. With this in mind, I have been conscious of the commitment and courage of the women to working in this way.

Art therapy has been crucial in enabling these women to find a voice, and reach a stage where they will continue to grow and develop.

BIBLIOGRAPHY

Corob, A. (1987). *Working with Depressed Women*. Aldershot: Gower.
Dickson, A. (1982). *A Woman in Your Own Right*. London: Quartet Books.
Ernst, S. and Goodison, L. (1981). *In Our Own Hands*. London: The Women's Press.
Houston, G. (1984). *The Red Book of Groups*. Rochester: Rochester Foundation.
Liebmann, M. (1986). *Art Therapy for Groups*. London: Croom Helm (now published by Routledge).
NEWPIN Information Pack.
Payne, H. (ed.) (1993). *Handbook of Inquiry in the Arts Therapies: One River, Many Currents*. London: Jessica Kingsley Publishers.

Reason, P. (ed.) (1988). *Human Inquiry in Action: Developments in new paradigm research*. London: Sage.

Reason, P. and Rowan, J. (eds) (1981). *Human Inquiry: A sourcebook of new paradigm research*. Chichester: John Wiley.

Chapter 12

Black on black art therapy
Dreaming in colour

Jean Campbell and Doris Abra Gaga

The issues of race, culture and therapy are varied, exciting and challenging to art therapists. These issues influence black and white therapists alike while working in a multi-racial context as art therapists.[1] What knowledge and value bases do we need to work in this area?

This chapter has been developed from an Art Therapy Race and Culture Group (ARC) meeting where members presented a number of case studies which they felt highlighted issues of working as therapists with black clients. On reading a transcript of Doris Gaga's case study a number of questions came to mind: What was happening in the therapeutic encounter between two black women, a client and her therapist? What was significant about that encounter, and how did it relate to current art therapy theory and practice?

This coincided with my being introduced to some reading by a family therapist colleague on 'narrative' or co-constructionist theory and therapy.[2] In a co-constructionist approach the client is considered to be the authority on their own experience. Meaning and understanding is seen as created in the dialogue between two people, the therapist and the client. However, this approach does not privilege the therapist's expert knowledge. This theoretical framework provides a good foundation for effective art therapy work in which issues of gender, race and the dilemma of power and racism can be worked with in an open way.

'Guess what. I had a dream and I was black in my dream. And the people in my dream were black and that was OK. I was so happy.'

These words were said by a black client to her black art therapist towards the end of an eighteen-month period of art therapy.

What story do you deduce from this? That the client didn't use to dream of herself and others as black and that she was unhappy about this? Or that she was keen to report a change in her inner life, reflected in her dreams? Both answers are true. Equally important, however, is that the words show a coming together or conflation of meanings; socio-political, historical, subjective and visual within the therapeutic encounter. It is this area which I wish to explore further – the therapeutic possibility of a black therapist working with a black client on their lived experience around race and colour, factors which influenced this particular therapeutic relationship, and also theoretical considerations.

THE THERAPEUTIC POSSIBILITIES: BLACK DEMONS AND WHITE ANGELS

Sally Skaife, in her paper on the 'Dialectics of Art Therapy' (1995: 2) makes liberal use of the work 'radical' in reference to both the potential and process of art therapy. 'Art therapy by its nature, is radical. It is about empowering people. By making art, people discover their ability to act and create originally. Art provided a mirror or comment on society. It reaches beyond the conventions of daily life.' In my experience this radical potential enables us to offer a particularly effective therapeutic experience to black clients whose problems are closely linked with negative life experiences around race and colour. This is because art therapy is unique, it is the only therapeutic approach which brings words and language, concrete visual images, colour and action together.

The word 'black' is suffused with many meanings. In the external world it encapsulates socio/political realities, culture and history. My starting point when writing this part of the chapter is familial and personal. 'Black' also describes states of mind, emotions and qualities of being which are part of the richness of language shared between all people of all colours. The negative, racist and wounding associations around blackness, which are compounded by direct experiences of abuse do seem to make it so much harder for us, as black people, to explore our inner world of shadow and darkness; for when we touch on psychic blackness, we also trigger hurt, indignation and anger caused by external reality. I am aware that when I work with a black client the colour and the words 'black' and its tonal opposite, 'white', can be transformed into powerful metaphors, hooks and containers of feelings and experiences. Part of our therapeutic task is to recover a positive sense of blackness.

With art therapy, a creative path is constructed along which both the black client and the therapist can travel. The therapeutic journey through words, images and stories involves identifying the source of the person's distress: she may need to acknowledge the personal/individual aspects of this, as well as that which may be a reflection of social pathology, for example racism. Both of these are equally important parts of her story and lived experience. Psychological theories which generalise show a denial of difference and personhood.

Being able to make images outside ourselves and 'take them in' helps to enhance the capacity to hold on to and come to terms with conflicting and contrasting experiences of ourselves. We can be both black demons and the purest of white angels, as well as grey and nondescript.

FACE TO FACE

It is also my belief that there are a number of very specific factors which come into play in black on black art therapy. These factors colour aspects of the therapeutic relationship such as identification and transference in unique and challenging ways.

The moment of a first meeting between me (a black female therapist) and a new client – black or white – is very poignant. Usually the clients will do a double-take – a moment of shock as they register my colour. Sometimes I read what I interpret as disbelief, or anxiety. Sometimes it's as if shutters go down and a part of the person withdraws. With black clients the shock sometimes disperses into a broad smile or guarded suspicion. Issues of transference, identification and questions about my authority as a therapist come into play before any words or images are shared. It could be said that the first 'image' to be explored is how we (client and therapist) are reflected in each other's eyes and what 'colour' may mean as part of that reflection.

With the black client who melts into a smile I return that recognition but it is also at that point that I remind myself that we will need to explore the ways in which we are different. For, without that separation, her 'story' – by that I mean all the ways in which she shows who she is – will be influenced by mine.

TRANSFERENCE AND IDENTIFICATION

Current writing on aspects of transference and identification where a black therapist works with a black client mostly relate to verbal psychotherapy (Thomas, 1992).

In art therapy, powerful images are created not only in dialogue but also in fact. When a black woman paints a positive image of her brown body I can appreciate just how hard she may have had to work to get to that point; it is after all likely that some aspects of her journey may echo mine. What I do not know, however, is this particular black woman's story.

It is part of my responsibility to open up as many channels and ways for the client to come to know herself; to keep our quest for new meanings alive; to feed the client's experience of herself as a creative being.

My interest in highlighting this particular issue of identification in black on black art therapy is a response to a recent event where a black colleague of mine was questioned about her motives for wanting to run a black women's art therapy group, something I find extraordinary.

In my experience, black art therapists are particularly alert to issues of identification. We are, after all, alert to the harmful effects of denial of personhood which permeates our stories and histories.

INTERNALISED RACISM

Internalised racism refers to the insidious seepage and absorption of negative images, beliefs and ideas about the nature of blackness and being a black person. It is largely unconscious.

Internalised racism can also pervert all aspects of the therapeutic relationship and can influence a potential black client's decision on whether or not to work with a black therapist.

> This internalising of racism and sexism operates between us insidiously and is tricky to tease out. It gets in the way of our being close, for if in some way the information (or misinformation) of our 'second class' nature has seeped in, then spending time with others with that same second class nature is bound to stimulate all our self-loathing and lead us to be suspicious of each other.[3]

As a black art therapist working with a black female client, however, the impact of racism as an aspect of 'societal transference' must also be addressed.[4] Such transference is born of historical and social experiences which shape assumptions and feelings which the client may have for the therapist and the therapist for the client. Racism and its internalisation disempowers, it polarises relationships into that of superiority and inferiority, it generates suspicion, distrust and narrow-mindedness. In art therapy with a black woman, experiences around gender also have to be addressed by both the client and the therapist. How are we in our therapeutic encounters, to promote trust, healing and understanding out of this complex web of material which is presented in image and words?

THE THEORETICAL GROUND

In my view current art therapy theory lacks the beliefs and understanding necessary to support work with black clients.

Critiques which highlight the limitations (and racist implications) of white, middle-class, Western ideology and treatment systems in relation to the mental health of people from other races and cultures (Fernando, 1991) have been noted by some art therapists. Waller (1993) makes reference to the work of Littlewood and Lipsedge (1982). 'One of the most telling conclusions of their current research is that mental illness can be an intelligible response to racism and a disadvantage.'[5] Earlier Lewin (1990) explored 'Transcultural Issues: Considerations on Language Power and Racism' which reminded us that as art therapists we do not operate in a political vacuum.

Classical psychoanalytic and psychotherapeutic theories and approaches provide ways to understand and work with some of what may be going on in a black woman's internal world. Contemporary feminist theories and approaches to psychotherapy have also helped to broaden awareness of the impact of gender issues in relation to how women experience both their 'internal' and 'external' lives (Ernst and Maguire 1987; Maguire, 1995).

SOCIAL CONSTRUCTIONISM: A NEW THEORETICAL GROUND FOR WORKING WITH BLACK WOMEN'S STORIES IN ART THERAPY

The growing body of writing from 'narrative' to 'co-construction' therapists (Anderson, Goolishan, Gergen, Kaye and Hoffman) offers coherent criticism of modern therapy theory and alternatives. Dogmatic *a priori* assumptions are not made by co-constructionist therapists. In analytic psychotherapy, the therapist enters with set ideas, which form a sieve or lens through which all the client communicates is filtered. In analytic therapy, the therapist's focus is on the internal world of the client which does not take into account her everyday life experience. The irony of such a position is that the purely analytic therapist fails to make maximum therapeutic use of some of the most unique and powerful attributes of art therapy: the capacity of the image to hold and generate multiple meanings, the permanence and concrete nature of the image which means both therapist and 'artist'/client can explore how it is reflected in their view.

> It is not only that the client's own reality will eventually give way to the therapist's, but all other interpretations will be excluded.[6]

> By contrast the social construction theorists see ideas, concepts and memories arising from social interchange and mediated through language. All knowledge . . . evolves in the space between people and the realm of the 'common world' or the 'common dance'. Only through the ongoing conversation with intimates does the individual develop a sense of identity or an inner voice.[7]

From the narrative/social constructionist position the therapist engages with the client in order to allow the narrative/story to unfold. This is from a position of 'not knowing' whereby the client is viewed as 'the expert'. It is in the telling of her story (the creation of multiple meanings) that new ideas about herself and what she could be emerges.

Such ideas speak volumes to me for art therapy with black clients. Firstly, the foundations of the therapeutic relationship and all that happens in practice support the idea of two 'equals' meeting. The implications of the 'inferiority' which is inherent to racism is given less of a foothold. Secondly, the potential for empowerment is increased because the client is at the heart of the therapy, not the therapist's beliefs.

Of specific importance to art therapy, however, is the way ideas sanction the generation of multiple meaning. We return again to this unique quality of art therapy – that through images an abundant wealth of ideas, meanings and expressions are generated. It is in the telling of her story, the creation of multiple meanings, that new ideas about herself and what she could be emerge.

For the black female client, then, much can be gained from engaging with therapy that allows her to generate new meanings and understandings of herself in the telling of her story both visually and verbally. Part of that process involves the therapist and client generating stories about how she came to know what she knows about who she is. Her internal or intra-psychic story is also part of that story, indeed it is the story she told herself for many years.

I was intrigued by the profusion of references to art forms in the writings – social construction therapy, references to dance, play and the art of therapy. It is as if there is an understanding that once such an open and spontaneous stance is taken, using words, language and conversation, it cannot avoid triggering a world of creativity and aesthetics. There remains, however, an equally rich field in art therapy which can be of particular use to the black client which, at the risk of appearing an advocate of New Age ideas, I shall refer to as the 'spiritual ground'.

In common with most art therapists, I too have experienced moments of intensity when I 'sit a while' in conversation with a client and their work, and where my soul is touched. I can find no psychotherapeutic theory to explain this. However, I believe clients also benefit from such moments – and that these moments are not just limited to art therapy. Recognition of this more spiritual aspect of art therapy may also be part of what enables the client to explore other aspects of spiritual life – who they are and how they have come to understand themselves in that way. Cherry Lawrence, a black art therapist with many years' experience in community mental health work, feels strongly that all those who work with black people need to take religion and spiritual beliefs on board. Most adults of West Indian origin for example would have absorbed from an early age a wealth of ideas from Christianity. They draw about 'good' and 'evil', punishment and redemption; being cursed and blessed have not only collective meaning but may also be part of the individual's way of talking about and under-standing what is wrong.

CASE REPORT

The following case report, written by Doris Gaga, illustrates much of what has been said. Rather than order it into a clinical presentation, with interpretations of interpretations, we offer it in more or less the same form (though shortened) as it was originally presented by Doris.

It shows how the client's story unfolds through images and words, and the involvement of the therapist in this process. The case study illustrates the unfolding 'internal' world of the client and her direct experience of racism.

The current debate in the art therapy world, centred around whether we are recognised as psychotherapists or remain art therapists, can be viewed as a crisis of identity. What is left out of the debate, however, are questions about how our practice meets the need of our clients. The push to be embraced under the mantle of 'classical psychotherapy' may hamper our ability to embrace other innovative theories, particularly those offered by feminism, as well as methods of therapeutic practice which will keep our work creative and fresh.

Dreaming in colour: case report

I was thinking of calling this case study 'Dreaming in Colour'. The case is that of a young, black woman who came to me after taking a severe overdose. It wasn't her intention to end it all; she was desperate for help and did not know where to go. The case was brought to me by a consultant psychiatrist who had seen this woman. Her mother came to Britain from Jamaica in the 1950s. She (the mother) had a very hard time; she became a single mother, could not cope and offered her daughter for fostering when she was three months old. The child went to a number of foster homes – all white. This was before social services had a policy of placing black children into black homes.[8]

Whilst at these foster homes, she experienced varying degrees of abusive relationships in the way the foster parents related to her. One foster family made some attempt to understand her cultural background but the father was physically abusive. Among other things, he once tried to drown her in a bath. With another family she recalled how, when they went to the cinema, the rest of the family would pretend that she was not with them. One foster parent would recite the rhyme, 'God is good, God is bright. He made Helen in the night, but forgot to paint her white.' When she experienced racist name-calling at school, she was told that it wasn't really important. There was no attempt made to understand her, so she withdrew into her own secret world. Perhaps it was her only protection. Social services were reluctant to believe her experiences; so she stopped telling her story and kept quiet. Even her own mother had no idea what was going on.

So she came to really hate herself and hate her colour. It got to a point where she started to put weight on, not losing weight again until she was an adolescent. She went into a phase of bulimia. The way she described it, she thought she was poison, poisonous and bad and she would try to vomit it up. It is interesting that there is little acknowledgement of black women experiencing eating disorders.

She was quite a determined woman, did very well in her 'A' levels, and went to university. Whilst there, she entered into a relationship with a white male who, in fact, was very abusive towards her – so recreating a pattern. When she attempted to end the relationship, he broke into her house and smashed her windows.

Around this time, she developed a skin disorder where she puffed up and her skin started cracking. She went from one doctor to another and no one knew what was wrong with her. There seemed to be no physiological basis for this and they felt it was psychosomatic. Perhaps something like – she was filled with so much self-loathing, she was trying to burst out of her skin. It was very severe and she was at death's door. In hospital the consultant dermatologist was derogatory towards her. Everything came to a climax and she overdosed. She was referred to a consultant psychiatrist.

Suspicious and guarded about any sort of figures of authority, she feared she would be locked away and never get out of hospital again. She felt vindicated when the psychiatrist agreed that the dermatologist had been racist. Yet although he came across sympathetically, he continually stressed that her absent father played a major role in her psychological condition. The remarks were made without awareness that in Jamaican culture, there are alternative family structures wherein it is not unusual for the father to be absent, with the mother taking on a patriarchal role. She tried to explain this to him but he would not budge. She became very angry and at the point of despair, feeling totally misunderstood. When this consultant came to see me, he referred to the client's mother as an 'Uncle Tom' figure. This made me very angry and I agreed to see this woman.

When she came in, she was quite guarded and suspicious but as the relationship progressed, she did say that she wanted to work with me and how relieved she was to find someone like me in such a rural setting. We carried on working. She made amazing pictures. She articulated herself through the images very well. For the first time, she was both listened to and able to relate to her experiences.

One of the things she spoke about was how, before she started art therapy, she would dream of herself and others as white. At the end of the art therapy she came in and said, 'Guess what? I had a dream and I was black in my dream and the people in my dream were black and that was OK. I was so happy.' She spoke about one of the things that made her decide to work with me: it was my clothes. She felt that anyone who could dress like that was OK. I think what happened was that I was able to provide a mirror for her as one black woman to another. This enabled her to internalise a different experience of herself; being black need not be terrible, awful or grotesque – which is how she had seen herself.

She made a sculpture of herself standing in front of and behind a mirror which represented before and after coming to therapy. In front of the mirror, she was this grotesque figure holding herself in. Behind the mirror she was a confident, self-assured woman. It's difficult to talk about this because her imagery was so powerful. She was very specific about her use of colour, each one had a meaning; white, for example, represented anger. I wondered how much of this was to do with her relationship with her foster parents. Her ex-partner was shown as a grotesque white man with a big stick beating her.

Helen had a somewhat circular way of going about things. At the beginning of therapy, she started an image of herself as a black silhouette and nothing else, locked in a brick wall. There was a door with a key which she couldn't reach on the other side. Towards the end of therapy, she made an image of herself on the other side of the wall with her door opened, having got hold of the key.

She made images of herself carrying burdens on her back, shouldering loads. It made me think about black people being referred to as having a chip on their shoulders. She also depicted herself lifting off the burdens. These changes in representation illustrate eighteen months of work by someone who articulated herself well through imagery. The imagery reflected what was happening to her internally; it demonstrated her consideration of every detail in terms of colour and position. I recall another image of Helen on a train which is going round and round (Figure 12.1). She is in the very last carriage. It has no doors or light, whereas everyone else's carriages have doors and handles.

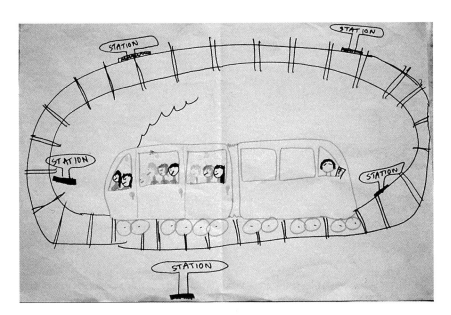

Figure 12.1 Untitled drawing

As Helen became more confident she was able to find ways of getting support and her ability to deal with difficulties increased. In the middle of all this, her mother became very seriously ill with septicaemia. Her class tutors were so insensitive to what was going on, they told her that she was having all these problems because she was unable to cope with academic pressure. This, despite the fact that on her engineering degree course she was the only woman, and the only black person.

When she talked about racism and the way it affected her life, the thing she said was most hurtful was the insidious kind of racism she experienced from the white so-called liberal teachers who openly talked about the black struggle but made no attempt to understand it. She said that the teacher who was overtly racist was quite honest about her abilities. He recognised that she was quite bright and had potential to do well.

Meanwhile the more 'liberal' ones had low expectations of her abilities; were convinced she wasn't able to achieve. She said that at first she couldn't understand what was happening. It was her mother who identified such attitudes as racist. As a small child, she couldn't understand that there was this layer, this hidden racism, which was outside of her awareness, and it was this she found difficult to deal with. Her foster parents did not realise it and therefore had denied her experience. Although they were painful and real, she began to doubt her own experiences. It was then, at the age of eleven, that her mother was able to help Helen acknowledge the abuse she had experienced and validated the pain caused by her experience of racism.

Despite the abuse and disadvantages experienced by Helen, she was able to retain her creativity and sense of self. Through image-making Helen found a voice, and an outlet for her pain and despair. Since she encountered so much denial and disbelief around this time, she began to disbelieve and doubt her own experiences and felt that there was something intrinsically wrong with her. She had difficulty in speaking of her life experience. But as she began to articulate in imagery, she became more articulate verbally. The imagery became a way to reflect upon her experience and really go through a journey of self-acceptance. That's what she left me with – 'Now I am black in my dreams'.

NOTES

1 In Britain the common use of the term 'black' refers to people of African/ Caribbean and South Asian origins. It has been pointed out that not all people from such backgrounds identify themselves as 'black' and that others who do not 'look' black choose to identify themselves as such (See Maria, 1995, and Brah, 1992). In this chapter equal weight is given to the cultural/psychological meaning of 'black' as positive self-identification aligned with political awareness. Its genesis is in the black power movement in 1960s USA, which turned the concept of black on its head, divested it of its pejorative connotations in

racialised discourses and transformed it into a confident expression of an assertive group identity (Brah, 1992: 127)

2 'Narrative' and 'co-construction' therapy refer to innovative developments in family therapy practice which are, in turn, based on the intellectual philosophical theories of how meaning evolves through shared language. From a postmodernist standpoint there is no such thing as a universal fixed truth; instead there are multiple world-views constantly being created through dialogue. Narratives/ stories, as lived experiences, are constructed in the telling/dialogue. Therapy involves a process of co-construction of the narrative and the meanings. Therapy becomes a dialogue-reflexive process of language and the social construction of meaning where therapist(s) and client(s) co-author a new story through conversation and joint reflection (Goolishan and Anderson, 1992; Hoffman, 1992; Epston *et al.*, 1992) quoted by Larner (1995: 191).

3 Hibbert and van Heeswyk, 1988: 85.
4 Kareem, 1992.
5 Waller, 1993: 6.
6 Gergen and Kaye, 1992: 172.
7 Hoffman, 1992: 8.
8 In Section 22 of the 1989 Children's Act, which came into force on 14 October 1991, adoption services are required to give 'due consideration' to the racial origins, cultural and religious heritage of the children when choosing appropriate families. Prior to this, adoption practice varied between agencies.

ACKNOWLEDGEMENT

Many thanks to Carol Halliwell and Cathy Ward for their help with this chapter.

BIBLIOGRAPHY

Anderson, H. and Goolishan, H. 1992. 'The Client is the Expert: A Not-Knowing Approach to Therapy', in S. McName and K. Gergen, (eds) *Therapy as Social Construction*. London: Sage.
Brah, A. 1992. 'Difference, Diversity and Differentiation', in J. Donald and A. Rattausi, *Race, Culture and Difference*. London: Sage.
Ernst, S. and Maguire, M. (eds) 1987. *Living With The Sphinx: Papers from The Women's Therapy Centre*. London: The Women's Press.
Fernando, S. 1991. *Mental Health, Race and Culture*. London: Mind Publications, MacMillan Press.
Gergen, K. J. and Kaye, J. 1992. 'Beyond Narrative in the Negotiation of Therapeutic Meaning', in S. McName and K. Gergen (eds) *Therapy as Social Construction*. London: Sage.
Hibbert, J. and Van Heeswyk, D. 1988. 'Black Women's Workshop', in S. Krzouski and P. Land (eds) 1988. *In Our Experience Workshops at the Women's Therapy Centre*. London: The Women's Press.
Hoffman, L. 1992. 'A Reflexive Stance for Family Therapy', in S. McName and K. Gergen (eds) *Therapy as Social Construction*. London: Sage.
Kareem, J. 1992. 'The Nafsiyat Intercultural Therapy Centre: Ideas and Experiences in Intercultural Therapy', in J. Kareem and R. Littlewood (eds) *Inter-Cultural Therapy: Themes Interpretations and Practice*. London: Blackwell Scientific Publications.

Larner, G. 1995. 'The Real as Illusion: Deconstructing Power in Family Therapy', *The Journal of Family Therapy*, vol. 17, May.

Lewin, M. 1990. 'Transcultural Issues: Considerations on Language, Power and Racism', *Inscape: The Journal of the British Association of Art Therapy*. Summer Issue.

Maguire, M. 1995. *Men, Women, Passion and Power – Gender Issues in Psychotherapy*. London: Routledge.

Mama, A. 1995. *Beyond the Masks: Race, Gender and Subjectivity*. London: Routledge.

Skaife, S. 1995. 'The Dialectics of Art Therapy', *Inscape: The Journal of the British Association of Art Therapy*. vol. 1.

Thomas, L. 1992. 'Racism and Psychotherapy: Working with Racism in the Consulting Room', in J. Kareem, and R. Littlewood (eds) *Intercultural Therapy: Themes Interpretations and Practice*. London: Blackwell Scientific Publications.

Waller, D. 1993. *Group Interactive Art Therapy*. London: Routledge.

Chapter 13

Many murders
Art therapy with a 'traditional' woman

Harriet Wadeson

If art were life, Paul would have died many excruciatingly painful deaths at the hands of his wife. In life, however, it was herself that she had attempted to kill. The daughter and wife of funeral directors, she had lived much of her life above the funeral parlour, with death ever present.

Conventional therapy would have probed early family relationships and childhood experiences, but my work with this client over a number of years dealt little with childhood and evolved a more contemporary focus, expanding her own personal issues to a feminist view of the impact of societal influences upon her life. Of particular significance was the nature of our therapeutic relationship, its non-traditional, more feminist components, and its essential place in her healing.

At fifty, Betty was a heavy-set woman with bleached hair, fashionably coiffed. She was always very well dressed, her attire set off with tasteful, expensive jewellery. Her facial expression was set and showed no display of feelings. Nor was there any variation of tone in her voice. Together these features gave the impression of her being very much held in.

Betty was referred to me for art therapy after her second serious suicide attempt resulting in a nine-day coma. In the hospital she cried in reaction to a picture she had drawn. Her psychiatrist was impressed with art's potential to unleash the feelings that had been trapped inside her and recommended art therapy as her primary treatment since the verbal therapy she had then and for the two years between suicide attempts elicited little more than defence and resistance.

HISTORY

Betty was the middle of three children, whose father was an undertaker in a small American Midwestern town. Her childhood home was an apartment over the funeral parlour where she had to remain quiet and where the phone ringing usually signalled a 'call of death'. Betty had lived all her life in the same area and today resides in a similar small town a few miles away. She had gone to college and was teaching at an elementary school when she met Paul, who was also in the funeral business. They married and lived over his funeral parlour for the first ten years of their marriage. He became much more successful than Betty's father, buying one funeral business after another in the surrounding small towns. Betty gave birth to three children, two boys and a girl. She was almost the 'traditional woman' stereotype. Her life consisted of being a wife, mother and housekeeper. She gave dinner parties and put effort into her cooking. With their increased wealth, they bought a house which Betty decorated and maintained. She also decorated the funeral parlours and later redecorated them and her home. Paul was a workaholic with little time for the family. He had become a prominent member of the community and was looked to for solace at times of death. He insisted that Betty support this image.

ART THERAPY

Betty's hospital records, which were sent to me shortly after I began seeing her, gave her a Borderline Personality diagnosis, partially based on the impulsiveness of her suicide attempts. My work with her did not bear out this diagnosis. She was also described as unable to stick with anything and unable to tolerate being alone, as described by her husband and former psychiatrist. Both these characteristics changed in the course of our work.

Because she lived in a small town, it was necessary for Betty to travel two hours by early-morning train to Chicago and then take a half-hour taxi ride to see me. The return train did not get her home until late afternoon so in effect it was necessary for her to devote a whole day to each of our appointments. As a result, I saw her for two-hour sessions initially every two weeks. She was also monitored for the effects of the anti-depressant medication on a monthly basis by a psychiatrist in her town.

Art-making served several purposes for Betty. First it was a significant vehicle for catharsis. This was a woman who had learned at an early age the danger of expressing her feelings. In a picture of a childhood memory, Betty drew herself 'cringing in terror' as her mother beat her older, rebellious sister for 'talking back'. She described her mother as a cold woman who showed no affection or tenderness toward her, and, as mentioned above, the children were required to be quiet at all times in order not to be heard by the mourners below. In her art Betty released feelings of frustration, rage, sadness, despair, and much later in the treatment hope and happiness. When she entered art therapy, she expressed anger only through an occasional sarcastic remark, distancing herself from emotional engagement with me. For example, in relation to my fee, 'what do the poor people do for therapy?' or to the distance from my office, 'when are you going to move to Denton (her town)?'

Another benefit of the art-making was that the communication through images enabled her to probe issues she avoided verbally. For example, upon beginning a session, if I asked her how she was feeling, she would respond 'fine' or 'not too bad'. In the course of the session it would come out that she was despairing, suicidal or furious. Her usual pattern was to begin by recounting activities of her children, 'John is interviewing for a new job' or 'Amy and Dan decided to have their wedding at the country club'. After listening and inquiring about her feelings in relation to the various events she described, I would suggest that she make some art. Often her picture would have nothing to do with what she had been recounting, but might be a picture of herself feeling torn apart, or one of her many murders or mutilations of her husband, followed by a much deeper exploration of her current state.

Another benefit was the fulfilment Betty felt from making art. After filling her life with family, she now took time for herself by making art. She converted her basement into a studio and spent many hours there in solitary pursuit of her own self-expression. As mentioned earlier, it was reported in her hospital records that she had been unable to spend time alone. Furthering her feelings of autonomy was the success of her art work. She began selling it and having shows, receiving commissions as well. The art she made at home was very different from the work in our sessions. She described the difference as her 'inside and outside art'. At home she painted landscapes and made country craft items. The pictures in our sessions were very raw and primitive.

THERAPEUTIC ISSUES

Not surprisingly, Betty's issues were rage at her husband and parents, letting go of her children, and low self-esteem. Most of her feelings around these issues were inaccessible to her prior to her suicide attempts. Her rage at Paul dominated others as the basis of her despair. She saw him as the cause of her misery. At her first session she drew him as a 'stick-in-the-mud' and described the many ways he squelched her. He would criticise her for being loud in a restaurant, pressure her to lose weight, and generally disparage her. He spent most of his time and energy at the funeral parlour, leaving the rearing of the children and the care of both their elderly parents to her. She felt constrained to be the perfect wife and mother to support his image in the community. She still harboured fury about his relationship, fifteen years in the past, with a friend of the family. She was convinced he had had an affair with her although he denied it. She felt doubly betrayed: with respect to his commitment to her and in requiring her to be perfect while he 'played around'. She said if she ever discovered that he had been unfaithful again she would kill both him and herself. She always resented his narrowness, his unwillingness to try new things (for instance travel, ethnic restaurants), and his sexual inhibition. During the course of the treatment there were marked changes in their relationship, as will be described below.

In her art, Betty vented her anger at Paul many times. She titled one picture 'The End of Mr. Perfect' and drew herself shooting him while his parents watched because they were responsible for his narrow, controlling nature. In another, she sliced him to bits with daggers, attacking his mouth and brain, because it was with them he berated and hurt her. In yet another she is performing surgery on his brain, putting in caring and understanding qualities. She depicted him as 'an ass' and gave herself a big foot 'kicking him in the ass'. In addition to relishing fantasies of vengeance in her art, she also expressed how he hurt her. In one he is a dragon breathing fire that envelops her, which she described as 'how he controls my life'. In it she is depicted with a broken heart and tears in her brain that never escaped. Her hands are raised to protect herself from the dragon. Her tongue is cut off because she was 'wrong' and no one listened to her. This is how she felt when she attempted suicide. In another she is precariously balanced on a tight rope, which Paul is shaking, representing her insecure position.

For most of the years of her marriage, Betty had denied herself, and had lived for her children who were now in their twenties. The oldest, John, was a continuous worry to her. He had a drinking problem, he left school, went from job to job, took up with a married woman and so on. She feared that 'he has my genes', in other words, instability. She was very close to her daughter, Amy, and remained very involved with all her children. An issue for her was coming to terms with her children becoming adults and this too was dealt with in therapy. Mixed with her feelings of loss was resentment toward them for all she had sacrificed of herself on their behalf. She also resented her elderly parents for the care she gave them and her siblings for leaving it all to her.

Low self-esteem, along with experiencing and expressing her feelings, was the most crucial issue for Betty. It was in this realm that a feminist approach and awareness were most helpful to her. She had tended to hide her self-doubts behind a mask of bravado and sarcasm on one hand or a stoic iciness on the other. She blamed her husband for undermining her confidence and for killing the spirit she had had as a young person.

THERAPEUTIC COURSE

In her first session Betty made a picture of how she felt when depressed – that no one heard her scream. She projected her own unawareness of her feelings outward. At an early session she drew herself as a wife and mother with many hands pulling at her. She reported that the pictures she drew in our sessions of her anger at Paul made her feel better toward him at home.

She realised that her suicide attempt resulted from her self-devaluation. Paul told people that it resulted from a chemical imbalance.

My response to her anger at having been squeezed into the role of wife and mother to the detriment of her own development was to help her see that all of society conspired to press her into this position. The repetition of this point of view throughout the several years of her therapy was important in releasing her from blaming herself for allowing this to happen.

As the art therapy progressed, Betty reported that she found painting therapeutic, otherwise she would be suicidal. She also noted that after about five months her attitude improved after 'griping' to me for two hours. She was feeling more confident and described her relationship with Paul as 'fairly compatible'. She was also deriving satisfaction from making art at home.

Six months into therapy and prior to the first marriage of one of her children, her second son, Brian, she became depressed. She felt like crying but couldn't and became afraid of her feelings. She painted a picture of drowning herself saying she could not handle everything – her kids, home and severe back problems she was having. She said she would wait until after the wedding, however, so as not to ruin it. She was fighting with Paul who was urging her to lose weight. She ate in defiance. She drew herself on a rollercoaster, feeling as though she would fall off, and as a witch, saying she was fat and wanted to withdraw. I was out of town for several weeks, and, despite seeing a counsellor in her psychiatrist's office, she became so depressed after the wedding that she almost went into hospital. It was only in retrospect that I saw how dependent on me she had become. She realised that she had been 'dead' before but now she was feeling her feelings. She made a picture of the loss of Brian's childhood.

During the next several months she improved rapidly. She went on a vacation and realised that she could now see the beauty in her surroundings. She spoke of rebirth, 'like coming out of the dead'. Her eyes were now open she said. There had been a 'dark veil over my feelings'.

Betty began selling her art. With my encouragement she took a trip alone away from the family for the first time to a painting workshop. She enjoyed her increasing independence. She reported feeling more and drew herself 'flowering' expressing herself. In her new independence from Paul, she no longer helped him with visiting the bereaved because 'death bothered me'. This was the first time in over a year of therapy that she spoke of funerals other than as a business. She drew a casket and said that before she had attempted suicide to end her misery. Now she saw it as 'distasteful'. She realised her children would miss her. She drew herself as a bird that was in a cage but now is free. She was no longer flaring up at Paul because she was letting her anger out.

The next summer, eighteen months into therapy, despite getting lots of commissions for art, winning a first prize in an art show, and enjoying redecorating her home, Betty became depressed again. Her picture expressed a fear of going 'down' again. She said she would kill herself if she was down all the time. Her anger toward Paul flared up again, and she made pictures of killing or hurting him. I encouraged her to beat cushions to enact her anger. She cried and drew herself buried. When I left for vacation, she had made arrangements to see someone in her psychiatrist's office regularly. Nevertheless she checked herself into the hospital. There she 'demanded' art supplies and cried a lot.

At this time Betty threatened Paul with a divorce, which changed their relationship considerably. She drew herself as a volcano. At the next session she drew herself 'wilting' from Paul's disparagement and above her 'clouds of doubt'. She said she went to hospital to 'disappear' and drew herself in a cell. She expressed her fear of being crazy and needing 'confinement'. This is how she felt when she tried to kill herself, she said. She recognised that her fears made the cell.

Once again Betty improved rapidly. She now saw herself as having 'talents' and reported better communication with Paul. Her art was selling even better, she was feeling more and was not 'analysing' everything, and she experienced herself as getting her own identity back. Her affect remained fairly flat, but she was able to express herself in art. She said, 'If people can't draw, how do they express themselves?' and 'I can't feel things until I draw them'.

Betty's relationship with Paul went up and down. Apparently her divorce threat scared him and he was now trying to change in the ways she wanted him to. Her independence empowered her. She started smoking after her hospitalisation to let Paul know she would do what she wanted. She began socialising more, but still hid her feelings behind a smile in social situations. Although she still got 'down' when Paul criticised her, she knew that she could come 'up'. They began marital counselling with a social worker in her psychiatrist's office.

As Betty began her third year of therapy, Amy became engaged. Our sessions became focused on her children. Betty had some well-founded anxieties about Amy's fiancé. She made art around the loss of her children as well as her resentment of them. At this time John was having drinking and job difficulties. Betty focused on trying to let go of her feelings of responsibility towards her children. She had dreams about losing them.

As the year ended she recognised that she was '100 per cent' better than the previous year. She had begun exercising and was about to begin teaching art to deprived children. She stood up to her parents and also insisted that Paul shoulder more of the burden for his own parents. She told her brother he would have to help more with her parents whose health was deteriorating. Paul was being more helpful, and she drew them with intertwined roots signifying understanding. She drew herself showing 'lots of growth this year, emerging from hell's pit'. She recognised that she had blamed Paul for everything instead of seeing some of her own weaknesses. Paul expressed his pride in her painting and he praised her for redecoration of the funeral home.

As Amy's wedding approached, we worked to prepare Betty to anticipate the realistic rather than the idealised feelings she might experience. She drew a volcano with the lava cooling and grass and trees growing from it. Although the wedding was a huge affair requiring much planning and arranging, she did well and noticed that she was calmer than Paul. Her expectations were realistic and she was prepared to let Amy live her life as she chose. She made a clay piece of the family. They were all involved but there was a door that allowed them to go in and out.

The children in the art class wrote, 'Betty's great'. In our sessions, Betty's own art expressions became fuller and more invested. She began to have more back problems and although she was told that her back pain was incurable, she became discouraged rather than depressed. She was tearful as she expressed her anger at God; her feelings were more accessible to her and their expression more possible for her.

After four years of therapy, Betty's moods had stabilised, she felt contented, and she no longer became suicidal. We decreased the sessions to monthly visits, but actually they were less frequent due to trips she took. Betty was now feeling more 'a part of things', life was 'fuller' and she was enjoying her children. Both sons were now working in the funeral business and Amy seemed happy in her marriage. Brian's wife was pregnant and Betty was looking forward to this new stage in her life. She drew herself with strong roots. She took her longest trip alone yet, for thirteen days to an art retreat, but came home earlier than the three weeks she had planned to be away because she missed Paul. She said, 'I'm comfortable with myself now'.

We agreed to have six-month 'check up' appointments the next year and then we met a year later to be sure she maintained her progress. In relation to her continuing back pain, she reported good and bad days, that she was sometimes discouraged but accepted her situation. She was feeling loved by her family and proudly said that Paul no longer gets away with squelching and controlling her. She summed up her progress by saying, 'I've worked too hard to crawl out of the pit to go back in'.

THERAPEUTIC RELATIONSHIP

In addition to becoming aware of long-pent-up feelings of rage and despair through the art-making process and expressing them strongly and safely in pictures, the nature of the therapeutic relationship was essential to Betty's recovery. As previously mentioned, frequently I validated her experience by reframing it in light of societal pressures on traditional women who came of age in the 1950s. Eventually such discussions helped her feel 'intelligent'.

Indirectly I served as a role model of an independent woman. Early on Betty said that she liked my directness and that I kept her on 'track'. She could talk to me better than other therapists she had seen, she said, and related how she withdrew from her relationship with her previous psychiatrist before her recent suicide attempt. After six months of art therapy she said that I brought her out of her depression, that I was her 'haven', and that she had talked to me more than to anyone in her life. She said that although she sometimes left our sessions drained, more often she felt exhilarated. Despite such positive comments and her fearing my vacations and getting worse during them, for the most part Betty's affect showed little attachment. Toward the end of her treatment Betty related that early on if I had moved to another part of the country she would have had to follow me, but now she would not have to.

Sometimes she complained about the three hours it took her to travel to my office and she wished I lived nearer to her. When she was angry with me for commenting on her early arrival to one session, I suggested she draw a picture of our relationship. In it I am picking her brain apart. She felt sad about it. I suggested she make a picture of how she would like our relationship to be. She drew a mother and child and said that she wanted me to protect her. At another session she spoke of wishing I would inject her brain with self-worth and kill off the part she had drawn as black, the problem part. She resented my vacations, sometimes becoming fearful. She said, 'I won't have the open space to say what I want when I come here'.

In many respects the therapeutic relationship was typical in the sense that Betty's positive transference imbued me with wisdom and power. For example, she said that she had learned a lot from me, becoming wise in dealing with Paul, in accepting him and recognising she could not actively change him.

Nevertheless, in other respects the therapeutic relationship was non-traditional. Particularly in the latter periods of therapy as Betty became more confident and the focus shifted to relationships with children and parents, I began to relate to her as one woman to another. Her children and parents were close in age to mine and, as relevant, I would share with her some of my own experiences of parenting and dealing with elderly parents. Towards the end we each became a grandmother within a couple of weeks of each other. Our now infrequent sessions would begin with exchanging photos of our granddaughters and discussing their developmental milestones. There was something very folksy and homey in this. I believe it was an important capstone of our relationship to move toward a more mutual, egalitarian interchange as two women entering a new phase of their lives. This sort of sharing expressed mutual respect and affection, and I believe, enhanced her feelings of self-worth.

At her last session, Betty said she would not be where she is today without her therapy with me by getting rid of or understanding her feelings. She was glad I 'was put on this earth' and wondered if I had helped everyone as much as I had helped her.

CONCLUSION

For this 'traditional' woman whose culture had taught her to serve her husband, children and parents and to deny her own needs and feelings, art therapy became both the key to unlock her awareness and the door through which her long-closed-off feelings could flow.

In executing many murders in her art, thus ventilating her anger over and over again at her husband, whom she saw as the chief source of her misery, she was eventually able to evolve a satisfactory relationship with him. Our relationship validated her feelings and helped her to see herself in the context of a society that conspired not only to mould her into a woman who lived for her family rather than for herself, but also to be unaware of any anger or resentment for living in this way.

There was an almost exclusive focus on the present with very little delving into the past, despite the considerable length of treatment. There were other 'neglects' as well. For example, Betty's suicide attempts must have been of considerable embarrassment to Paul in his role as minister to mourners. Although he explained the cause as a chemical imbalance, had he actually had to arrange her funeral due to suicide, it probably would have been mortifying for him. Betty never acknowledged that her suicide attempts may have been an unconscious desire for vengeance toward Paul. In the eyes of the community he seemed so caring and sensitive. However, her suicide would show him as being uncaring and insensitive to his own family.

Another departure from 'traditional' therapy was the folksy woman-to-woman relationship we evolved toward the end as we exchanged grandmother stories. I believe this evolution aided in the growth of Betty's self-esteem.

To sum up, my work with this 'traditional woman' illustrates a feminist art therapy that helps the client to understand her development in the matrix of the societal pressures that have impacted on her, gives her space to express her feelings freely and safely, and provides a therapeutic relationship in which she feels validated and esteemed.

Chapter 14

A tasty drop of dragon's blood
Self-identity, sexuality and motherhood

Susan Hogan

This chapter will examine one woman's struggle to come to terms with the experience of giving birth, the death of one of her twin babies, issues surrounding her sexuality, and her changed sense of her sexuality as a result of childbirth. It also explores her reactions both to societal role expectations and her own feelings of a changed self-identity as a result of motherhood.

Although the chapter will examine one woman's story in particular, many of the issues raised are of common concern, particularly those connected with birth practices and medical intervention. The case study is relevant to the experience of many women.

Jay had hoped to have a home birth but was rushed into hospital to have an episiotomy. Many of her drawings and paintings explore her feelings about this ordeal.

BEREAVEMENT AND LOSS

The experience of loss is felt in various ways. Reactions to loss can include shock, a feeling of numbness, disbelief, anxiety, sadness, relief, despair, loneliness, anger and guilt. What exactly is felt when, and over what length of time, can vary tremendously from person to person. Physical experiences often accompany emotions, such as appetite disturbances, forgetfulness, a sharper or heightened sense of reality, lack of energy, breathlessness, over-sensitivity to noise, a feeling of hollowness of the abdomen or tightness of the chest (Littlewood 1992).

Research on bereaved parents has found that preoccupation with the image of the dead baby is common, along with a strong desire to hold the dead baby – a desire which is frequently thwarted by hospital practice.[1]

BIRTH PRACTICES AND CULTURAL ASSUMPTIONS

Feminist theorists have pointed out how the increasing use of technology in childbirth has resulted in midwifery, a traditionally female occupation, becoming taken over by obstetrics which is dominated by men. It is obstetricians who oversee surgical interventions such as caesarean section or episiotomy. Fear of litigation because of a delayed medical intervention and professional territorialism lead obstetricians to perform medical interventions which many commentators feel are unnecessary.[2]

The experience of enduring surgery during the act of giving birth can provoke many of those feelings commonly associated with a death. This is not surprising since there is a tremendous societal expectation of women's reproductive and mothering capabilities as well as a huge mythology surrounding women's fecundity. Giving birth to a large extent is still considered a 'natural' function of womanhood. There is a very real sense of loss felt by women who are subject to such medical intervention.

A parallel might be seen between the expectation of 'natural' birth capabilities and the expectation of female orgasm in penetrative sex:

> Orgasm has been set up by our culture as something women should strive for, a gift men must offer women and the proof of sexual success for both partners. Sex researchers ... all assume that orgasm is the measure of sexual satisfaction ... For most women orgasm does not have this central role.[3]

The theorist Luce Irigaray suggests that women are more subject to an all-over body eroticism; although such generalisations about women's sexuality may be viewed with suspicion, just as women are supposed to achieve orgasm in successful sexual relations, we are also assumed to crave the experiences of pregnancy and birth in our maturation as women. The considerable ambivalence of many women towards the idea of pregnancy and motherhood is not often acknowledged.

The consequence of medical intervention is that many women are left feeling guilty and inadequate because they have been unable to fulfil what is seen by many as a biological imperative requiring no technical aid. Anger is also frequently felt by women following a caesarean or episiotomy because they allowed others (usually men) to control an event which should be (as prevailing ideology would have it) the woman's glorious moment of self-realisation – the most important experience in our lives. It is the loss of control of the birth that is frustrating and humiliating for so many women.

Many women decide to have a home or a 'natural' birth or use a birthing centre. This requires a large investment of time and energy and/or cash. The decision to have a home birth entails making extra arrangements, and requires considerable strength of purpose, as the prospective mother may encounter opposition or misinformation from doctors or from family members who will need to be persuaded. She may have to put extra effort into getting fit for the birth and the birth environment must be planned. An actively involved partner or a close and supportive friend is also a prerequisite.

For women (such as my client Jay) who make the decision to take charge of their own birth and the birth environment, being rushed into hospital at the last minute, away from the carefully prepared and anticipated birth environment and away from supportive family and friends, is disorienting and can represent bitter failure.

Caesarean section (where an incision is made through the abdominal wall of the woman into the uterus and the baby is removed through the abdomen) should only be performed where loss of life would otherwise seem inevitable. However it is increasingly being used unnecessarily on a routine basis for breach presentations and premature births.[4] Such interventions are associated with considerable post-operative discomfort, infection, feeding difficulties and emotional distress.[5]

An episiotomy is an incision into the perineum (the area between the vagina and the anus) to enlarge the opening through which the baby will pass. It is usually performed just before the appearance of the baby's head. Episiotomies are mistakenly performed in order to decrease the amount of time spent in labour, despite lack of evidence that it speeds up the birth.[6] Giving birth in a squatting or semi-sitting position can relieve tension on the perineum and avoid the need for this intervention.[7]

The effects of undergoing an episiotomy, both emotional and physical, can last a long time. The operation can cause discomfort during intercourse which can create stress in a couple's relationship at a time when the woman is in extra need of support, for many months. The episiotomy can involve intense pain both during the cutting and the stitching.[8]

Caesarean section and episiotomy rob women of both the experience of giving birth and the feeling of being in control of the event. Guilt is a common reaction (both for those who planned a 'natural' birth as well as those who did not); rage is another reaction. Women are frequently left feeling that they just couldn't get it right.

CASE STUDY: DRAGON'S BLOOD A TASTY DROP[9]

It is clear that Jay is a woman who has suffered multiple loss. The 'birth and death' (as she referred to it) triggered off issues of self-identity, dependence and independence, sexuality and childhood sexual abuse.

Jay presented herself for art therapy in an eighteen-week closed group in 1992 conducted in Sydney by myself and co-facilitated by a USA-trained therapist. This account has been written in the way it has to privilege Jay's story, rather than illustrate a theoretical position.[10]

Jay completed a number of images before experiencing the 'birth and death' and prior to starting the group. These were made with the intention of getting used to the idea of having twins and feeling good about it. She described the drawings as happy and expectant. At the time that the pencil sketches were completed Jay was preparing herself for the birth by becoming physically fit. She was eating well, resting, relaxing and reading – novels as well as books about childbirth. She described herself as feeling good about her body in general and good about her shape.

In early drawings made prior to starting the group but after the birth Jay depicted the two birth experiences – pushing the live baby, Bruno, out which she described as 'fantastic' and the other birth of the dead baby, Eric. Jay described this image as showing her 'disorientation and agony'.

In response to this image, which was completed at home (Figure 14.1), she describes her disappointment with the birth process and she reflected upon the experience of the birth and her expectations of it. Jay and her partner, Leo, had planned for a home birth and had installed a water tank in their lounge room and had an open fire alight on the day of the birth. Jay described the room as 'gorgeous'. Family members and friends had been invited for the event. However, all their plans were dashed when on first examination Jay was told that she would have to go into hospital, though by this time she was well into the birth having reached a dilation of the cervix of 8cm (birth proceeds usually at 10cm). Jay said that she was feeling very good about the labour, very relaxed, and felt that she had gone a long way already on her own and without too much pain. Given the absence of extreme pain Jay was anticipating the rest of the birth going well. She was not told why she was being taken into hospital.

Jay was rushed into hospital and given three consecutive ultra-sounds. By now Jay felt anxiety, an anxiety she was unable to quash despite her efforts to stay relaxed. Running through her mind were the thoughts 'keep calm – we don't want a caesarean – keep calm relax – hold it all – it's fine', the fear of medical intervention providing the impetus not to panic. The first ultra-sound machine was faulty and the second did not pick up the second heartbeat so a third, bigger and more intimidating, machine was brought in. This was the point at which she was told that one of the babies might be dead, but that they were not yet certain, in order to prepare her for the result of the third ultra-sound (this was about one hour before Bruno's birth).

Jay described the member of nursing staff who performed the ultra-sound as 'not interested in me at all'. She described the ultra-sound jelly being smeared over her belly and her feeling that the person doing it just wanted to get it over and done with as quickly as possible, as she did too. It was this person, with whom she had no rapport, who broke the news that one of the babies was dead. On the ultra-sound it was possible to see Eric's skull moving which meant that the bone had lost integrity – the baby was already decomposing.

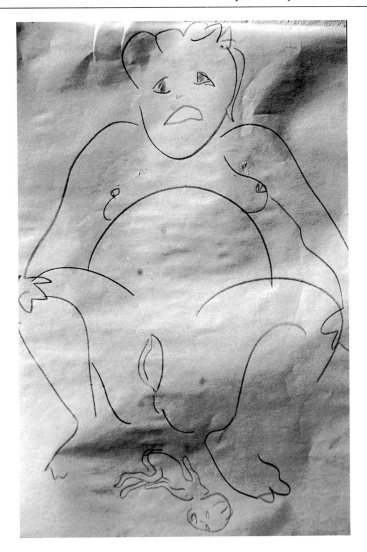

Figure 14.1

Jay expressed her sense of disappointment that she had not been given the chance to push Bruno out. Her labour had just started its final stage when her doctor turned to her midwife and said that he was going to get the baby out and 'cut'. Jay described this as a horrible moment and said that she felt robbed of the experience of pushing. Pushing she described as 'an extraordinary experience – it's like being an animal – it's like things moving through you – it's a force that is so uncontrollable – I was revelling in it'.

Jay felt betrayed, undefended and let down. Her partner, Leo, she described as 'pretty much out of it by then' and her midwife she felt 'didn't hold up'. The midwife had been taken aback by the whole thing. Her partner she had cut off from because she was trying to keep calm and seeing Leo looking distraught was not helping her. To keep relaxed, Jay avoided eye contact with him, though he was next to her.

The first picture made in the group depicted the shape of her belly. The text written on the drawing 'Oh it's a boy' indicates her shock that she had been expecting two boys. In this session she expressed her feelings that she had not yet come to terms with being married. Although she had known after 21 weeks of pregnancy that she had been expecting twins she had not known their gender. She expressed her sense of shock that she could have produced two boys – her least preferred choice. She said that the idea of living with a man and two boys would have been too much in terms of 'male presence'. She said that she didn't like the image.

This painting (Figure 14.2) produced in week two illustrates what she described as a 'kind of compost heap' representing a raw looking mish-mash of her past hurts. She described the compost heap as a pregnant stack with blood dribbling out of it. During the birth she had lost a lot of blood and the picture reminded her of that. She described the experience of losing blood as very disturbing (and emphasised that she had lost a lot of blood), yet at the same time it had felt like a 'function' of having a dead baby. The blood loss added a poignancy to having a dead child and also

Figure 14.2

added a melodramatic quality that she felt was inappropriate. The blood had a disturbing effect on the people in the delivery room who looked visibly upset by the amount of blood. Jay associated blood with car accidents or disasters – whereas she felt that the baby's death was more like an energy that had gone out. When Jay talked about the image she mixed up the babies' names. The red lines she described as 'tracks of sorrow' which run past the photos of the dead baby, Eric, and into the heap or belly.

In the corner of the picture she describes her 'mind chatter' which she described as her guilty feelings, her feelings of obligation and her propensity to judge herself harshly. She felt that she SHOULD be coping better by this point (two months after the birth and death) and SHOULD be getting on with life, and SHOULD be feeling more resolved.

Jay also made a charcoal drawing in the same week, of herself immersed, and decorporealised in 'the shower of grief' which she now felt might be half over.

Another quick charcoal sketch produced in the second art therapy session is of the dead baby Eric who is portrayed after the moment of birth when he had flopped out lifeless (she had not seen Bruno emerge as she had been on all fours for his delivery). Jay described her strong sense of wanting to reach down and get him. In this reaching down Jay expresses her sense of wanting him to be alive and her wanting to be able to spend more time with him. The reaching down also represents her feeling of disbelief – the hands reaching down are 'impotent', unable to give him life.

She depicts her hand wearing the wedding ring which confirms that it is her hand reaching down. The ring also denotes her new status as a wife and a mother – a mother of twins. The latter status she describes as 'shattered' at this moment of reaching down and knowing that Eric was dead. Her emphasis on the hand reaching down being hers 'rather than the hand of God' seems to indicate her sense of responsibility. Her uncertainty seemed clear in the way that she described the image. She felt that he was a normal healthy baby (he had not died because he was damaged in some way – brain damaged or disabled) but he 'had chosen to leave'. Jay expressed her sense that that moment changed her future – that her life would have been completely different had he lived.

In this sketch of Bruno (Figure 14.3) she described him as 'just full of life' and 'just taking up all of the space'. She said of the image 'everything about him is coming at you' and he is 'very present with a big smile'. The yellow represents his energy and his aliveness. She described her feeling of being suffocated by the drawing when she first did it but then later coming to like it. The picture represents both her altered sense of space and her feelings of need for a space in which to grieve. Jay told us that her motivation for coming to art therapy had been very much concerned with creating a space in which to express her grief as she felt that it was unfair both on herself and on Bruno to grieve with him around. She described her

Figure 14.3

experience of being with baby Bruno and wanting to be with him without weeping, and yet she was constantly reminded of the death of the other baby by his presence.

In the third art therapy session Jay made an image which seemed to embody a sense of fear or foreboding. The drawing (Figure 14.4) was precipitated by a quotation Jay had read about bats of sorrow landing in one's hair and she expressed a feeling of disgust about this prospect. She described her portrait of herself as frightened and described her sense that

Figure 14.4

it was all getting too much for her. The mood in the picture she explained as 'don't come near me'.

As well as expressing her feelings of not coping in this picture, she seems to be imparting a sense of self-loathing, perhaps linked to her feeling that she was languishing in her sorrow. However it later emerged that hair is an important symbol of her sexuality, though she did not talk about this at the time. The 'don't come near me' therefore may refer to her lack of sexual relations with her partner at the time, or a feeling that grieving and sex were incompatible, or to incidents in her childhood.

Completed in the same week, Figure 14.5 portrays Jay carrying wood to a bonfire. She discussed how she felt that repressed feelings burn the body and of her desire to rid her body of her own grief – to show it, allow it, get it over with. The clock represents the time it takes to express grief and her desire to give herself the time to express the sorrow. She expressed her wish not to end up old and unresolved about Eric's death (actually she talked mostly about 'the grief' which may encompass more than the death).

Jay described her depiction of the baby's body as 'disturbing', saying that it has a 'looseness' and a 'craziness' about it. The body would seem to be rotting or putrefying with steam coming off it. She then talked about the results of the post-mortem examination which indicated that Eric had started to decompose in her womb. She said that she had read that babies that die in the womb 'rot down real quick'. Though the corporeal depiction of Eric clearly revolted her, his spirit is also depicted in the top right-hand corner of the image flying upwards.

Figure 14.5

The next image completed depicts a woman laying with her legs open who seems to be covering up or touching her vagina. It conveys more about Jay's feelings about the birth. She described the drawing as disturbing. Jay thought that the figure in the image looked as though she was stitching herself up. She talked about the 'openness' and 'rawness' of birth. She said of the image that she is a woman of the world expressing the grief of many women. She talked of the grief of child loss not being acknowledged around the world. She then went on to talk about meeting some women who had had caesareans and who as a result did not feel like proper women. She expressed anger about the treatment of women, particularly in relation to their feelings of guilt and lack of support, and said that it was shameful and evil. Jay talked about how the death had stifled her motivation, her sense of fulfilment and her self-confidence. She described the loss of the baby as affecting her self-image and her capacity to learn.

Also produced in week three, Figure 14.6 reveals Jay's anger. The text reads 'baton down those hatches' and the hammer represents the forces oppressing women. She described the image as depicting rage and anger, but also being about reason or judgement. The repressing forces are seen as not only hammering down but also making judgements about women.

The next image (Figure 14.7) denotes more about Jay's feelings towards the experience of the births. It refers to having twins and also to having three ultra-sounds. The text, 'physician heal thyself', refers to Jay's anger

Figure 14.6

about the doctors and the medical environment. However, she described the emergency staff as sensitive as they allowed the dead baby Eric to remain in the room for eight hours or more before he was taken for the post-mortem examination. However, an overnight stay in hospital with Bruno proved to be extremely unpleasant because Jay got no privacy and because the lighting could not be dimmed. An attempt to breast-feed Bruno had to be made in the dark or in full lighting. Jay found the stay exhausting and expressed her feeling that the notion of the hospital being about health or healing was 'totally screwed up'.

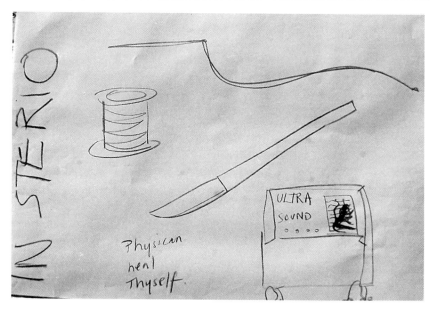

Figure 14.7

Jay described her feelings of shock about the birth experience. She had put a lot of effort into being prepared and described herself as a 'model pregnant twin pregnant woman' in other words that she had felt proud. She had walked for an hour and a half each day and then done forty minutes of exercise as well as paying attention to her diet. She described herself as feeling physically and psychologically well prepared.

In the same session Jay produced a drawing of a figure holding a baby while a man floats with his legs apart. In response to this charcoal sketch Jay talked about how the dead baby Eric had reminded her of a Biafran child, when he was returned to her after the post-mortem having been cut and stitched up. She expressed a desire to situate her experience in a global perspective and the circle she described as representing the world. Apparent in the picture are what she describes as the 'the hands of grief' and a womb. The baby she said 'doesn't want to know', reflecting again perhaps her sense that Eric had chosen to die. She described the figure with legs apart as a 'fat cat male who's saying "shhhhhhhh don't speak about it"' (the text is written over his mouth). She also commented that this figure reminded her of her father. The figure represents her wavering feelings about men on several levels – how men react to the death of children globally with reference to famines that they are 'fat cats' making money while children starve. It also refers to her perception that men have difficulty in accepting and expressing grief. This is also the first clear allusion to her childhood sexual abuse where the 'Shhhhhhhh don't speak about it' had quite sinister implications.

In the fourth week of art therapy Jay made a collage which is characterised by things being within other things. The bull depicted refers to Jay's father (a Taurus) and inside him is a unicorn. In a pastoral scene is a prickly sea anemone. In the left-hand corner of the picture are a variety of cloaks which refer to her different personae. She described her personae as a matter of choice – 'what shall I be wearing today?' – the coat of anger, the coat of grief, the coat of sadness or the coat of fears. They were mantles that could be put on or off and felt to her slightly manufactured.

In week five Jay executed a painting of an underwater scene in which a large crustacean sits with matter growing on its edge. The shapes depicted were very womb-like.

Jay responded to the contents of a drawing made in the same session (Figure 14.8). One aspect of the figure on the right is stoic and 'grounded' (illustrated by the lead boots) and another part of it is 'hysterical' (indicated by the flapping hands). The figure on the left represents her self-control and the other shows her 'horror' and 'disbelief' of her experience. The episiotomy is also depicted as the stitching on the womb-like shape.

In the same week Jay also drew an image which she described as elucidating her denial of her body as well as her willpower. She depicted herself holding above her head a plank or iron bar which represented her life but is also a reference to some sort of meditation or martial arts practice. The iron bar or plank is held, balanced, for long periods of time

Figure 14.8

by dint of sheer willpower. She notes the cups of tea, which are balanced on the plank or bar. She mentioned that her partner (who was otherwise absent in the pictures) was very good at producing cups of tea.

Jay said of the bar that it represented a sense of her 'holding it all together', yet it also had what she described as a 'flaying arms quality to it', representing her wish that she had more arms! On the bar are balanced all the things which punctuate her time: tired eyes, cups of tea, a book, a womb, both babies, a TV set, a 'dick and balls', and a mouth. Jay noted that she had not given herself a mouth. Although she had been weeping quite a lot at the time she felt that she was holding the grief in her body. Jay described a definite sense that whilst she was making an outward expression of her grief that somehow it didn't feel 'like it was moving'.

Jay then talked about the difficulty of coping with a crying baby. Her feelings of fatigue at this time would trigger feelings of grief and she said, 'I don't know whether I was crying because I didn't know what to do with a crying baby or whether I was crying because of the dead baby'. Jay described herself as feeling both fear and relief – a fear that she would not have been able to cope with the care of another infant and a relief that she only had one child to look after. This feeling alternated with one of confidence that she would have coped because she felt herself to be a capable woman. Jay also questioned whether she hadn't in some way caused the death herself.

In week six Jay produced an interesting self-portrait (Figure 14.9). The text reads 'shaky shaky girl bird woman dead girl bird'. She described the picture as depicting herself as an eight-year-old. She talked about all of her recent experiences as being touched by a more general and more encompassing sadness. Jay said that she hadn't previously been able to acknowledge that she lived with sadness. She explained that she regarded herself as a reasonably 'up' sort of person (Jay was quite extrovert) and yet that her experiences were edged with sadness and longing. She thought that the picture had a quality of being 'out of control'. Jay described the recent grief experiences as triggering off feelings from the past – from a world she'd left – that of being molested by her father as a young child. She described her father as representing part of the oppressive forces depicted in an earlier image. However, the grief, she felt, even went beyond her childhood abuse.

Jay then made a series of drawings, which she described as being very real to her experience (Figure 14.10). They show her reaching into a black hole touching the grief. She described the arms as being 'useless arms [that] will never stretch that long' referring to her sense of futility. The text accompanying the piece reads: 'Black mess in a hole is in me . . . I want to reach in and touch him, get him hold him, I want to reach in and hold him, bring him up so that I can see him and love him'. These images mark a turning point in the art therapy sessions because Jay felt that she had

Figure 14.9

contacted her grief. At this time she started to stick the pictures up on her wall at home after the sessions and write poems to accompany them:

Black missing
a hole
is he in there
or is that what he left?
a sad
grey weeping silent

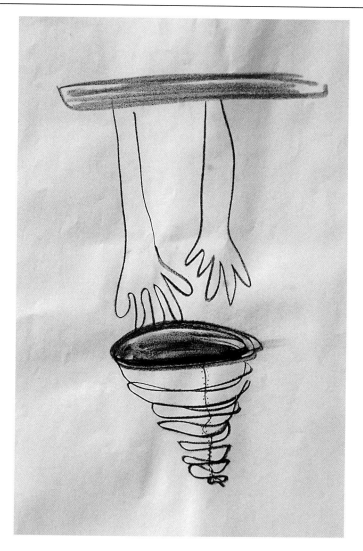

Figure 14.10

Produced in the same week Jay described Figure 14.11 as her holding her heart which has turned out looking more like an aggressive dagger than a heart. In this picture Jay noted the black hole of the womb echoing the black hole of her mouth. On the drawing she has written 'empty womb – wild top spinning craziness – hearts on hold'.

Tensions between Jay and her spouse on the subject of work are reflected in Figure 14.12. The image shows Jay going about her daily work and depicts her doing somersaults, standing on her head, and back-bending and then not having all this activity acknowledged as work by her

Figure 14.11

partner – the *real* work is something that only happens outside. The picture refers to her conflicts with Leo about whose work is the real work, and who needs to get sleep, and who gets up in the night to change Bruno. Jay's anger was very evident when she talked about an incident in which she asked Leo to get up in the night to change Bruno and he refused. Jay also expressed her absolute amazement that Leo could sleep while the baby cried.

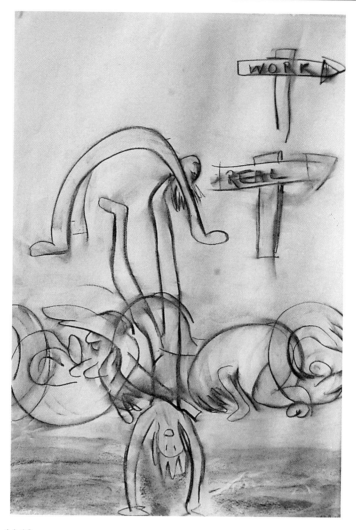

Figure 14.12

In Figure 14.13 the black hole of the womb becomes the black hole of the mouth. The dead baby is sucking. Jay wrote a poem to accompany the piece:

A dead baby sucking
Its little body curled up
in my heart
his arm laying flat
his fingers never touched my skin
too much too much mouthing
the blackness within . . .

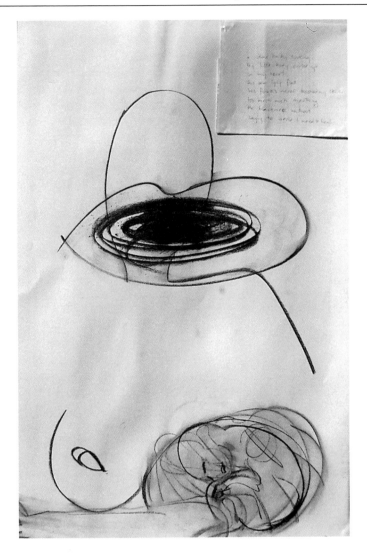

Figure 14.13

Jay also produced an image in the same session of Leo going off to work in the car while Jay holds the dead baby Eric. Both pictures reflect a strong sense of her holding the grief and being protective of it. She described herself as being in her 'special domain' as holder of the grief, expressing her unwillingness to get into the car with Leo. In this she felt that there might be a denial, on her part, of Leo's feelings of grief.

Jay produced a large image (Figure 14.14) which exemplifies the patterns that she sees emerging in her life. She has divided the page up into

Figure 14.14

small squares which contain almost a visual summary of the issues addressed in the art therapy sessions up to that date. She identified the content of most of the squares: a watch referring to the quality of her time; a flight of steps which, she said, ask the question 'has it been an uplifting experience?' The stairs are also a reference to her decreased mobility and the difficulties of access caused by her 'hauling a bloody pram around'. The box containing a car referred to her partner going off to work and to her experience of social isolation and being housebound as well as to the different roles adopted by herself and her partner and the value placed on their respective work. In another box the text 'an attack of heart' refers to her father's heart attack. Of the bottom right-hand square which is entirely black, she said that 'this felt like this was him', referring to her father and the abuse which was possibly committed in the dark. In another section the stitched womb is represented; another part shows her weight lifting with the dead baby (fourth along on the third row down) and she described this image as a 'muscle building arm holding Eric'. This has several possible meanings with reference to her previous work. She said of the image that Bruno was getting very heavy and that she wanted to 'work out' to build her strength. The muscle-building arm might also be referring to grief work as well as to the strength that it had taken to keep going; also depicted are tired eyes representing sleepless nights; sleep; in another of the squares is 'the black hole of grief'; a further section shows cups of tea which represent her partner's presence (as the tea maker) and also life's distractions; Bruno appears; an image of Jay on the road; arms going into a box which she described as Eric's coffin.

Jay decided to pick the content of one of the sections of the larger drawing to explore further. The image produced depicts arms stretched out to a box and the text reads 'father or son' illustrating her confusion as to whom she was grieving for. Jay described the aching of her heart caused by Eric's death and her anger that her father's fatal heart attack had prevented him from seeing his grandchild – she felt 'ripped off' (again this could have a double meaning referring also to her childhood).

The next image made in week seven (Figure 14.15) elaborates on the contents of another of the boxes. The picture refers to the famous photograph of the girl in Vietnam running naked and terrified away from a USA napalm attack. Jay described the girl as representing terror and horror and it was her outstretched arms that Jay felt that she had been drawing for most of the time. The picture may be viewed in two different ways (like a *trompe-l'œil*). The second way of seeing the picture portrays the girl as run over and lying flattened by the passing truck. This too has metaphoric and analogous possibilities – the most literal that Jay was feeling flattened by her experience.

Made in the same session (week seven), Jay produced a quickly executed charcoal sketch which represents her ability to exercise choice

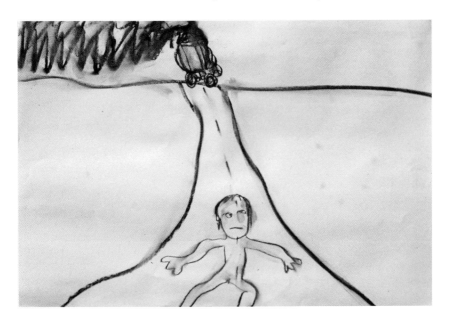

Figure 14.15

about how she wishes to live. On the left is the 'tea cup of distraction' and on the right is a plant pot which is symbolic of her taking action (she had just been out and bought plants for her house). The half-finished figure standing on one leg is Jay finding herself in an unstable position.

The next image made is an image of balance (looking not dissimilar to the scales of justice) which depicts Jay with two nests with a baby in each. Bruno's nest she describes as having integrity and Eric's she sees as falling apart. She saw them as being very much the same except for the breath that divides life from death.

On the left-hand side of Jay's following image were depicted all the distractions in Jay's life. The footprints represent the steps that she was making towards 'the sacred or the more spiritual side of her life'. In the altar she places herself.

Jay's next image is quite ambiguous. In it a snake is whispering (the snake she associates with a prophetic feminine aspect of herself) and a dog is eating part of her womb which she says may be diseased or may be left over from the birth – she is not sure. Jay thought that the dog was a helper.

Completed in colour in the tenth week of art therapy, Figure 14.16 denotes Jay's dramatic emergence from depression. This is an image that Jay described as big and powerful. It depicts a spiritual 'Venus' with arms outstretched breaking through a barrier or dome and gaining access to another space or realm and being transformed in the process. The Venus is straddling the chalice and is buoyant and being pushed upwards. Jay noted that whilst she has breasts she has no vagina. Jay expressed her pleasure in her use of colour and agreed that the drawing was quite celebratory. The text accompanying the piece reads:

> The cup of essence straddled, brings
> woman heated bursting forth green,
> coming up for air,
> parting madness and timidity . . .
> looking for her own face, her own glorious space,
> part the lips that fold . . .
> here she comes under world woman
> at last . . .

Drawn in the same week, Figure 14.17 depicts the colourful 'chalice' (representing blood and the womb) being held by big hands. Jay said that she is holding on to the bowl but not yet drinking – she can see it but not yet taste it. Jay felt that this picture had integrity and that it was intact. The text accompanying the image reads 'Not the cup of distraction – the stitched womb – rich full my lips are dry – my mouth salivates – I'm touching but I haven't got a hold'.

Figure 14.16

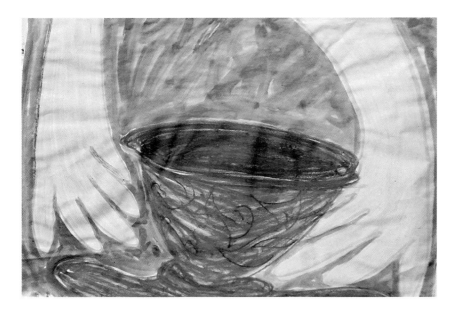

Figure 14.17

Also produced in the tenth week was a drawing which refers to the Third World and women having to walk for miles to fetch water. The text reads 'developing world woman balancing precious fluid on a ten mile walk – will she be nourished or only serve it to others? A giant dead baby holds the chalice with reverence while another woman drinks – life's not too far – my teat tastes sweet'. Jay had cut out and framed the drawing of Bruno from this session because she liked it.

Figure 14.18, completed in week eleven, depicts a number of pillars upon which are placed various aspects of Jay's life. There is a chalice which she described as symbolic of her spiritual questing, the tea cup of distraction appears, a monkey in the customary position of dead Eric also appears and the headless woman has a head created by the negative space. The lack of a body Jay described as reflecting her experience. The stitching at the top of the drawing refers to the episiotomy. The wedding ring reappears. The tap refers to the 'tapping' of Jay's emotions which she felt to be 'dripping'.

Jay's ensuing drawing depicts an incident which triggered very strong emotions. She was visiting a woman who had four children, including twins, and they were joined by another woman, a neighbour, who was subsequently introduced. Her friend introduced Jay and Bruno to the neighbour and then her friend was introduced with the *twins*. Jay was stunned by this because she still thought of Bruno as being a twin. Jay described the incident as being typical of her emotionality at that time – a

Figure 14.18

small incident, in this case a gauche introduction, causing a huge emotional response. On the drawing she had written the different women's views and opinions about children and child birth:

Oh what lovely twins
Oh I'm trying to have a baby
But I miscarried
Oh, I've got to get going, to pick
up the other two
Oh he died probably a week before the birth
maybe more
Oh Oh Oh
Do you think he'll miss his dead twin?
Do you think that if I breathe in this air of
babies I'll get pregnant?
Do you think I'll only make babies?
Oh Oh Oh.

Figure 14.19 appeared to frighten Jay. The image reminded her of a Sydney Nolan mask (the Ned Kelly series of paintings being very well known in Australia) and it shows a figure who has been body-building holding the dead baby and making a 'hush' gesture with her fingers. Jay referred to the figure as herself, saying, 'keep it in the blocked mouth'. She described the

Figure 14.19

drawing as 'spooky' because of the way the figure in it is keeping quiet and because of the contained quality of the figure which she described as not quite human.

On the left-hand side of the picture separated by a bar (as seen in earlier images) are the objects of distraction including the pram and Bruno. It seemed clear that these were things distracting Jay from her sense of grief. She talked in this session about her need to have her feelings of grief validated.

The next image, completed in the same week, is of a headless woman. In this case the head is obliterated, again expressing a sense of covering up or repressing feelings. The woman in the picture is shown in a twisted pose hanging from two pieces of rope. Jay said that the image expressed her anger, disgust and a general feeling of being 'pissed off'. It is a specific reference to a billboard advertising campaign in Australia for women's sports underwear. The poster in question depicts a woman in a contorted pose with most of her head and body cut off by the frame of the photograph. Jay described the advertisement as outrageous and as soft porn. Although the image could be seen as saying that women can be strong and active she felt that the image was primarily about bondage and objectification. The text reads, 'no pain – no strain without feeling no life' (again a double meaning which could refer to Jay's sense of blocked and unacknowledged emotion). The bondage she also associated with having a baby with her all the time and to her experience of spending protracted periods of time indoors on her own. She mentioned that she had started watching day-time television (Perry Mason) which gave her the feeling that she was not getting on with life, and this in turn made her feel anxious. Jay said that she did not like television much anyway. Perry Mason reminded her of her father but also of a forthcoming legal situation involving her partner.

In the following session (week twelve) Jay depicted the dragon (Figure 14.20) which is symbolic of a forthcoming legal case which concerned Jay's partner in particular (and of which she did not disclose details to the group). The picture exemplifies the various positions that she found herself in with regard to this legal issue. Jay is pictured as a maiden in distress and also as George the dragon slayer. She also depicts herself as having magic powers and attempting to change the situation by casting spells. She is also Little Boy Blue who is asleep having forgotten entirely about the situation and who she felt was unwilling to take control. She perceived that these manifestations of her self-image fluctuated and that she could actively choose to be in one position or role with respect to any problem. The dragon therefore became representative of any potential difficulty. Jay said that she had really wanted to make an image of herself actively slaying the dragon.

The next image produced illustrated Jay's increasing interest in personal spirituality. A yellow shape is about to be led into a castle accessible

Figure 14.20

through an open door. A row of spears which represents the castle's defences falls away. Steps lead to the front door, while something is about to enter. Through the windows can be seen glimpses of herself and (from left to right) the grief, part of her body and her anger.

Embodying a spirit of optimism, Figure 14.21 is a positive affirmation of the family. It depicts the slayed dragon which was the expected outcome of the then looming court case. The figures in the picture are suffused with a bright light and a sense of peace. The dead baby Eric is represented by this sense of peace and by the yellow light and the family is therefore complete. Jay said that she felt more resolved about Eric's death after making this picture which she referred to thenceforth as the 'family picture'.

Jay was absent in week thirteen and the following week she produced six images in one session. The first image (Figure 14.22) reveals the successful outcome of the legal issue. The dragon has 'hit the dust' and the family are having a real celebration with cups of dragon's blood.

The next image (Figure 14.23) Jay describes as having more of a spiritual quality to it, even though the chalice is being filled by a tea pot (Jay laughed at this). The text on this picture reads 'Dragons blood a tasty drop'.

A further quicker sketch produced in the same week shows 'screamy hands' with which Jay wanted to contextualise her experiences into the larger sphere of life and death. The text 'There's always a bigger picture' is written on the page.

Figure 14.21

Figure 14.22

Figure 14.23

A further picture is a declaration about Jay's sexuality. This portrays Jay with a baby's dummy. The dummy may be a sex aid or it may be for plugging herself up – she thought that the idea of the dummy being a marital aid was very funny. Jay felt that the image expressed a 'profaning' of the maternal role. She felt that motherhood as a notion was placed on a pedestal of purity which is cut off from the physical and sexual aspects of being a woman, and that the divide between motherhood and sexuality as perceived by society is an artificial one. She felt that the picture challenged the notion of motherhood as sacred. Jay liked the picture's iconoclastic quality.

Jay described the experience of making Figure 14.24 as extraordinary. She explained that the image was about sexuality and motherhood. The drawing shows a woman sitting on top of the world. She is sitting with her legs open looking up at a bottle that she is about to plunge into herself as a dildo.

Jay described her experience of sex and her experience of herself as a sexual being as having been quite changed by the experience of mothering. She felt that the change was astonishing. Jay described her conflicting thoughts about sexuality and motherhood. On the one hand, pregnancy and motherhood denote prior sexual activity but, on the other, Jay felt that she had been transformed into a non-sexual being who was seen as not being in need of physical contact. She also said that this lack of need was indeed true insofar as she felt tired a lot of the time. However, Jay said that

Figure 14.24

she'd been astonished at how much sensual contact she had with the baby. This contact was fairly constant as she was breast-feeding Bruno. She described her pleasure in feeding him to sleep and feeling his little hand stroking her breast. Jay remembered something she had read by Germaine Greer and agreed that she was experiencing more ongoing 'sexuality and sensuality' with her child than with her partner because of her continuing contact with the child.

Jay talked about penetrative sex feeling uncomfortable even after the episiotomy had healed. She described the experience of episiotomy as a 'mutilation' and as a 'kind of rape'.

Also created in the same week was a rendering of a doorway or a vagina which expressed Jay's desire to profane the maternal role (or at least some of the fantasy surrounding it). She recounted that when she had been very pregnant she had wanted to dress up as the Madonna and be photographed. Jay said that she had been very proud of her huge belly and that the photographs ware about claiming a certain sort of sacredness as well as being challenging. The text on the piece reads:

Inside is Mary
She's wearing a suspender belt
she's embarrassed to come out
the space not coloured is
a woman any woman
by non presence creating

the phallus
like any hole or doorway
something to go through.

Jay liked the idea of the Madonna in a suspender belt. Again she expressed the desire to knock the notion of motherhood off its abstract and idealised pedestal but without denigrating it.

The following week (week fifteen) Jay made an image of a sitting room which contains the 'perfect couch' (which represents her sense of being able to get what she wants in terms of material comfort). The light coming from the lamp she described as symbolic of illumination and focus. The wall-shelves delineate different sets of choices in Jay's life. Each shelf contains a row of options, for example, a shelf of knickers referring to different types of sexuality (G-strings, cottontails, boxer shorts are arranged on the shelf). On other shelves are different types of houses, various countries (where and how does she want to live?) and different types of books (what kind of intellectual stimulus does she want?). The top shelf contains a row of cups and chalices. Jay was preoccupied with prioritising choices at the time that this image was made and with choosing a new self-identity. The eternity symbol in the drawing hovers in mid-air and represents both life and death. Its relationship to the shelves of choices is ambiguous.

The totemic doll or monster completed in week sixteen (Figure 14.25) is compressed into a space too small for it. The shading on the left of the image is symbolic of the womb. Jay's reactions to the image were quite different in the group session and in her review after the group. When she first completed the image she felt that it could be the dead baby Eric in his coffin. Also figured is her partner, Leo, being hit by a hammer on the head (Jay had arrived at the session late feeling angry because Leo had forgotten to return at an appointed time to take over the child-care and release the car for her use). However, in the review she saw the doll as herself and as exemplifying her changed conception of her sense of personal space.

Jay saw the doll as representing her sense of having to give up her feeling of individual space because of caring for Bruno. This awareness of space she described as radically altered because of her experience of motherhood. She talked about her body feeling 'extended' and accessible. Jay found that this was draining. She also experienced much internal resistance to letting go and just relaxing with her new state of availability. Sometimes she experienced a claustrophobia and need to escape from the situation which manifested itself with strong physical sensations. On the other hand, Jay expressed her surprise at just how much she had been able to allow her body to become an extension of Bruno. She regarded her independence as being a strong part of her self-identity yet she regarded herself as an extension of Bruno rather than the reverse. She found this a

Figure 14.25

challenge to her sense of self-identity and her notion of independence. Jay felt that her primary experience of motherhood, that of selflessness, is grossly underestimated and understated in our culture.

In week seventeen Jay made several quick drawings on a roll of paper which indicate her feeling of being out of control. In one image she is portrayed as immersed in a whirlpool of grief and in another she is compressed. She then made an image that indicated where she wanted to be, safe in a womb being fed from the tea cup and the chalice intravenously.[11] Having felt unsafe and unstable, the drawing depicts Jay receiving comfort and nourishment.

In the final week (eighteen) participants made images to give to other group members. Jay kept one image which depicts her wearing dancing shoes and without hair (she had long hair). She felt that the image was of her feeling good about herself doing her dance.

CONCLUDING NOTE

Jay went on to join a support group for women, feeling that she was no longer in need of 'therapy' at the close of the art therapy group. She is keen for her story to be told.

ACKNOWLEDGEMENTS

Particular thanks are due to Jay for her agreement to this publication and for allowing her work to be photographed and for allowing me to tape-record our review session together. Many thanks to my co-therapist, Suzanne Calomeris, for photographing the work and producing a set of slides for my use.

NOTES

1 Bowlby, 1981: 122–3.
2 Illich 1977.
3 Kitzinger 1985: 80 cited in Llewelyn and Osborne 1990: 85.
4 Rakusen 1971: 438.
5 Rakusen 1971: 438.
6 Rakusen 1971: 433.
7 There is no evidence to suggest that there is a correlation between increase in episiotomy rates and decreasing rates of perineal tearing (Chalmers, cited in Rakusen 1971: 434).
8 Rakusen argues that this procedure is frequently carried out with insufficient pain relief (1971: 434).
9 This case study draws upon the notes of the two art therapists facilitating the group as well as a tape-recorded review of all of the sessions with the client. I have tried as far as possible to use the same style of language and words that Jay (a pseudonym) used herself in the sessions to ensure maximum authenticity. The reader will note that the case study is written from Jay's point of view rather than my own as a facilitator. The emphasis is on Jay's experience rather than on my and my colleague's therapeutic interventions. It must be remembered that all case studies are 'constructed'. This case study has attempted to privilege the client's voice.
10 Jay was very focused on getting the most out of the sessions and interacted little with other group members during the art-making part of the session. However, in the second half of sessions she sensitively asked questions about other group members' work and gave her own response to it. Jay felt comfortable about taking up time in the group and was forthright about talking about her images. Because she had experienced a death the group seemed to be particularly willing to give Jay space and time in the group. The insistence of her need was respected and acknowledged by the group.
11 In Jay's therapy the chalice represents the goblet from which the congregation sips. It is full of her blood (a symbol of her fecundity) and/or a symbol of her womb (and her coming to terms with her episiotomy) and then of dragon's blood or spiritual nourishment. It also merges with the 'tea cup of distraction'. The latter starts off as a self-criticism – a sense of Jay wasting her time (as well as a symbol of Leo's presence) and ends up as a symbol of self-acceptance through Jay allowing everyday experiences to become more 'sacred'. The meaningfulness of her role is articulated here. The chalice functions in the case study to illustrate how one reoccurring symbol can contain many meanings and serves as a good indicator of Jay's state of mind.

BIBLIOGRAPHY

Berger, P. L. and Luckmann, T. 1967. *The Social Construction of Reality*. Harmondsworth: Penguin.

Bowlby, J. 1981. *Attachment and Loss*, vol. 3. Harmondsworth: Penguin.

Farsides, C. 1994. 'Autonomy, Responsibility and Midwifery', in Budd, S. and Sharma, U. (eds) *The Healing Bond: The Patient–Practitioner Relationship and Therapeutic Responsibility*. London: Routledge.

Illich, I. 1977. *Limits to Medicine: Medical Nemesis and the Expropriation of Health*. Harmondsworth: Penguin.

Kübler-Ross, E. 1973. *On Death and Dying*. London: Routledge.

Littlewood, J. 1992. *Aspects of Grief: Bereavement in Adult Life*. London: Routledge.

Llewelyn, S. and Osborne, K. 1990. *Women's Lives*. London: Routledge.

Lupton, D. 1994. *Medicine as Culture: Illness, Disease and the Body in Western Societies*. London: Sage.

Mitchell, R. 1975. *Depression*. Harmondsworth: Penguin.

Parkes, C. 1975. *Bereavement: Studies of Grief in Adult Life*. London: Tavistock.

Pitt, S. 1994. 'Midwifery and Medicine: Discourses on Childbirth 1945–1974'. 'Work-in-Progress in the History of Medicine' conference. University of Aberdeen, October 1994, unpublished paper supplied by author.

Rakusen, J. 1971. *Our Bodies Ourselves: A Health Book by and for Women*. Harmondsworth: Penguin.

Rakusen, J. and Davidson, N. 1982. *Out of Our Hands: What Technology Does to Pregnancy*. London: Pan.

Riley, D. 1982. *War in the Nursery: Theories of the Child and the Mother*. London: Virago.

Rowe, D. 1987. *Beyond Fear*. London: Fontana.

Sulieman, S. (ed.) 1986. *The Female Body in Western Culture*. Cambridge, MA: Harvard University Press.

Ussher, M. and Nicolson, P. (eds) 1992. *Gender Issues in Clinical Psychology*. London: Routledge.

Index